The

Age

of

Access

The Age of
Access

The New Culture of Hypercapitalism,
Where All of Life
Is a Paid-for Experience

Jeremy Rifkin

Jeremy P. Tarcher / Putnam

a member of Penguin Putnam Inc.

New York

Most Tarcher/Putnam books are available at special quantity discounts for bulk purchase for sales promotions, premiums, fund-raising, and educational needs. Special books or book excerpts also can be created to fit specific needs. For details, write Putnam Special Markets, 375 Hudson Street, New York, NY 10014.

Jeremy P. Tarcher/Putnam
a member of
Penguin Putnam Inc.
375 Hudson Street
New York, NY 10014
www.penguinputnam.com

First Trade Paperback Edition 2001

The Library of Congress Cataloged the hardcover edition as follows

Rifkin, Jeremy.
The age of access: The new culture of hypercapitalism,
where all of life is a paid-for experience / by Jeremy Rifkin.
    p.   cm.
ISBN 1-58542-018-2
ISBN 1-58542-082-4 (Paperback edition)
1. Electronic commerce.   2. Electronic commerce—Social aspects.   3. Electronic
data interchange.   4. Internet (Computer network)—Economic aspects.
5. Business—Computer network resources.   I. Title.
HF5548.32.R54 2000
650'.0285'4678—dc21   99-054028

Printed in the United States of America
1 3 5 7 9 10 8 6 4 2

Book design by Ralph Fowler

Acknowledgments

I would like to thank Jon Akland, who assisted me as researcher for *The Age of Access*. Jon was always able to locate just the right research we were looking for throughout the long process of putting this book together. I am grateful for his watchful eye on the many details that went into preparing the manuscript. Controlling and organizing the sheer volume of information that was assembled during the course of this project was a formidable task. Jon handled the effort with great care and efficiency.

I'd also like to thank Jerry Rosenbloom, Sheldon Rovin, and Scott Koerwer at the Wharton School, as well as David Noble and Steve Samuel for their many helpful comments on early drafts of the manuscript. I'd like to especially thank my old friend and colleague Ted Howard who spent many days wrestling with various versions of the manuscript and providing me with insightful and invaluable commentary.

I'd also like to thank my father-in-law, Ted Grunewald, for his many constructive ideas as well as his help in preparing some vital research that was used in the course of writing the book.

Laura Martino's research and fact-checking also contributed greatly to the book and is much appreciated. Thanks go also to Clara Mack, Joyce

Wooten, Eric Schoenfield, and Anna Awimbo for all of their painstaking efforts in preparing the manuscript.

I'd also like to thank my wife, Carol Grunewald, for the many hours of fruitful conversation that helped focus some of the ideas in the book.

I'd also like to thank my good friend and publisher Jeremy Tarcher for his important critique of the first draft of the manuscript, which helped provide direction to the project. And thanks to Joel Fotinos, my publisher, for believing in the project from the outset and for shepherding it through the process at Putnam. I'd also like to extend my appreciation to Cathy Fox at Putnam for making sure that the book receives a wide audience in countries around the world. Thanks to Kim Seidman for her outstanding copyediting of the manuscript. Thanks go also to my agent, Jim Stein, who is always the first to champion a new book idea and who makes sure that the project happens.

Finally, I'd like to thank my editor, Mitch Horowitz. This is the second book we have worked on together. It truly has been a joint collaboration. His editorial presence pervades virtually every page of the book. I have very much enjoyed sharing ideas at every stage of this project and appreciate the keen intellect, as well as grace and wit, that he brought to the effort.

Contents

The Next

Capitalist

Frontier

Entering
the Age of
Access

The role of property is changing radically. The implications for society are enormous and far-reaching. For the whole of the Modern Age, property and markets have been synonymous. Indeed, the capitalist economy is founded on the very idea of exchanging property in markets. The word *market* first appeared in the English language in the twelfth century and referred to the physical space set aside for sellers and buyers to exchange goods and livestock. By the late eighteenth century, the term had become separated from any geographic reference and was being used to describe the abstract process of selling and buying things.[1] So much of the world we know has been bound up in the process of selling and buying things in the marketplace that we can't imagine any other way of structuring human affairs. The marketplace is a pervasive force in our lives. We all are deeply affected by its moods and swings. Its well-being becomes a measure of our own. If markets are healthy, we feel buoyed. If they weaken, we despair. The marketplace is our guide and counselor and sometimes the bane of our existence.

Some of a small child's first encounters are likely to be in the marketplace. What youngster hasn't peered into a shop window and asked sheepishly, "How much is that?" From an early age, we learn that virtually everything has a price and everything is for sale. When we're older, we're introduced to the dark side of the market with the warning *caveat emptor,* "let the buyer beware." We live by the rules of the invisible hand of the market and continually hone our lives to the task of buying cheap and selling dear. We are taught that acquiring and accumulating property are integral parts of our earthly sojourn and that who we are is, at least to some degree, a reflection of what we own. Our very notions about the way the world works are based, in large part, on what we have come to regard as the primordial urge to exchange goods with one another and become propertied members of society.

We embrace the marketplace with an unswerving devotion. We sing its praises and admonish its detractors. Who hasn't defended the virtues of property and markets with passionate abandon at one time or another? Ideas about individual freedom, inalienable rights, and the social contract all are figments of this indivisible and essential social convention.

Now the foundation of modern life is beginning to disintegrate. The institution which once drove men to ideological battles, revolutions, and wars is slowly dying out in the wake of a new constellation of economic realities that is moving society to rethink the kinds of bonds and boundaries that will define human relations in the coming century.

In the new era, markets are making way for networks, and ownership is steadily being replaced by access. Companies and consumers are beginning to abandon the central reality of modern economic life—the market exchange of property between sellers and buyers. This doesn't mean property disappears in the coming Age of Access. Quite the contrary. Property continues to exist but is far less likely to be exchanged in markets. Instead, suppliers hold on to property in the new economy and lease, rent, or charge an admission fee, subscription, or membership dues for its short-term use. The exchange of property between sellers and buyers—the most important feature of the modern market system—gives way to short-term access between servers and clients operating in a network relationship. Markets remain but play an increasingly diminished role in human affairs.

In the network economy, both physical and intellectual property are more likely to be accessed by businesses rather than exchanged. Ownership of physical capital, however, once the heart of the industrial way of life, becomes increasingly marginal to the economic process. It is more likely to be regarded by companies as a mere expense of operation rather than an asset, and something to borrow rather than to own. Intellectual capital, on the other hand, is the driving force of the new era, and much coveted. Concepts, ideas, and images—not things—are the real items of value in the new economy. Wealth is no longer vested in physical capital but rather in human imagination and creativity. Intellectual capital, it should be pointed out, is rarely exchanged. Instead, it is closely held by the suppliers and leased or licensed to other parties for their limited use.

Businesses already are well along the way toward the transition from ownership to access. They are selling off their real estate, shrinking their inventories, leasing their equipment, and outsourcing their activities in a life-or-death race to rid themselves of every conceivable kind of physical property. Owning things, lots of things, is considered outdated and out of place in the more ephemeral, fast-paced economy of the new century. In the contemporary commercial world, most everything needed to run the physical business itself is borrowed.

Where the market used to boast sellers and buyers, now the talk is more of suppliers and users. In the network economy, market transactions are giving way to strategic alliances, cosourcing, and gain-sharing agreements. Many companies no longer sell things to one another but rather pool and share their collective resources, creating vast supplier-user networks that comanage each other's businesses.

Not surprising, the new means of organizing economic life brings with it different ways of concentrating economic power in fewer corporate hands. In the era of markets, institutions that amassed physical capital exercised increasing control over the exchange of goods between sellers and buyers. In the era of networks, suppliers who amass valuable intellectual capital are beginning to exercise control over the conditions and terms by which users secure access to critical ideas, knowledge, and expertise.

Commercial success in the access economy depends less on individual market exchanges of goods and more on establishing long-term commercial relationships. A case in point is the changing relationship between goods and the services that accompany them. Whereas for most of the Industrial Age the emphasis was on selling goods and attaching free service warranties to the products as an incentive to buy, now the relationship between goods and services is being reversed. An increasing number of businesses literally give away their products for free in the hopes of entering into long-term service relationships with clients.

Consumers, too, are just beginning to make the shift from ownership to access. While cheap, durable goods will continue to be bought and sold in the market, more costly items like appliances, automobiles, and homes increasingly will be held by suppliers and accessed by consumers in the form of short-term leases, rentals, memberships, and other service arrangements.

It is likely that for a growing number of enterprises and consumers, the very idea of ownership will seem limited, even old-fashioned, twenty-five years from now. Ownership simply is too slow an institution to adjust to the near warp speed of a nanosecond culture. Ownership is based on the idea that possessing a physical asset or piece of property over an extended period of time is valuable. "To have," "to hold," and "to accumulate" are cherished concepts. Now, however, the speed of technological innovation and the dizzying pace of economic activity often make the notion of ownership problematic. In a world of customized production, continuous innovation and upgrades, and ever narrowing product life cycles, everything becomes almost immediately outdated. To have, to hold, and to accumulate in an economy in which change itself is the only constant makes less and less sense.

The Age of Access, then, is governed by a whole new set of business assumptions that are very different from those used to manage a market era. In the new world, markets give way to networks, sellers and buyers are replaced by suppliers and users, and virtually everything is accessed.

The shift from a propertied regime based on the idea of broadly distributed ownership to an access regime based on securing short-term limited use of assets controlled by networks of suppliers changes fundamentally our notions of how economic power is to be exercised in the years ahead. Because our political institutions and laws are steeped in market-based property relations, the shift from ownership to access also portends profound changes in the way we will govern ourselves in the new century. Perhaps even more important, in a world where personal ownership of property has long been regarded as an extension of one's very being and the "measure of a man," its waning significance in commerce suggests a formidable change in the way future generations will perceive of human nature. Indeed, a world structured around access relationships is likely to produce a very different kind of human being.

The changes taking place in the structuring of economic relationships are part of an even larger transformation occurring in the nature of the capitalist system. We are making a long-term shift from industrial production to cultural production. More and more cutting-edge commerce in the future will involve the marketing of a vast array of cultural experiences rather than of just traditional industrial-based goods and services. Global travel and tourism, theme cities and parks, destination entertainment centers, wellness, fashion and cuisine, professional sports and games, gambling, music, film, television, the virtual worlds of cyberspace, and electronically mediated entertainment of every kind are fast becoming the center of a new hypercapitalism that trades in access to cultural experiences.

The metamorphosis from industrial production to cultural capitalism is being accompanied by an equally significant shift from the work ethic to the play ethic. While the industrial era was characterized by the commodification of work, the Age of Access is about, above all else, the commodification of play—namely the marketing of cultural resources including rituals, the arts, festivals, social movements, spiritual and fraternal activity, and civic engagement in the form of paid-for personal entertainment. The struggle between the cultural sphere and the commercial sphere to control both access to and the content of play is one of the defining elements of the coming era.

Transnational media companies with communications networks that span the globe are mining local cultural resources in every part of the world and repackaging them as cultural commodities and entertainments. The top fifth of the world's population now spends almost as much of its income accessing cultural experiences as on buying manufactured goods and basic services. We are making the transition into what economists call an "experience" economy—a world in which each person's own life becomes, in effect, a commercial market. In business circles, the new operative term is the "lifetime value" (LTV) of the customer, the theoretical measure of how much a human being is worth if every moment of his or her life were to be commodified in one form or another in the commercial sphere. In the new era, people purchase their very existence in small commercial segments.

Between Two Worlds

Cultural production is beginning to eclipse physical production in world commerce and trade. The old giants of the Industrial Age—Exxon, General Motors, USX, and Sears—are giving way to the new giants of cultural capitalism—Viacom, Time Warner, Disney, Sony, Seagram, Microsoft, News Corporation, General Electric, Bertelsmann A.G., and PolyGram. These transnational media companies are using the new digital revolution in communications to connect the world and in the process are pulling the cultural sphere inexorably into the commercial sphere, where it is being commodified in the form of customized cultural experiences, mass commercial spectacles, and personal entertainment.

In the Industrial Age, when producing goods was the most important form of economic activity, being propertied was critical to physical survival and success. In the new era, where cultural production is increasingly becoming the dominant form of economic activity, securing access to the many cultural resources and experiences that nurture one's psychological existence becomes just as important as holding on to property.

The transformation from the old economic era to the new has been long in the making. The process started earlier in the twentieth century with the shift in emphasis from manufacturing goods to providing basic services. Now the commercial sphere is making an equally important shift from being service-related to experience-oriented. Cultural production represents the final stage of the capitalist way of life, whose essential mission has always been to bring more and more human activity into the commercial arena. The progression in economic priorities from manufacturing goods to providing basic services to commodifying human relationships and finally to selling access to cultural experiences is testimony to the single-minded determination of the commercial sphere to make all relations economic ones.

The commodification of human culture is bringing with it a fundamental change in the nature of employment. In the Industrial Age, human labor was engaged in the production of goods and the performance of basic services. In the Age of Access, intelligent machines—in the form of software and "wetware"—increasingly replace human labor in the agri-culture, manufacturing, and service sectors. Farms, factories, and many white-collar service industries are quickly becoming automated. More and more physical and mental labor, from menial repetitive tasks to highly conceptual professional work, will be done by thinking machines in the twenty-first century. The cheapest workers in the world likely will be not as cheap as the technology coming online to replace them. By the middle decades of the twenty-first century, the commercial sphere will have the technological wherewithal and organizational capacity to provide goods and basic services for an expanding human population using a fraction of the workforce presently employed. Perhaps as little as 5 percent of the adult population will be needed to manage and operate the traditional in-dustrial sphere by the year 2050. Near-workerless farms, factories, and of-fices will be the norm in every country. New employment opportunities will exist, for the most part, but in paid cultural work in the commercial arena. As more and more of people's personal lives become paid-for expe-riences, millions of other people will become employed in the commercial sphere to service cultural needs and desires.

The capitalist journey, which began with the commodification of space and material, is ending with the commodification of human time and duration. The selling of the culture in the form of more and more paid-for human activity is quickly leading to a world where pecuniary kinds of human relationships are substituting for traditional social rela-tionships. Imagine a world where virtually every activity outside the confines of family relations is a paid-for experience, a world in which tra-ditional reciprocal obligations and expectations—mediated by feelings of faith, empathy, and solidarity—are replaced by contractual relations in the form of paid memberships, subscriptions, admission charges, retain-ers, and fees.

Think for a moment how much of our daily interactions with our fel-low human beings already are bound up in strictly commercial relation-ships. We increasingly buy others' time, their regard and affection, their sympathy and attention. We buy enlightenment and play, grooming and grace, and everything in between—even the passing of time itself is on the clock. Life is becoming more and more commodified, and communica-tions, communion, and commerce are becoming indistinguishable.

Even in a fully mature market economy, remember, commerce is still periodic. Sellers and buyers come together for a brief moment to negotiate a transfer of goods and services, and then they go their separate ways. The rest of their time is free of market considerations and commerce. Cultural time—noncommodified time—still exists. In a hypercapitalist economy, however, steeped in access relationships, virtually all of our time is commodified. For example, when a customer buys a car, the real-time relationship with the dealer is short lived. If a client secures access to the same vehicle in the form of a lease, his relationship with the supplier is continuous and uninterrupted for the duration of the agreement. Suppliers say they prefer "commodifying relationships" with their customers because they provide them with ongoing connections that are renewable and, at least in theory, perpetual. When everyone is embedded in commercial networks of one sort or another and in continuous association by way of paid leases, partnerships, subscriptions, and retainer fees, all time is commercial time. Cultural time wanes, leaving humanity with only commercial bonds to hold civilization together. This is the crisis of postmodernity.

In the 1980s and 1990s, deregulation of government functions and services was the rage. In less than twenty years, the global marketplace successfully absorbed large parts of what formerly was the government sphere—including mass transportation, utilities, and telecommunications—into the commercial realm. Now the economy has turned its attention to the last remaining independent sphere of human activity: the culture itself. Cultural rituals, community events, social gatherings, the arts, sports and games, social movements, and civic engagements all are being encroached upon by the commercial sphere. The great issue at hand in the coming years is whether civilization can survive with a greatly reduced government and cultural sphere and where only the commercial sphere is left as the primary mediator of human life.

In this book, we will examine the many structural changes that are laying the conceptual groundwork and organizational base for the Age of Access. The shift from markets to networks and from ownership to access, the marginalization of physical property and the ascendance of intellectual property, and the increasing commodification of human relationships are slowly leading us out of an era in which the exchange of property is the critical function of the economy and into a new world in which the purchase of lived experiences becomes the consummate commodity.

The transformation from industrial to cultural capitalism already is challenging many of our most basic assumptions about what constitutes human society. Old institutions grounded in property relations, market exchanges, and material accumulation are slowly being uprooted to make room for an era in which culture becomes the most important commercial resource, time and attention become the most valuable possession, and each individual's own life becomes the ultimate market.

The Clash of Culture and Commerce

We are journeying into a new period in which more and more human experience is purchased in the form of access to multifaceted networks in cyberspace. These electronic networks, within which an increasing number of people spend much of their day-to-day experience, are controlled by a few powerful transnational media companies who own the pipelines over which people communicate with one another and who control much of the cultural content that makes up the paid-for experiences of a postmodern world. There is no precedent in history for this kind of overarching control of human communications. Giant media conglomerates and their content providers become the "gatekeepers" who determine the conditions and terms upon which hundreds of millions of human beings secure access to one another in the coming era. It is a new form of global commercial monopoly—one exercised over the lived experiences of a large percentage of the human population on earth. In a world in which access to human culture is increasingly commodified and mediated by global corporations, questions of institutional power and freedom become more salient than ever before.

The absorption of the cultural sphere into the commercial sphere signals a fundamental change in human relationships with troubling consequences for the future of society. From the beginning of human civilization to now, culture has always preceded markets. People create communities, construct elaborate codes of social conduct, reproduce shared meaning and values, and build social trust in the form of social capital. Only when social trust and social exchange are well developed do communities engage in commerce and trade. The point is, the commercial sphere always has been derivative of and dependent on the cultural sphere. That's because culture is the wellspring from which agreed-upon behavioral norms are generated. It is those behavioral norms, in turn, that create a trusting environment within which commerce and trade can take place. When the commercial sphere begins to devour the cultural sphere—as we will explore further in part II—it threatens to destroy the very social foundations that give rise to commercial relations.

Restoring a proper balance between the cultural realm and the commercial realm is likely to be one of the most important challenges of the coming Age of Access. Cultural resources risk overexploitation and depletion at the hands of commerce just as natural resources did during the Industrial Age. Finding a sustainable way to preserve and enhance the rich cultural diversity that is the lifeblood of civilization in a global network economy increasingly based on paid access to commodified cultural experiences is one of the primary political tasks of the new century.

Proteans and Proletarians

The Age of Access also is bringing with it a new type of human being. The young people of the new "protean" generation are far more comfortable conducting business and engaging in social activity in the worlds of electronic commerce and cyberspace, and they adapt easily to the many simulated worlds that make up the cultural economy. Theirs is a world that is more theatrical than ideological and oriented more to a play ethos than to a work ethos. For them, access already is a way of life, and while property is important, being connected is even more important. The people of the twenty-first century are as likely to perceive themselves as nodes embedded in networks of shared interests as they are to perceive themselves as autonomous agents in a Darwinian world of competitive survival. For them, personal freedom has less to do with the right of possession and the ability to exclude others and more to do with the right to be included in webs of mutual relationships. They are the first generation of the Age of Access.

Just as the printing press altered human consciousness over the past several hundred years, the computer will likely have a similar affect on consciousness over the next two centuries. Psychologists and sociologists already are beginning to note a change taking place in cognitive development among youngsters in the so-called "dot-com" generation. A small but increasing number of young people who are growing up in front of computer screens and spending much of their time in chat rooms and simulated environments appear to be developing what psychologists call "multiple personas"—short-lived fragmented frames of consciousness, each used to negotiate whatever virtual world or network they happen to be in at any particular moment of time. Some observers worry that the dot-commers may begin to experience reality as little more than shifting story lines and entertainments and that they might lack both the deeply anchored socializing experience and extended attention span necessary to form a coherent frame of reference for understanding and adapting to the world around them.

Others see the development in a more positive light, as a freeing up of the human consciousness to be more playful, flexible, and even transient in order to accommodate the fast-moving and ever changing realities people experience. Today's children, they argue, are growing up in a world of networks and connectivity in which combative notions of mine and thine, so characteristic of a propertied market economy, are giving way to a more interdependent and embedded means of perceiving reality—one more cooperative than competitive and more wedded to systems thinking and consensus building.

In truth, it's far too early to know where the new consciousness will lead. On the one hand, the commercial forces are both powerful and seductive and already are bringing large numbers of dot-commers into the new worlds of cultural production. On the other hand, many young people are using their newfound senses of relatedness and connectivity to challenge an unbridled commercial ethic and create new communities of shared interests. Whether the forces of cultural commerce ultimately prevail or a renewed cultural realm is able to strike a balance between the two spheres is an open question.

The generation gap is being accompanied by an equally profound economic and social gap. While ⅕ of the world's population is migrating to cyberspace and access relationships, the rest of humanity still is caught up in the world of physical scarcity. For the poor, life remains a daily struggle for survival, and being propertied is an immediate preoccupation—and, for some, only a distant goal. Their world is far removed from fiber-optic cables, satellite uplinks, cellular phones, computer screens, and cyberspace networks. Although difficult for many of us to comprehend, more than half of the human race has never made a phone call.

The gap between the possessed and the dispossessed is wide, but the gap between the connected and the disconnected is even wider. The world is fast developing into two distinct civilizations—those living inside the electronic gates of cyberspace and those living on the outside. The new global digital communications networks, because they are so all-encompassing and comprehensive, have the effect of creating a new and totalizing social space, a second earthly sphere above the terra mater, suspended in the ether of cyberspace. The migration of human commerce and social life to the realm of cyberspace isolates one part of the human population from the rest in ways never before imaginable. The separation of humanity into two different spheres of existence—the so-called digital divide—represents a defining moment in history. When one segment of the human population is no longer able even to communicate with the other in time and space, the question of access takes on a political import of historic proportions. The great divide, in the coming age, is between those whose lives are increasingly taken up in cyberspace and those who will never have access to this powerful new realm of human existence. It is this basic schism that will determine much of the political struggle in the years ahead.

The shifts from geography to cyberspace, industrial to cultural capitalism, and ownership to access are going to force a wholesale rethinking of the social contract. Bear in mind that the modern notion of property as private, exclusive, and exchangeable in the marketplace has been the core institution of the Industrial Age. It has dictated the terms of daily life, informed political discourse, and been used to gauge the status of a human being. Now, after several hundred years of being the dominant organizing paradigm of civilization, the market regime, which brought sellers and buyers together to exchange property, is beginning to deconstruct. On the horizon looms the Age of Access—an era that will bring with it a new way of thinking about commercial relations, political engagement, and how we regard ourselves at the deepest level of human consciousness.

The very thought of leaving markets and the exchange of property behind—of advancing a conceptual change in the structuring of human relationships away from ownership and toward access—is as inconceivable to many people today as the enclosure and privatization of land and labor into property relations must have been more than half a millennium ago. Still, a portion of humanity already has embarked on this new journey. Those people are moving more and more of their affairs from the geographic confines of the marketplace to the temporal realm of cyberspace. In this new world that trades in information and services, in consciousness and lived experience, in which the material gives way to the immaterial and commodifying time becomes more important than expropriating space, the conventional notions of property relations and markets, which came to define the industrial way of life, become increasingly less relevant.

The notion of access and networks, however, is becoming ever important and is beginning to redefine our social dynamics as powerfully as did the idea of property and markets at the dawn of the modern era. Until recently, the word *access* was heard only occasionally and generally was confined to questions of admittance to physical spaces. In 1990, however, the eighth edition of the *Concise Oxford Dictionary* listed *access* as a verb for the first time, signaling its new, more expansive use in human discourse. Now, *access* is one of the most-used terms in social life. When people hear the word *access,* they are likely to think of openings to whole new worlds of possibilities and opportunities. Access has become the ticket to advancement and personal fulfillment and as powerful as the democratic vision was to earlier generations. It is a highly charged word, full of political significance. Access is, after all, about distinctions and divisions, about who is to be included and who is to be excluded. Access is becoming a potent conceptual tool for rethinking our worldview as well as our economic view, making it the single most powerful metaphor of the coming age.

When Markets
Give Way to
Networks

Musing over the kind of world electricity would bring, Nathaniel Hawthorne wrote in 1851, "Is it a fact . . . that, by means of electricity, the world of matter has become a great nerve, vibrating thousands of miles in a breathless point of time? Rather, the round globe is a vast head, a brain, instinct with intelligence! Or, shall we say, it is itself a thought, nothing but thought, and no longer the substance which we deemed it!"[1]

Hawthorne's vision is now becoming reality with the coming together of microelectronics, computers, and telecommunications into a single integrated communications grid, a kind of global nervous system enveloping the world. The shift from analog to digital forms of communication has hurried the convergence process along. Modern technologies make possible a new way to conduct business, what economists call a "network approach" to economic life.

The new commerce occurs in cyberspace, an electronic medium far removed from the geographically bound marketplace. The shift in primary commerce from geography to cyberspace represents one of the great changes in human organization and needs to be properly understood, as it brings with it vast changes in the very nature of human perception and social intercourse. Nowhere are those changes likely to have a bigger impact than on our notions of property. Whereas in a geographically based economy, sellers and buyers exchange physical goods and services, in cyberspace, servers and clients are more likely to exchange information, knowledge, experience, and even fantasies. In the former realm, the goal is transferring property, while in the new realm, the goal is providing access to one's daily existence.

The repositioning of primary commerce in cyberspace and the transition to a network-based global economy are made possible by the proliferation of global electronic networks, the most important being the Internet. The Pentagon created the Internet in the late 1960s. Anxious to save money on the costs of providing expensive new supercomputers to academic and defense-contracting researchers, the Pentagon began exploring ways to share computers among people who were separated by time and space. Top brass at the Department of Defense (DOD) were concerned also about the potential vulnerability to attack of centrally controlled communications operations. They were looking for a new kind of decentralized communication medium that could route messages to large numbers of researchers in a variety of ways and could continue to function even if part of the system were destroyed. The answer came in the form of the ARPANET, developed by the DOD's Advanced Research Projects Agency.

The first host computer came online in 1969. By 1988, more than 60,000 host computers were connected.[2] Other networks followed closely on the heels of ARPANET. The National Science Foundation created NSFnet to connect its supercomputer sites at major universities with researchers around the country. When ARPANET was shut down in 1990, NSFnet became the main vehicle for connecting computers. The NSFnet opened up access to an increasing number of people and eventually metamorphosed into what we now call the Internet. Other government agencies created their own networks. The Department of Energy established ESnet, and the National Aeronautics and Space Administration (NASA) went online with NSInet. Private networks also were put in place in the 1980s. Among the pioneers were IBM, GTE, and AT&T.[3] Designed for both internal use and real-time communications with suppliers and customers, these private networks began to lay the groundwork for the emergence of an electronically mediated network-based economy.

The Internet is a network of networks, and its messages can be sent via telephone wires, cable, and satellites. In a society weaned on the notion of ownership, says author James Gleick, "the hardest fact to grasp . . . is this: [The Internet] isn't a thing, it isn't an entity; it isn't an organization. No one owns it; no one runs it. It is simply Everyone's Computers, Connected."[4]

Today, more than 200 million people around the world have access to the Internet, according to the U.S. Department of Commerce, and forecasters estimate that by the year 2005, more than 1 billion human beings will enjoy access.[5] In 1998, the Internet economy generated more than $301 billion in revenue and created more than 1.2 million jobs. According to a study conducted by the University of Texas, the network economy is growing at an average of 174.5 percent a year and is now doubling in size every nine months.[6]

Corporate networks also are proliferating. In 1989, less than 10 percent of U.S. companies were connected to networks. By 1993, more than 60 percent of American businesses were online.[7] EDS boasts the world's largest corporate data network. The system, which cost $1 billion to install, connects 400,000 desktop computers and terminals to ninety-five data centers. The EDSnet routes 51.2 million transactions and data transfers every day and can store 49.7 trillion pieces of data, more than forty-five times the amount of information housed at the Library of Congress.[8]

In 1998, American companies were doing more than $43 billion worth of business with one another online. Forrester Research, a market research firm in Cambridge, Massachusetts, estimates that by the year 2003, business sales online will reach $1.3 trillion, or 9.4 percent of all business sales.[9]

The Connected Economy

The essential feature of commercial business in cyberspace is connectedness. Electronic networks, by their very nature, break down boundaries and walls. Unlike the geographic marketplace of the industrial era—which was based on the idea of sovereign and autonomous sellers and buyers engaging in discrete transactions, each independent of the other—the cyberspace economy brings enterprises together in deep webs of mutually interdependent relationships, where they share activities and pursuits. Kevin Kelly, editor at large of *Wired* magazine, speaks for many enthusiasts when he suggests that "the central act of the coming era is to connect everything to everything." Kelly foresees a future where "all matter, big and small, will be linked into vast webs of networks at many levels."[10] Already, businesses are connecting with suppliers and customers to share intangible resources in the form of information and expertise, as well as physical resources, with the conviction that by pooling their strengths, each firm can better optimize its own objectives.

This kind of network approach to commercial relations is a far cry from Adam Smith's dictum, which held sway for the better part of the industrial revolution. In *The Wealth of Nations*, published in 1776, the Scottish economist argued:

> *Every individual is continually exerting himself to find out the most advantageous employment for whatever capital he can command. It is his own advantage, indeed, and not that of society which he has in view. But the study of his own advantage naturally, or rather necessarily, leads him to prefer that employment which is most advantageous to the society.*[11]

In Smith's world, the market game is predicated on the ability to amass and hold property and to exclude others.

Self-interest dictates a different course in a network economy. By embedding one's own firm in a network of mutually beneficial reciprocal relationships designed to optimize the collective effort, each individual firm's success is more likely to be guaranteed—what some in the business community refer to as a win-win strategy.

Sociologist Manuel Castells of the University of California at Berkeley identifies five major kinds of networks in the new global network economy: supplier networks, in which firms subcontract for a range of inputs from design operations to the manufacturing of component parts; producer networks, made up of companies that pool their production facilities, financial resources, and human resources to expand their portfolios of goods and services, broaden geographic markets, and reduce up-front risk costs; customer networks, which link together manufacturers, distributors, marketing channels, value-added resellers, and end users; standard coalitions, which bring together as many firms as possible in a given field with the purpose of binding them to the technical standards established by an industry leader; and technology cooperation networks, which allow firms to share valuable knowledge and expertise in the research and development of product lines.[12]

The first thing to understand about a network-based global economy is that it both drives and is driven by a dramatic acceleration in technological innovation. Because production processes, equipment, and goods and services all become obsolete faster in an electronically mediated environment, long-term ownership becomes less palatable, while short-term access becomes a more frequent option. Sped-up innovation and product turnover dictate the terms of the new network economy. The process is demanding and relentless.

This narrowing of product life cycles is a direct result of Moore's Law. Gordon Moore, an electrical engineer and the founder of Intel, predicted early on that the processing power of computer chips would continue to double every eighteen months, while the cost of producing the chips would hold constant or decrease. Moore's Law was subsequently extended to include computer memory, data storage capacity, and telecommunications.[13]

Moore's prediction has proved remarkably accurate. Computing power continues to increase, even as the prices of computers and chips continue to fall. Personal computers that retailed for more than $3,000 a decade ago now can be purchased for less than $1,000, despite the fact that the computing power in each machine has risen dramatically. Now, chips are embedded in thousands of products from greeting cards to washing machines, making everything around us smarter and more information intensive.[14]

Moore's Law is wreaking havoc on product life cycles. "Smart" products containing computer chips are far more time sensitive than traditional products; they are constantly evolving and maturing, taking on new tasks and assignments with each new passage and in each successive generation.[15] As products come alive with information and animated with continual feedback, the pressure to upgrade and innovate increases. University of California marketing professor Rashi Glazer notes that "to the extent that a product is far along the information-intensiveness continuum, it becomes both more necessary and easier to change the offering."[16] The more interactive the information-rich product is with its environment—with feedback loops—the more likely the process itself will suggest innovative ways to make the product more effective. Although the research and development costs for upgrading the information component may be high, the actual production cost of embedding that new information in each product coming off the line is relatively low. "The result," says Glazer, "is a more rapid evolution in the basic product form and a shift in emphasis toward successive *generations* of the product, with the life cycle of any one generation or 'version' . . . assuming less importance."[17]

Product life cycles are narrowing in every industry. It took Chrysler fifty-four months, with a workforce of 3,100 people, to develop and manufacture its K-car in the late 1970s and early 1980s. A few years later, Chrysler developed its Neon automobile in less than thirty-three months, with a workforce of only 700 people. Today Chrysler's research and development division can deliver a new car in less than two years. Auto makers envision that within less than a decade, they will be able to build and deliver custom-made, defect-free cars in only three days.[18]

In 1986, the average development time for a new pharmaceutical product was ten years. The new generation of information-rich biotechnology-based pharmaceuticals is being developed and readied for market in four to seven years. At the same time, the useful life of pharmaceutical products is declining. For example, injectable cephalosporins for bacterial infections were introduced into the market in the mid 1960s. Twelve years later, sales of the second generation of this product surpassed the first. Sales of the fourth generation of the product, however, eclipsed the third generation in less than a year.[19]

Electromechanical products like typewriters, electrical switches, and automotive subsystem controls used to last for decades in the market. Their successors now have an average life span of less than three to five years before being overtaken by newer versions and models. Workstations used to last for a decade or more. Now their life span is less than twenty-four months.[20]

Japanese electronic companies' consumer products now average a mere three-month life cycle. Sony introduced a staggering 5,000 new products in 1995.[21] The dizzying proliferation of new products with shorter life spans led Microsoft's chief technology officer, Nathan Myhrvold, to quip, "No matter how good your product, you are only eighteen months away from failure."[22] Staying ahead of the competition often means competing against yourself. Intel, for example, works on three generations of chips concurrently. While one chip is still in production, a second generation of chips is being readied for production and a third generation is being designed.[23] The Honeywell corporation has slashed its product development time by 60 percent while reducing its labor hours by 5 to 10 percent. Xerox has cut its product development time by 50 percent.[24]

Sun Microsystems chief technology officer Eric Schmidt says that research and development is now measured in "web weeks." He estimates that 20 percent of the knowledge generated inside his company becomes obsolete within less than a year.[25] Wim Roelandts, chief of Hewlett-Packard's computer systems organization, observes that most of his company's revenues are derived from products that didn't exist a year ago.[26] Even more traditional consumer items, which used to create long-term customer loyalty, are falling by the wayside. More than 90 percent of Miller Brewing Company's revenue comes from new beers that didn't exist even two years ago.[27]

According to futurists Alvin and Heidi Toffler, "Economies of speed replace economies of scale" in the new hypercompetitive marketplace.[28] Being first to market allows companies to command higher prices and profit margins. Even a few months of lead time over competitors can mean the difference between success and failure. The faster a product goes to market, the longer its life span. By reducing research and development time, the firm extends the product's duration in the market, allowing the company to recoup its investment and hopefully turn a profit before the product becomes obsolete.

Of course, the narrowing of product life cycles has its counterpart in the shorter attention spans of consumers. With thousands of new products whizzing in and out of the marketplace at an ever quickening pace, it's only natural to expect a quickening of consumer impatience and a narrowing of consumer attention as well. The interval between desire and gratification is quickly approaching simultaneity as consumers come to expect a greater array of novel products and services at near breakneck speed. Today, consumers all along the line, including end-use consumers, barely have time to experience a new technology, product, or service before its upgraded successor becomes available. In this kind of hypercommercial environment, the very idea of ownership seems a bit out of place. Why assume ownership of a technology or product that's likely to be outdated even before it's paid for? In the new network economy, short-term access to goods and services—in the form of leases, rentals, and the like—becomes an increasingly attractive alternative to purchase and long-term ownership.

Shorter process and product life cycles and the increasing costs of sophisticated high-tech research and development—as well as the additional marketing costs involved in the launch of new product lines—have led many firms to come together to share strategic information as well as to pool resources and share costs as a way both to stay ahead of the game and to ensure against losses in an increasingly mercurial, volatile, and fast-paced cyberspace economy. Sharing the losses of failed processes and technologies provides a kind of collective insurance, allowing all the players to stay in the game.

A network economy differs substantially, then, from both traditional markets and hierarchical organizations. Walter Powell, director of the Social and Behavioral Sciences Research Institute of the University of Arizona, points out that market transactions generally prevail when the exchange itself is simple, direct, and nonrepetitive in nature and brings with it few transaction-specific investments. In markets, little trust is required between sellers and buyers. Rather, legally binding contracts ensure that the transfer of the product will be honored or that the promise of service will be rendered. Market transactions are fleeting encounters generally devoid of future commitments. They reflect Adam Smith's notion of self-interested parties trying to exact maximum advantage in a competitive and often antagonistic setting.

More complex exchanges generally favor hierarchical structures of organization. Servicing extended geographic markets with mass-produced goods requires greater control of inputs and tighter coordination of production processes and distribution mechanisms. Formal hierarchies, with clear divisions of authority, allow information to flow up the chain of command and decision making to flow down the line with the minimum of disruptions. Hierarchical organizations work best in periods of steady and stable markets but are woefully inadequate in periods of flux. Their administrative procedures are far too rigid to adjust to rapid changes in market conditions.

Networks, on the other hand, are far more flexible and better suited to the volatile nature of the new global economy. Cooperation and team approaches to problem solving allow the partners to respond more quickly to changes in the external environment. While the players give up a degree of autonomy and sovereignty, the spontaneity and creativity that flow from network-based collaboration give them a collective edge in the new, more demanding high-tech economy. Because networks involve complex channels of communications, diverse perspectives, parallel processing of information, continuous feedback, and reward thinking "outside the box," the players are more likely to make new connections, generate new ideas, create new scenarios, and implement new action plans in what is becoming a hypercommercial environment. Time Warner's Walter Isaacson captured the significance of the shift in the capitalist organization when he observed that "the old establishment was a club. The new establishment is a network."[29]

The Hollywood Organizational Model

The Hollywood culture industries have had a long experience with network-based approaches to organization and, for that reason, are fast becoming the prototype for the reorganization of the rest of the capitalist system along network lines. To begin with, the entertainment industry has to deal with the risks that accompany products with a truncated life cycle. Each film is a unique experience that has to find a quick audience if the production company is to recoup its investment, making a network approach to doing business a matter of necessity.

That's not always been the case, however. The early film industry relied on the kind of "Fordist" manufacturing principles that were in vogue across a wide range of industries in the 1920s. So-called "formula" films were produced like automobiles coming off an assembly line. One of the pioneers of the field, the Universal Film Manufacturing Company, produced more than 250 films in a single year. In the early years, films were actually sold by the foot rather than by content, reflecting the bias toward a mass-production mode of operation.[30]

By the early 1930s, a handful of studio giants—including Warner Brothers, Paramount, Metro-Goldwyn-Mayer, and Twentieth Century Fox—controlled the film industry. Their organizations were hierarchically structured and designed to oversee and regulate every aspect of the production process, from scripts to distribution. Professor Michael Storper of the University of California at Los Angeles School of Public Policy and Social Research explains how the system operated.

The major studios had permanent staffs of writers and production plan-
ners who were assigned to produce formula scripts in volume and
push them through the production system. Production crews and stars
were assembled in teams charged with making as many as thirty films
per year. Studios had large departments to make sets, operate sound
stages and film labs, and carry out marketing and distribution. A prod-
uct would move from department to department in assembly-line fash-
ion. . . . The internal organization—or technical division of labor—in
each phase of the labor process became increasingly similar to that of
true mass production, where routinization and task fragmentation were
the guiding principles.[31]

In 1944, the big studios earned 73 percent of all domestic cinema
rentals and owned or leased 4,424 theaters, or nearly one out of every four
movie houses in the country. Moviegoing peaked in 1946, with more than
90 million tickets sold per week.[32]

In the late 1940s and early 1950s, the film industry was hit with two
external shocks that forced it to reorganize along the network baselines
currently in practice. The U.S. Supreme Court—in a landmark antitrust
case—forced the major studios to divest themselves of their cinema
chains. No longer able to exercise control over the end user at the box office, film companies saw their revenues decline. The advent of television
further cut into film company profits. Millions of former moviegoers preferred to stay home and be entertained for free. Box office receipts fell by
40 percent between 1946 and 1956, and the film audience declined by 50
percent. The gross revenues of the ten leading film companies declined by
26 percent, and profit declined by 50 percent.[33]

Faced with increasing competition from the new medium of television, the film industry responded by changing their approach to filmmak-
ing. Realizing they couldn't successfully compete with a free medium
pumping out similar formulaic cultural products, the studio leaders
began to experiment with making fewer, more entertaining films, each a
unique product that could vie for viewer attention. The new films were
called "spectaculars"—later "blockbusters"—and they moved the film industry from mass production to customized production oriented toward
creating a "movie experience" each time the moviegoer walked into the
theater.

The new genre of films was more elaborate and expensive, and because each film was a unique product and therefore untested in the marketplace, large sums of money had to be invested in advertising and promotion. In short, the increasing cost involved in making fewer, more differentiated films brought with it greater financial risks and less sure returns on investments.

The network system of film production emerged in the 1950s partially in response to the need to bring together diverse talent to each unique film project and to pool risks in case any one product failed at the box office. The studio giants began to contract out for talent and services on a project-to-project basis. Independent production companies, made up of artisans and artists formerly under contract at the big studios, began to proliferate. Today, the remaining studio giants rarely produce films inhouse. Instead, they act as financial investors, providing seed money to independent producers in return for the right to distribute the end product at movie houses and later on television and video.

Every film production brings together a team of specialized production companies and independent contractors, each with its own expertise, along with the talent. Together, the parties constitute a short-lived network enterprise whose life span will be limited to the duration of the project. Scripting, casting, set design, cinematography, costuming, sound mixing and mastering, editing, and film processing all are done by independent agents working in temporary partnership with an independent production company. By assembling expertise from a number of specialized companies, producers can find exactly the right combination of skills needed to make the specific film project a success. Independent contractors, in turn, minimize their risks by engaging in a number of projects simultaneously across industry lines. It's not unusual for a special-effects company, for example, to be working in several temporary networks at once, performing specialized tasks on any given day on a film, in a television commercial, or on location at a live stage event. At the same time, overall labor costs are kept at a minimum by utilizing skills on an "as needed" basis or by contract for the completion of specific services. From 1979 to 1995, the number of entertainment-related films tripled in Southern California. Most of the firms in the film industry, however, employ fewer than ten people.[34] Independent production companies, which produced only 28 percent of all U.S. films in 1960, were making 58 percent of the films just two decades later, while the majors were producing fewer than 31 percent of the films.[35]

It should be emphasized, however, that although the network approach to commercial organization has brought an increasing number of smaller firms into the industry, the major studios and entertainment companies still exercise control over much of the process by their abilities to partially finance production and to control distribution of the product. In fact, film industry analysts Asu Aksoy and Kevin Robins make the point that vertical disintegration and the shift to network forms of organization were consciously pursued goals to allow the studio giants to better generate product while minimizing financial risks. The key to maintaining effective control over the industry, say Aksoy and Robins, has always revolved around controlling access to the distribution channels.

> By holding on to their power as national and international distribution networks, the majors were able to use their financial muscle to dominate the film business and to squeeze or to use the independent production companies.[36]

Robins and Aksoy contend that industry statistics are often misleading. Despite the fact that independent film companies produce the bulk of new films, the majors still reap most of the profit. In 1990, for example, the top five companies earned 69.7 percent of the box office returns.[37] The network approach to organizing commerce—as we will see repeatedly throughout the book—allows the biggest transnational companies to rid themselves of physical plants, equipment, and talent by creating strategic relationships with suppliers to produce content. In a world of increasing competition, more diversified products and services, and shorter product life cycles, companies stay on top by controlling finance and distribution channels while pushing off onto smaller entities the burdens of ownership and management of physical assets.

The Hollywood network approach to commercial organization is leading the way toward a new network-based economy in cyberspace, just as General Motors' hierarchical form of organization did at the onset of the second industrial revolution in the 1920s. In an article entitled "Why Every Business Will Be Like Show Business" in *Inc.* magazine, Joel Kotkin writes:

> Hollywood [has mutated] from an industry of classic huge vertically integrated corporations into the world's best example of a network econ-

omy. . . . Eventually, every knowledge-intensive industry will end up in the same flattened atomized state. Hollywood just has gotten there first.[38]

The Hollywood organizational model is quickly being adopted by a number of the cutting-edge industries of the twenty-first century. Andy Grove, former chairman of Intel, compares the software industry to the theater, where directors, actors, musicians, writers, technicians, and financial backers are brought together for a brief moment of time to create a new production. Even though the number of successes are few and far between, says Grove, the process also creates smash hits.[39] In his book *Jamming: The Art and Discipline of Business Creativity,* John Kao of the Harvard Business School urges CEOs to integrate the Hollywood network model into their long-term strategic plans. "You need to act like today's version of a Hollywood studio," says Kao.[40]

In the new network-based economy, Max Weber's idea of "organization" as a relatively fixed structure with set rules and procedures begins to disintegrate. In the fast-changing world of electronic commerce, enterprises have to be far more protean in nature, able to change shape and form at a moment's notice to accommodate new economic conditions. In geographic markets, structure still counts. In cyberspace, however, boundaries fall and process replaces structure as the standard operating procedure for survival. Organization becomes as ephemeral and fleeting as the electronic medium in which business is conducted.

Management consultant Tom Peters aptly describes the new network approach to commerce. In the future, says Peters, "networks of bits and pieces of companies will come together to exploit a market opportunity, perhaps stay together for a couple of years (though changing shape, dramatically, several times in the process), then dissolve, never to exist again in the same form."[41]

Everywhere in the world, companies large and small are in a frenzied scramble to become part of expanding commercial networks. In the Age of Access, a company's biggest concern is not being included in the commercial webs and relationships that create economic opportunities. Having access to networks is becoming as important in cyberspace commerce as enjoying market advantage was in the industrial era. Being left out of the loop can mean instant failure in this new world of ever changing alliances.

A final point needs to be made about the Hollywood organizational model that is too often glossed over or missed altogether in discussions of management strategies. It's no mere coincidence that other industries try to model the way the entertainment industry is organized. The cultural industries—including the recording industry, the arts, television, and radio—commodify, package, and market experiences as opposed to physical products or services. Their stock and trade is selling short-term access to simulated worlds and altered states of consciousness. The fact is, they are an ideal organizational model for a global economy that is metamorphosing from commodifying goods and services to commodifying cultural experience itself.

In cyberspace, the relationships between suppliers and users increasingly resemble the kinds of relationships that the culture industries have forged with audiences over the years. We are entering a more cerebral period of capitalism whose product is access to time and mind. The manufacture and transfer of physical goods between sellers and buyers (property), while still part of our day-to-day reality, especially in geographically based markets, will continue to migrate to the second tier of economic activity. The first tier will increasingly be made up of the selling and buying of human experiences. The movie industry is the front-runner in a new era in which each consumer's life experience will be commodified and transformed into an unending series of theatrical moments, dramatic events, and personal transformations. As the rest of the economy begins to make the shift from geographic markets to cyberspace and from selling goods and services to commodifying whole areas of human experiences, the Hollywood studio model of organization will increasingly be looked to as a standard for organizing commercial activity.[42]

Chapter Three

The Weightless
Economy

The physical economy is shrinking. If the industrial era was character-ized by the amassing of physical capital and property, the new era prizes intangible forms of power bound up in bundles of information and intellectual assets. The fact is, physical products, which for so long were a measure of wealth in the industrial world, are dematerializing.

In October 1996, Alan Greenspan, the chairman of the Federal Reserve Board, took note of a powerful change taking place in the U.S. and global economies—their increasing weightlessness. New, lighter construction materials, miniaturization, the substitution of information for physical content, and the expanding role of services all are contributing to a shrinkage in the physicality of economic output. He observed that "while the weight of current economic output is probably only modestly higher than it was half a century ago, value added adjusted for price change has risen well over threefold."[1] According to the Organization for Economic Cooperation and Development, the average weight of a real dollar of U.S. exports halved between 1990 and 1996.[2]

In her book, *The Weightless World,* Diane Coyle reminds us that until recently, nations measured exports against imports based on sheer weight. Incredibly, the British government was still using weight to measure the value of exports versus imports as late as 1985. Even computer imports were being assessed by weight. Today the idea of measuring the value of computers based on weight would be considered daffy, when a birthday greeting card with a microchip contains more computer power than existed in the whole world in 1945.

Computers are among the countless physical items that are dematerializing and heading toward weightlessness. We need only recall that the original IBM personal computer, introduced in 1981, weighed 44.3 pounds. A 1995 Macintosh Power Book 5300C, by contrast, weighs a mere 6.2 pounds and has more than 500 times more brainpower.[3] Or consider the fact that a few pounds of fiber-optic cable has more transmission capability than a ton of copper.[4]

Shrinking Real Estate

Products aren't the only things dematerializing in the new weightless world of electronic commerce. Real estate also is shrinking. Companies have introduced a spate of new innovative designs to better accommodate the more open network type of organizational structure. In offices, private space is disappearing. The idea of enclosed industrial offices walled off from fellow workers went well with a hierarchical form of corporate organization. In a network environment, however, private space gives over to social space. Project teams working together, continually sharing information, knowledge, and expertise, require open areas that encourage face-to-face communication. In the new office setting, possession of private space and the ability to exclude others—hallmarks of an ownership mentality—are anathema to the corporate mission. In the Age of Access, a premium is placed on having immediate and open-ended access to colleagues.

Many companies have designed the new office space to encourage networking within the company. At Procter and Gamble's new facility north of Cincinnati, members of teams work together in open cubicles—sometimes called "harbors." Files are on wheels to allow for greater mobility. Special meeting rooms and large areas are strategically placed to facilitate brainstorming sessions. Even the corridors have been made wider and have couches to encourage "pickup" conversation. J. P. Jones, Procter and Gamble's research and development vice president for over-the-counter health-care products, says the network approach to open spaces will likely result in a 20 to 30 percent gain in productivity because "data sharing is immediate, and higher-quality decisions are made faster."[5]

Management also is implementing other ideas to reduce office space. Many companies like IBM have literally eliminated personal desk space altogether and sent their employees packing. Workers are given cell phones and laptops and encouraged to spend their time more efficiently working out of their homes or in their clients' offices. IBM and other companies also have introduced hoteling. Employees can reserve workstations, offices, or meeting rooms by calling ahead. Some hoteling operations run like real hotels. At Ernst and Young's Washington office, a concierge is always on duty to "take care of guests." Upon arrival, employees will find their names on the doors, and files and any supplies they might have requested on their desks. Their phone numbers have been forwarded, and digitized photos of their children or spouses are there to greet them on the computer screens.[6] IBM now has more than 20,000 sales and service personnel around the country who use shared offices in a hoteling arrangement. A study published in the *Harvard Business Review* found that by shifting to hoteling, closing down unutilized offices, and moving to less expensive locations, IBM has saved $1.4 billion in its real estate expenses.[7]

The dematerialization of office space is being hurried along also by the shift from paper files to electronic storage. Although the paperless office is not yet in sight, forecasters predict that more than 50 percent of all data will be electronically stored by the year 2005.[8]

Finally, companies continue to flatten their organizational structures and replace blue- and white-collar workers with intelligent technologies, reducing both their workforces and their real-estate needs. A British study suggests that physical facilities will shrink by at least 25 percent in the coming years as firms make the transitions to electronic commerce and to a network approach to organizational activity.[9]

Just-in-Time Inventory

Physical assets, in the form of property, are shrinking or disappearing altogether at every stage and in every corner of the capitalist system. Take, for example, inventory. Companies used to have giant warehouses stocked with material goods. Now, electronic scanners at the point of sale transmit instant up-to-the-moment information on reorders to suppliers, who then manufacture the products in hours or days and deliver them directly to the retailers, bypassing the warehouses altogether.

Using electronic data to monitor and track consumers and production schedules, GE has been able to create a state-of-the-art just-in-time inventory process, saving the company the high cost of maintaining large inventories and warehouses to stock their product lines. Between 1987 and 1997, the company closed twenty-six of its thirty-four warehouses in the U.S. and replaced twenty-five customer-service centers with one central hub.[10]

Japan's National Bicycle Company has leaped ahead of just-in-time inventory with its customized made-to-order system. A customer can enter a retail showroom and, with the assistance of a computer-aided design system, be fitted to the size and shape of bicycle best suited to his physiology. The buyer can design his own bike by choosing among different types of brakes, chains, tires, and derailleurs. The information is electronically transmitted to the factory, where the made-to-order bicycle is manufactured, assembled, and shipped in less than three hours.[11] With made-to-order systems, inventory and warehouses are eliminated.

In May 1999, Universal Music, a unit of the Seagram company, and Sony Music Entertainment both announced that they would be distributing music online in digital form. Sony will use Microsoft's Windows Media 4.0 to upload singles of some of its most popular recording artists, including Mariah Carey, Celine Dion, and Will Smith. According to Marketing Tracking International (MTI), a research consulting firm, digital distribution of music over the Internet will exceed $4 billion and account for more than 8 percent of all recorded music sold in the world by the year 2004. By the year 2010, MTI projects that more than 20 percent of all music sold will be by way of digital distribution over the Internet.[12]

Digital distribution of music to consumers, via the Internet, allows recording companies to do away with suppliers, warehouses, inventories, distributors, and shippers, saving on the costs of handling a physical version of the recording. The electronic transmission of music products is still another example of the new weightless capitalism that is emerging in the cyberspace economy.

Electronic commerce is growing even faster than its most ardent supporters had predicted. The number of commercial sites on the Internet has ballooned from 2,000 in 1995 to more than 400,000 in 1998. Equally impressive is the fact that 46 percent of online stores are actually making money.[13] Their success can be attributed to the increase in consumer traffic in cyberspace. In 1995 only 14.3 million people were browsing the Web. By the end of 1997, however, more than 41 million people were shopping in the electronic aisles.[14]

Cyberspace commerce already is posing a significant threat to the nation's retail stores. Many retailers are finding it increasingly difficult to compete with virtual stores that have fewer or no physical assets, little or no inventory or real estate, and therefore greatly reduced overhead costs. Holding property of all kinds is a hindrance for a growing number of retailers in the new era of near weightless commerce. Not surprising, retail sales have been steadily declining in recent years as customers are making fewer visits to the stores and more purchases online. In the early 1980s, shoppers averaged more than 1.5 hours per visit at the shopping mall. By the 1990s, the average had dropped to 71 minutes and the number of stores visited declined from 3.6 to 2.6. Meanwhile, electronic purchases by credit cards jumped 30 percent during roughly the same period.[15] Anxious not to be left behind, many of the nation's best-known retailers like Macy's are entering the electronic shopping market with twenty-four-hour cable TV shopping channels and with online ordering.

Toys "R" Us, the giant toy retailer, suddenly awoke to the power of e-commerce when a small online retailer called eToy shot out of nowhere during Christmas 1998 to claim a significant share of the peak season toy business. So giddy were prospective investors over the potential success of the upstart e-commerce company that eToy scored a market cap of $7.8 billion on its first trading day in May 1999, leaving Toys "R" Us in the dust at $5.6 billion. Worried that his company might face serious and sustained long-term losses and even extinction, Toys "R" Us CEO Robert C. Nakasone responded in kind, entering into a partnership with Benchmark Capital, a Silicon Valley venture capitalist company, to finance an $80 million online business of his own.[16]

Although trend forecasters are quick to point out that large numbers of consumers will continue to buy at department stores and malls, because they both prefer to see and handle the merchandise and enjoy browsing as a recreational activity, there is a growing realization that the retail market will likely contract in the wake of increasing electronic commerce in cyberspace. Quite simply, convenience and cheaper prices are likely to favor the new marketspace. That being the case, it's also likely that many of the shopping centers built to accommodate the highway culture of the post–World War II era will suffer a marked decline in traffic, forcing them either to close their doors or to shift to selling entertainment and other kinds of experiential commodities.

What is becoming increasingly apparent is that commercial real estate, once the centerpiece of the private-property regime and long regarded as a bellwether of the health of the capitalist system, is less a measure of prosperity in the Age of Access—at least in some industries—and more often an obstacle in the pursuit of profit. In the era of geographically based markets, entrepreneurs of every stripe and color at least agreed on one thing: that commercial success was largely determined by location, location, location! The fact that real estate is now regarded more as a burden for some businesses and a thing to shrink, shed, or avoid says much about the nature of the transition from an era based on geographic markets to one based on cyberspace networks.

The Dematerialization of Money

Money, too, is dematerializing in the new wired economy. Recall that in the early stages of exchange, money was solid and often bulky. Natives of West Africa used iron bars as money in the eighteenth century. Cultures in both Africa and Europe used cattle as a source of money. The very term *cattle* comes from the same root as *chattel* and *capital* and remains a medium of exchange even today among some peoples. Salt and linen cloth also have been used as money. The phrase "a piece of India" referred to the amount of cotton cloth (from the Indies) that was equivalent to the price of a slave, and was used by slave traders as a medium of exchange.[17] Tobacco, sugar, cocoa, and fur pelts also were popular forms of money among colonial traders and natives in the New World. Copper, gold, and silver have been the most durable and popular forms of money and have been used for coinage through much of Western history.

The increased pace and volume of trade and commerce in the mercantile era of the sixteenth and seventeenth centuries led to the introduction of lighter, more flexible currency in the form of promissory notes and bills. Checks were introduced in the first half of the twentieth century, and credit cards in the second half, making money even more mobile and less material.

In the new cyberspace economy, money is becoming even less physical. Every day, more than $1.9 trillion passes through electronic networks in New York City. Every two weeks, observes Walter Joel Kurtzman in his book *The Death of Money*, "the annual product of the world passes through the network in New York" without ever taking concrete form—a far different reality from the time, just a short while ago, when gold bars were being transferred from bank to bank and country to country to back up trade and currency exchanges.[18] The new dematerialized form of money, notes Kurtzman, is "nothing more than an assemblage of ones and zeros, the fundamental units of computing . . . that are piped through miles of wire, pumped over fiber-optic highways, bounced off satellites, and beamed from one microwave relay station to another."[19] Kurtzman likens this new money to a shadow. "Its cool-gray shape can be seen but not touched. It has no tactile dimension, no heft or weight. . . . Money," he says, "is now an image."[20]

The final dematerialization of money is the result of two developments—one political, the other technical. On August 15, 1971, President Richard Nixon closed the "gold window," ending the relationship between money and valuable metal. The value of the dollar, which long had been linked to the amount of gold in a country's reserves—in the U.S.'s case, the gold stored at Fort Knox—was decoupled and allowed to be traded without any tangible wealth in the form of gold to back it up.[21]

The new cyberspace economy also is creating the technology for a cash-free society. ATM machines, smart cards, and digital cash are remaking the rules of the money game. Businesses and consumers are increasingly exchanging goods and services and conducting a full range of business transactions electronically. Private forms of electronic cash with names like Digicash, Bitbux, Cybercash, Netbills, E-Cash, and Netchex are proliferating.[22] Meanwhile, we are seeing the emergence of the "soft bank," says William J. Mitchell, dean of the School of Architecture and Planning at the Massachusetts Institute of Technology, "a round-the-clock facility, accessible from indefinitely many locations, and providing electronically mediated withdrawals, deposits, bill payments, check cashing, point-of-sale transactions, travelers' checks, loan applications, statements, and whatever other financial services the banking industry can dream up and sell."[23]

In a global economy that is increasingly weightless, the money used to negotiate market transactions and other financial arrangements is likewise dematerializing into electronic bits capable of traveling at the speed of light in the form of pure information. Today, less than 10 percent of the American money supply is still in the form of currency. If all the coins and bills currently circulating were added up, it would amount to less than $400 billion. Much of that is no longer circulating in the United States but rather in other countries.[24] In another twenty-five years or so, hard material currency is likely to be regarded as an historical oddity, part of a bygone era where economic activity itself was far more physical in nature and material in form.

No More Savings

The dematerialization of money has gone hand in glove with the decline in savings and the rise in personal debt. The steady growth in the production of goods and services over the course of the past century has led to a number of innovations in commercial credit designed to spark greater consumption. The result has been that at the end of the century, Americans were saving far less of their income than they were at the beginning of the century. Property in the form of personal savings is fast becoming an anachronism in an era of ever accelerated economic activity where quick turnover, not accumulation, is the prevailing ethos.

Consumer credit first became a popular mechanism for financing purchases in the 1880s. Department stores like A. T. Stewart in New York City and Wanamaker's in Philadelphia began the practice of granting their better customers "charge privileges." In the first decade of the twentieth century, department stores began to introduce "installment clubs" to sell more expensive items like phonographs, sewing machines, and pianos. Customers could pay off their purchases in monthly installments over an extended period of time.[25] "Charge it" soon became a popular refrain in stores across the country. One credit analyst at the time mused that "Charge it" was the modern Aladdin's lamp. "Armed with these precious words an American citizen can go downtown with an empty pocketbook and return home reeking with luxury."[26]

By the mid-1920s, Americans were up to their ears in consumer debt. Marshall Field's in Chicago increased its charge accounts to 180,000, nearly double the figure at the beginning of the decade. Stores like Abraham & Straus and Lord & Taylor reported that 45 to 70 percent of their total retail business was from charge operations.[27]

The middle class, large numbers of which had eschewed even the notion of installment buying a decade earlier, had been won over to the new financing schemes, purchasing automobiles, washing machines, refrigerators, and dishwashers on credit.[28] Three-quarters of all the automobiles sold in 1925 were paid for by installment credit.[29] Between 1925 and 1930, private debt in the United States increased by 21 percent.[30] By 1932, 60 percent of the furniture, household appliances, and automobiles sold were bought on installment credit, as well as 75 percent of the radios and other electronic equipment.[31]

In 1928, National City Bank became the first commercial bank in the country to make personal loans. On the first day of business, more than 500 customers descended on the bank. Another 2,500 people applied for loans within the next three days, inaugurating a new era of personal lending. The press heralded the development as "a milestone in the democratization of credit."[32]

Consumer debt increased even more rapidly in the 1950s with the introduction of credit cards. In 1949, Alfred Bloomingdale introduced the Diners Club card, allowing customers to charge their meals, hotels, and other travel expenses at establishments across the country. In 1958, American Express and Carte Blanche joined the credit card race. These early cards, however, did not allow for revolving credit and the running up of account balances. Then, in 1958, Bank of America and Chase Manhattan Bank entered the field and introduced revolving credit. Bank Americard changed its name to Visa in 1976, and MasterCharge became MasterCard in 1980. By 1980, 52 million Americans counted themselves as cardholders.[33]

Credit cards have revolutionized the way Americans—and increasingly, other nations—relate to the marketplace. In an era of shorter product life cycles, quicker product turnovers, and ever more diverse product lines, revolving credit card debt has been the mechanism that has allowed millions of consumers to accelerate their purchases while paying exorbitant interest rates for the privilege of postponing their payments on goods and services purchased previously. According to a study conducted by the Consumer Federation of America, some 56 to 60 million households have credit card debt of more than $6,000 and pay more than $1,000 a year in interest and fees on that debt. The typical household burdened by debt has an annual disposable income of less than $20,000 and credit card debts of more than $10,000.[34]

Personal savings—one of the key measures of a private property regime—is disappearing as millions of consumers continue to spend beyond their incomes, with the help of credit cards. Today, according to the Federal Reserve Board, Americans are literally spending more than they are taking in, marking the first time since the Great Depression that the country has experienced a negative savings rate.[35] Consider that in 1944, Americans saved 25.5 percent of their after-tax income. In the early 1990s, the figure dropped to a savings rate of 6 percent of after-tax income. By October 1998, Americans were spending .2 percent more than they earned. Japanese households, in contrast, currently save 30 percent of their after-tax income.[36]

In addition, credit card companies continue to lower their lending requirements to bring more customers in, while extending credit lines to their existing customers. In 1996, consumers had available $1.2 trillion in used and unused credit lines on their cards.[37] At the same time, consumer credit has been growing at a 9 percent annual rate.[38] In 1998, total revolving credit was $531.1 billion, up from $503.8 billion twelve months earlier.[39]

Meanwhile, the standard of living of the average American family hasn't gone up appreciably since the late 1970s.[40] Despite this fact, Americans appear comfortable with the idea of spending more than they take in, as evidenced by the fact that while the Federal Reserve Board was reporting a negative family savings rate in 1999, both the University of Michigan and Conference Board surveys continued to show high consumer confidence. Some of that confidence, economists observe, can be attributed to the record gains in the stock market, which give Americans the feeling of being well off, despite negative savings. Still, says Lester Thurow, the former dean of MIT's Sloan School of Management, we need to remember that 90 percent of the gains in the stock market have gone to the top 10 percent of households, while the bottom 60 percent of Americans have not benefited at all from the bull market, as they own no stock.[41] Obviously, some other factor must account for the high consumer confidence existing alongside a negative savings rate.

The fact of the matter is, Americans—and increasingly, consumers in Europe and elsewhere—are becoming used to the idea of turning over their income to immediate consumption and living with less accumulated savings. As long as they can continue to enjoy access to credit lines, they see no compelling need to hold on to their income in the form of property-tied savings. This, at least, was the conclusion of a panel formed by Congress to look into the issue. It concluded that "unprecedented access" to consumer credit has turned many Americans from savers to debtors.[42] Even the filing of bankruptcy, once considered among the more shameful experiences that can befall a person in a propertied society, has lost its stigma. According to the American Bankruptcy Institute, 1.35 million Americans filed for bankruptcy in 1997, a 20 percent increase over the year before and a 145 percent increase over ten years earlier, when 549,831 Americans filed for bankruptcy.[43]

In a new era, where holding property, in all of its various forms, becomes less important than securing short-term access to commercial opportunities, savings also become less important to hold on to. As long as consumers are willing to transform earned income into immediate consumption, and as long as the banking system is willing to extend credit lines fast enough to keep up with production, argue some economists, savings is not all that important and may even be a drag on the growth of the economy. Although personal savings rates still remain somewhat higher in Europe, Asia, and Latin America than in the U.S., credit card companies and banks project that more and more consumers will be won over to credit card use by the early decades of the twenty-first century as they make the shift from propertied savings to short-term access to credit lines.

A Borrowed Existence

The dematerialization of property and money; the scramble to shrink office space, avoid inventories, and shed real estate; and the disappearance of personal savings are being accompanied by an even greater change. Physical capital itself, the most important type of property in the capitalist system and the wellspring upon which the entire edifice has been built, is likewise being eclipsed and relegated to a secondary status in many industries. When we think of physical capital, what comes to mind are the tools, machines, equipment, and factories that provide the infrastructure and operating capacity to produce goods and deliver services. A new generation of management consultants and economists, however, is counseling corporate clients to avoid amassing physical capital wherever possible. Business consultant and former Harvard Business School professor Stan Davis, and Christopher Meyer, director of the Ernst & Young Center for Business Innovation, say rather bluntly, "We need to walk away from the idea that owning or even controlling capital is a necessary resource for fulfilling market needs."[44] Davis and Meyer, like others, believe that in a fast-paced network economy, "it often doesn't pay to own capital equipment. . . . Ownership can prove to be an albatross, the sheer weight of which will hinder the firm's ability to move swiftly out of one business line and into another."[45] Davis and Meyer understand that in the new economy, "capital as inventory of capacity must give way to 'just-in-time' capital as access to the use of capacity."[46] Their first axiom about capital is "Use it, don't own it."[47] Columnist Thomas Stewart, writing in *Fortune* magazine, sums up the new sentiment that separates the old guard of the industrial economy from the new entrepreneurs and corporate leaders of the network economy: "One could say that businesses are moving to one side or the other of a dividing line: asset owners vs. asset renters."[48]

"Neither a borrower nor a lender be" might have been sound advice for a propertied age. In the Age of Access, however, the wisdom of an earlier era is literally turned on its head. Jean Baptiste Say, Adam Smith, David Ricardo, and the other classical economists of modern capitalism would be dumbstruck by such a thought. Nonetheless, a new kind of capitalism is journeying to the center stage of world history, as different in its operating assumptions as industrial capitalism was from its predecessor, the mercantile economy of the sixteenth and seventeenth centuries.

Many companies, for example, no longer think of purchasing capital equipment but rather borrow the physical capital they need in the form of a lease and charge it as a short-term expense, a cost of doing business. Today, nearly ⅓ of all the business machines, equipment, and transportation fleets in the U.S. are leased rather than owned. Translated into dollars, that means that of the $582.1 billion of investment in equipment made in 1997, nearly $180 billion was in the form of leases.[49] Virtually every type of business capital is now being leased, including industrial and office equipment, transportation equipment, real estate, machine tools, electronic production and control equipment, construction equipment, factories, office space, retail stores, freight cars, airplanes, tankers, automobiles, pipelines, X-ray equipment, computers, printers, and even dairy cows.[50] Eighty percent of American companies lease all or some of their equipment from more than 2,000 leasing companies.[51]

Leasing dates back to the beginning of human commerce but has come to play a significant role in the modern capitalist system only since the 1950s. More than 5,000 years ago, Sumerian princes and palace priests leased out "sacred land" to peasant farmers in exchange for a fee of approximately 1/7 of the harvest. Ship leases were common in ancient Persia, as was the leasing of dams and irrigation canals.[52]

In Babylonia, oxen were leased, and strict contracts regulating the relationship and responsibilities of the leasing parties were rigidly enforced. If an ox were killed by a lion, the owner would have to assume the loss. If, however, the leased ox were to die because of maltreatment, the lessee was held liable. If God had smitten the ox, the lessee would "swear himself freed before God—thereby transferring the liability to the lessor."[53]

The first leasing statute enacted in Britain in 1284—the Statute of Wales—allowed for land, houses, and chattel to be leased. Leasing as a vehicle to secure expensive capital equipment became prevalent in England first during the early development of railroads. Many railroad companies leased tracks from the company that laid the lines, and later leased rail cars as well. One of the earliest lessors, the Birmingham Wagon company, began leasing wagon cars in 1854. By 1862, more than two dozen wagon companies were competing with the Birmingham company in a lucrative leasing trade. In the last years of the nineteenth century, leasing was extended to a range of capital equipment, including looms for the cotton textile industry, telephone systems, electricity and gas meters, and transport vehicles.[54]

Leasing moved from the backwaters of capital investment to center stage after World War II. Often unable to secure conventional financing, entrepreneurs took to leasing. In a period of expanding business opportunities, companies saw leasing as a way to free up needed cash for their other operations. In addition, since equipment leases were not loans, they could appear on the books as operating expenses rather than fixed debt, making the company's financial picture look better. The lessors also bene-fited. Because lessors were not banks, they were not regulated by the government and could charge a high rate of return to compensate for the higher lending risks attached to leasing arrangements.[55]

Equipment manufacturers like IBM, Burroughs, Singer, NCR, and Olivetti began to offer their own leasing programs to customers in the late 1950s and early 1960s. In 1971, the U.S. banking laws were amended, allowing banks to establish holding companies that could own other kinds of financial-service businesses, including leasing companies. The entrance of the banking community into the leasing arena greatly enhanced its credibility as a financial institution, adding still further impetus to leasing as a new way to do business.[56]

Companies say that the principal reason they choose leasing over buying is that it allows them to be flexible in fast-changing markets and when faced with technological obsolescence.[57] "We can keep ahead of technology by not owning it and replacing it quickly at the termination of the lease and getting something newer," says David J. Burns, corporate comptroller at Timex, Inc., in Middlebury, Connecticut.[58] Many leases allow the lessee to cancel existing leases and upgrade equipment without any penalty.

Companies lease also for convenience. The lessor generally is responsible for upkeep and maintenance and sometimes is responsible for administration and management of the equipment and facilities as well. "These days," says former Bell Atlantic Capital CEO Robert Stubbs, "we're asset managers rather than just financing companies."[59]

Leasing has become a worldwide phenomenon. In fact, more than half the world's leasing is done by companies in Europe and Japan.[60] Leasing industries now exist in more than eighty countries. In a number of countries, leasing market penetration is approaching that of the United States. In Korea, 23 percent of all new capital equipment is leased. In Brazil, the figure is 20 percent; in Great Britain 19 percent; in Germany 15.9 percent; in Ireland 42.5 percent; in Canada 12.8 percent; in Italy 10.8 percent; in Sweden 20 percent; and in the Philippines 20 percent.[61]

One of the fastest growing areas in leasing is sale-leaseback arrangements. Companies are literally selling off their own facilities, then leasing them back from real-estate investment trust companies. Sale-leaseback contracts have mushroomed across the U.S. and are now finding fertile ground in many other countries.

Motel 6 negotiated a sale-leaseback of 288 of its locations—a total of 33,000 rooms—for $1.1 billion. The buyers included U.S. Realty, Norton Herrick & Sunder, and Phillip Morris.[62] Retail chains like Borders Books and Music, Eckerd, and Office Max are also negotiating sale-leaseback arrangements for many of their locations around the country.[63] Auto distributorships are doing the same. Potamkin sold the real estate to eight out of its eleven dealerships in November 1997 to Kimco-Auto Fund for $50 million, and leased them back under favorable long-term contracts. Allen Potamkin, co-chairman of the Potamkin chain, called the sale-leaseback a win-win situation. "This makes me more liquid. I'm a better credit risk to my lenders. I have more cash to expand, and I still control the business," said Potamkin.[64]

Many of the nation's leading utility companies also have entered into sale-leaseback arrangements, selling off their entire generating facilities to second parties and leasing them back. In effect, the utility becomes the manager of another company's physical plant and operating capital.

U.S. companies still own more than $1.7 trillion in property—or 70 percent of all the commercial property in the country. Michael Silver, the president of Equis, a real-estate consulting business in Chicago that manages large portfolios for Chrysler, Coca-Cola, and NationsBank, among others, asks CEOs to "think about what you could do releasing all that capital." Silver says that with sale-leasebacks, "you can shrink brick and mortar by selling to a hungry marketplace, and with what's remaining, you can lease—and lease flexibly."[65]

Outsourcing Ownership

Companies in every field and across every industry are racing to divest themselves of assets that are not strictly related to their core missions. The new thinking in the business community is "When in doubt, farm it out." If an asset or process isn't absolutely essential to advancing the primary goals of the company, it's best to turn it over to an outside contractor. In the emerging network economy, outsourcing is becoming a near religion.

Outsourcing is an agreement to contract with another party to perform functions or services that previously were done in-house—in other words, to substitute internal ownership of physical capital and operations with access to needed resources and processes from outside suppliers.

Ross Perot often is credited with pioneering the concept in the 1960s when his EDS corporation began to contract with government agencies and corporate clients to handle their data processing services out of house. Today, outsourcing has become the organizational centerpiece of an emerging network economy. Companies are stripping down their physical assets and functions, flattening out their corporate hierarchies, and connecting their operations to suppliers in increasingly intricate shared networks and relationships. The new computer, software, and telecommunications technologies allow firms to create a near seamless web between their own operations and outsource companies. Electronic data processing and instant feedback loops keep users and suppliers in constant communication, making possible the idea of an extended company of servers and clients working together to maintain day-to-day operations in real time.

As advances in electronic technologies continue to reduce the transaction costs involved in outsourcing, more and more firms are likely to hand over much of their internal non-core operations to other parties. Outsourcing, says the Outsourcing Institute, "is nothing less than a basic redefinition of the corporation."[66] The old idea of autonomous, boundaried business enterprises is giving way to the notion of multiple partners embedded deep in one another's operations and engaged in both formal and informal reciprocal relationships.

The maintenance and repair of computer equipment, training, applications development, consulting, and engineering all are being outsourced by a growing number of companies. Much of corporate operations also is being outsourced, including mailroom functions, printing and reprographics, records management, supply and inventory, and administrative systems. In customer services, companies are outsourcing telephone customer support. In the finance area, payroll processing, taxes, purchasing, and general accounting likewise are moving out of house and being handled by outsourcers. In human resource management, recruiting, staffing, training, and relocation of employees are being done by outside parties. In sales and marketing programs, advertising, direct mail, and telemarketing are being put in the hands of specialized marketing companies. In real estate and physical plants, companies are outsourcing security, facilities maintenance, and food services. In transportation, companies are letting contractors manage fleet maintenance and operations.[67]

Companies cite several advantages to outsourcing their business operations. Outsourcing allows the firm to focus more on what it does to make money and lets others handle support functions that, while critical to the maintenance of the organization, are not revenue producing. Second, by outsourcing operations, firms gain access to suppliers who, by virtue of their specialized expertise, can provide world-class services at reduced costs. Outsourcing reduces the need to buy expensive equipment and build extensive infrastructure for operations that are peripheral to the revenue-generating mission of the company. Finally, like leasing, outsourcing provides companies with the flexibility they need in fast-changing markets characterized by ever shorter product life cycles. Being stuck with outdated plants, obsolete equipment, and antiquated business systems and processes is a prescription for failure. By shifting from long-term ownership to short-term access through outsourcing, companies stay a leg up on the competition.

The outsourcing business is booming. Dun and Bradstreet estimates that there are currently more than 146,000 companies in the United States in the outsourcing business.[68] Outsourcing is expected to top 300 billion in revenue by the end of the year 2000.[69] Of the 1.6 million companies using outsourcing services of one kind or another, the largest group of firms employs fewer than ten people.[70] Large companies, however, also are outsourcing more of their internal operations. Three out of ten U.S. industrial companies already outsource more than half of their production activity.[71]

Outsourcing is not simply an American phenomenon. Two-thirds of companies worldwide are currently outsourcing one or more primary internal business processes. For example, more than 60 percent of Japanese companies engage in business-process outsourcing.[72]

Nowhere has outsourcing had a more significant impact than in manufacturing. In an industry where commercial prowess has long been measured by the ownership of physical capital, the rules of the capitalist game have been fundamentally changed. In less than a decade, some of the biggest names in the manufacturing sector have successfully metamorphosed into design studios and distribution houses, leaving plant and property behind and handing over the manufacturing to outside contractors.[73] The new supercontractors are giant manufacturing outsourcers that operate factories and manage supply networks all over the world.

The future in manufacturing lies with supercontractors like Ingram, the Santa Ana, California, outsourcer that churns out custom-made batches of computers emblazoned with logos ranging from IBM to Compaq. Just a few years ago, the very idea of a single factory manufacturing competitors' brands on the same assembly line would have been unimaginable. Today, it is becoming commonplace. Ingram is a full-service contractor. It will manufacture and distribute—under contract with retailers—directly to the end-use customer and will even bill, answer customer inquiries in the name of its clients, and set up and manage their Web sites. Sitting in the midst of Ingram's giant warehouse that's "big enough to house a fleet of jets," technology reporter Saul Hansell mused in a recent article in the *New York Times* that "here . . . is a glimpse of the future of American industry, where manufacturers don't make anything and retailers don't touch the goods they sell."[74]

In the new network economy what is really being bought and sold are ideas and images. The physical embodiment of these ideas and images becomes increasingly secondary to the economic process. If the industrial marketplace was characterized by the exchange of things, the network economy is characterized by access to concepts, carried inside physical forms.

Nike is perhaps the best example of the new commercial forces at work. Nike is, for all intents and purposes, a virtual company. While the public is likely to think of the company as a manufacturer of athletic footwear, in point of fact, the company is really a research and design studio with a sophisticated marketing formula and distribution mechanism. Although it is the world's leading manufacturer of athletic shoes, Nike owns no factories, machines, equipment, or real estate to speak of. Instead, it has established an extensive network of suppliers—which it calls "production partners"—in Southeast Asia who produce its hundreds of designer shoes and other gear. Nike also outsources much of its advertising and marketing operations. Indeed, the company's success in the 1990s is attributable in no small measure to the innovative advertising campaigns of Weiden and Kennedy, the advertising firm that helped make Nike the most coveted gym shoe in the world.[75]

Nike sells concepts. The company contracts with anonymous manufacturers in Southeast Asia to produce the physical forms of its concepts.

This new type of network approach to doing business, with its emphasis on nameless suppliers to produce the physical products, can sometimes result in the exploitation of workers.

Nike is one of scores of virtual "manufacturers" who have been subjected to lawsuits, boycotts, and public condemnation for engaging in unfair labor practices. Recently, worker protests at their overseas contractor plants led to media reports of widespread physical and sexual abuse of workers, inhumane working conditions, hazardous work environments, low wages, and quota systems for hiring of personnel. More than 450,000 Asian workers produce Nike's celebrated shoe lines. Although Nike's revenues in the U.S. alone were more than $4 billion in 1998, workers in its subcontracting plants in Vietnam were making between $1.60 and $2.25 in wages per day, less than it costs to provide three basic meals. In some of the plants, girls as young as thirteen were working more than sixty hours per week, and many were sexually molested. Unfortunately, the deplorable working conditions in outsourcing plants often are never detected because the corporate supply networks are closely guarded and kept hidden from the public.[76]

The outsourcing fervor has provided opportunities for new kinds of companies to create specialized niche markets. Norrell, an Atlanta-based firm that started as a small employment agency in 1961 and by the late 1980s had grown into a major temporary employment agency with local franchises around the country, took on outsourcing backroom operations in the 1990s. The company contracted with Sears in 1990 to take over the giant department store's switchboard, secretarial, photocopying, shipping, and receiving departments. In 1992, Norrell signed on with IBM in a $75 million outsourcing arrangement in which it would manage Big Blue's secretarial pools, process their office and travel expenses, and handle calls for their marketing and field-support divisions. As part of the deal, IBM was given a 5 percent equity holding in Norrell. Currently, more than 3,000 Norrell employees work at IBM, doing jobs that previously required 3,750 IBM workers. Norrell manages similar backroom outsourcing operations for other corporate leaders, including MCI, Bell Atlantic, UPS, and Equitable.[77]

While these kinds of outsourcing arrangements appear innocuous, they oftentimes mask a more covert agenda. Outsourcing has become a favored management tool to weaken the power of organized labor. By contracting services out to non-union shops, or hiring non-unionized companies to administer services on-site, companies can avoid collective bargaining agreements. Much of the decline of the trade union movement in the United States and countries around the world in recent years is directly attributable to the outsourcing phenomenon.

Recently, outsourcing has begun to migrate to cyberspace. EDS, the outsourcing pioneer, is negotiating with companies to manage their electronic commerce. EDS's Dallas-based c20 Internet consulting and services division entered into a $30 million agreement with Hachette Filipacchi Magazines, whose publications include *Road and Track* and *Travel Holiday,* to oversee the company's commercial Web sites. Under the agreement, the New York publisher won't have to pay anything up front. Instead, EDS will get a share of the media company's revenues generated from online sales of auto accessories, vacation packages, and cookbooks. The deal struck by Hachette and EDS for cosourcing—as opposed to more conventional outsourcing—represents the next wave in network relationships in cyberspace. Hachette's president, Jim Dochery, says of the agreement:

> *We were paying them for a while to develop and host our sites, but then a lightbulb went off in both places. We had the content and advertisements, but not the technology. And they had no content. This way, they don't pay for content, and we don't pay for technology. Everybody makes out on the deal.*[78]

In the Hachette/EDS deal, the traditional seller-buyer relationship was replaced by a supplier-user partnership. No capital or property of any kind exchanged hands. Each became a supplier as well as a user of the other's assets in this cosourcing arrangement. Each gained access to the other's core competencies and revenue-generating practices. It was the fusing together of both companies' core missions that created a new business opportunity. In this case, as in countless other partnerships that are forming in the new network economy and in cyberspace, access, not ownership, is the ultimate key to commercial success.

In the Age of Access, notes manufacturing consultant Earl Hall, "a manufacturing company [and for that manner any other company] will not be an isolated facility of production, but rather a node in the complex network of suppliers, customers, engineering, and other service functions."[79] Securing access to others in the new network economy means sharing information and building trust between parties who formerly engaged each other in adversarial terms as sellers and buyers. In their book, *The Virtual Corporation,* management consultant William Davidow and journalist Michael Malone argue that "The virtual corporation will appear less a discrete enterprise and more an ever-varying cluster of common activities in the midst of a vast fabric of relationships."[80]

Because a market-oriented private-property regime, by its very nature, organizes economic activity into mine and thine, it is increasingly out of place in a network-based economy, where commercial success is increasingly measured by the idea of what is mine is yours and what is yours is mine. It is the sharing of economic activity that is the defining feature of network-based commerce.

Intangible Assets

The dramatic change from ownership to leasing of physical capital and outsourcing of operations, in less than forty years, represents a sea change in the history of modern capitalism. Microsoft is a good example of the new logic at work in the emerging network economy—a logic that eschews long-term ownership of property in favor of short-term access to productive capital. Like other new high-tech companies, Microsoft spends most of its energy on creating intangible assets. Contrast the market capitalization and balance sheets of Microsoft with those of an older company like IBM. IBM's total market capitalization in November 1996 was $70.7 billion, and Microsoft's was $85.5 billion. On the other hand, IBM owned $16.6 billion in plants, equipment, and property, while Microsoft's fixed assets were a mere $930 million. Investors, however, were willing to pay more for Microsoft stock, despite the fact that it has far fewer fixed assets to its name—the traditional way of measuring the overall value of a company's stock.[81] Clearly, what investors are paying for when they purchase Microsoft stock are its intangible assets, the goodwill, ideas, talent, and expertise of the people who make up the company. Author and journalist Fred Moody put it best in an article in the *New York Times Magazine* when he wrote that "Microsoft's only factory asset is the human imagination."[82] So we see once again that the new commerce of the twenty-first century favors "lighter" companies, where value is measured in ideas rather than in hard physical assets.

The shift in value from tangible to intangible assets is beginning to show up across the global economy. Margaret Blair of the Brookings Institution found that whereas in 1982 tangible assets—property, plants, and equipment—of mining and manufacturing companies accounted for 62.3 percent of the enterprises' market value, ten years later, tangible assets had dropped to 37.9 percent of the market values of the same companies.[83] Leif Edvinsson, the director of intellectual capital for Skandia AFS, the Swedish financial-services company, estimates that for most companies the ratio of intellectual to physical and financial capital is between five to one and sixteen to one.[84]

The difference between market value and book value is called the Q ratio and was developed by economist and Nobel Laureate James Tobin of Yale University more than thirty years ago. In the days when physical assets made a difference, the Q ratio served as a barometer of whether a particular stock was overpriced and therefore ripe for a downward adjustment. Today, many of the best performing companies in the world have extraordinarily high Q ratios but are still considered good investments because of their intangible assets, which are immeasurable but are a more accurate gauge of the companies' future performance. Look at General Motors. Here's a company with $178 billion in sales in 1997, making it the number-one revenue-producing firm in the world. Its market capitalization, however, is less than half that amount. GM is the classic example of the old-fashioned company with large amounts of funds tied up in factory, machines, equipment, warehouses, and other fixed assets. On its balance sheet, GM appears healthy. It owns a lot of property. In the reality of the new global economy, however, GM's physical assets are a liability. Chrysler, on the other hand, which has divested itself of most of its property—by outsourcing to suppliers—and is more of a design studio and marketing channel, looks less prosperous on paper but is making a handsome profit in the marketplace. (It's interesting to note that although GM is number one in sales revenue in the world, its stock market value does not even earn it a slot in the top forty companies on the New York Stock Exchange.)[85]

The growing disparity between book value and market value is even more pronounced in other industrial sectors. Consider DreamWorks SKG, the film production company owned jointly by Steven Spielberg, Jeffrey Katzenberg, and David Geffen. The first public offering of the new company's stock was valued at $2 billion despite the fact that the enterprise had not a single piece of property to its name.[86] Again, investors were willing to pay to grab hold of a piece of the talent and expertise of the founders. George Gilder suggests we think of the gap between a company's market value and book value as the "index of the entrepreneurial dynamite in a capital stock."[87] In other words, investors are gambling on the future potential earnings of the company and basing their investment decisions on a host of intangible assets that are difficult to measure by conventional accounting standards.

In the future, says management consultant Adrian Slywotzky, the race is likely to go to the new weightless companies who are unencumbered by ownership of large amounts of property. "For a lot of asset-intensive businesses, like real estate, chemicals, or steel, making money will be tougher," argues Slywotzky, because so much of their worth is tied up in physical property and all kinds of physical assets.[88]

The transition from an economy in which wealth and success are measured in terms of ownership of physical capital to one where success is measured increasingly by control of ideas in the form of intellectual and intangible capital is beginning to undermine conventional accounting practices. In a network economy, because ideas and talent often are more important than plant and material, but also are more difficult to quantify, commercial judgments can become far more subjective and risky. The problem, says Judy Lewent, the chief financial officer of Merck and Company, is that "the accounting system doesn't capture anything, really."[89]

The traditional corporate balance sheet reports on the flow of funds and goods through the enterprise. It gives a picture of the fixed assets and property owned by the company as well as the various outstanding claims against the firm. Classical accounting procedures work well in an economy that produces and trades primarily in physical things between sellers and buyers. But in an economy in which exchanging goods is less important than sharing access to services and experiences between servers and clients, the old-fashioned double-entry bookkeeping is inadequate.

The new information-based industries—finance, entertainment, communications, business services, and education—already make up more than 25 percent of the U.S. economy. Much of their value is tied up in intangible assets and therefore not accurately presented in their accounting. The life-science industries—agricultural biotechnology, fiber, construction materials, energy, and pharmaceuticals—also rely far more on intangible assets, especially intellectual property and scientific know-how, and account for an additional 15 percent of the economy.[90] Together, the information sciences and life sciences—computers and genes—will dominate much of the commercial life of the twenty-first century. Both are based less on ownership of physical property and more on access to valuable information, be it embedded in software or wetware. How, for example, would the old accounting procedures measure the value of owning, in the form of intellectual property, the 140,000 or so genes that make up the blueprint of the human race?

The problem, then, says venture capitalist William Davidow, is that "information-age accountants are faced with a difficult challenge: live with the old system and distort the truth, or develop a new system fraught with the dangers of measuring intangibles." Davidow believes that "what we need . . . is a totally different system for measuring business."[91] It should be noted that most financial analysts, accountants, and managers are reluctant to introduce new accounting procedures to better reflect the contributions of intangible assets to a firm's profile because their values are subjective and open to misinterpretation and misuse as well as fraudulent reporting, and could subject the company to external audits or shareholder litigation.

The obstacles notwithstanding, some economists and business forecasters have begun to take on the new accounting task. Leif Edvinsson and Michael Malone have put together a prototype intellectual-capital reporting model based on the one currently being used by Edvinsson's own company, Skandia. They admit that their model "fails to capture many of the characteristics that make companies a success, including employee morale, dynamic and forward-thinking leadership, and an environment that supports innovation and creativity."[92] And they are quick to point out that is not intended to be a substitute for traditional bookkeeping but rather a complement that can provide a more transparent picture of the true worth of a company.

In the new accounting models of the network-based economy, physical capital is going to steadily migrate from the assets side of the ledger to the expense column, where they will be listed as a cost of operation, while intangible forms of capital will increasingly find their way onto the assets page.

Mind over Matter

The struggle to redefine our methods of accounting is reflective of the larger changes taking place as we make the transition from an era characterized by physical power to one based on mental acumen. The industrial era was a world of brute strength, of body and brawn. We fashioned giant tools to unearth, expropriate, and transform the physical world into material goods. It was an age in which we measured our accomplishments by height, weight, and grade in the sure conviction that "bigger is better." We poured concrete over every available space, creating a great industrial floor between ourselves and the natural world. We laid highways across great expanses. We built up to the sky and out to the horizon, making large swaths of the natural world a propertied domain. The pungent smell of burning fuel, the sight of industrial exhaust darkening the skies, and the unrelenting sounds of machines hissing, belching, and clanging day and night all were reminders of the grand experiment underway to remake the physical world in our own image. We reconstituted nature in the form of accumulated pieces of physical property, and each individual became a minor god, an overseer of his or her own little private Eden, each stocked with reworked mementos taken from the original creation.

In an era of property and markets steeped in material values, being omnipresent was the godlike goal. Being able to inflate one's physical presence by expropriating as much material existence as possible is what every propertied person yearned for. It was indeed, to quote Madonna, a "material world."

The new era, by contrast, is more immaterial and cerebral. It is a world of platonic forms; of ideas, images, and archetypes; of concepts and fictions. If the people of the industrial era were preoccupied with expropriating and reshaping matter, the first generation of the Age of Access is far more interested in manipulating mind. In the era of access and networks, where ideas are the grist for commerce, being all-knowing is the godlike goal. To be able to expand one's mental presence, to be universally connected so as to affect and shape human consciousness itself, is what motivates commercial activity in every industry.

We all live by ideas and thoughts as well as by bread and wine. If the industrial era nourished our physical being, the Age of Access feeds our mental, emotional, and spiritual being. While controlling the exchange of goods characterized the age just passing, controlling the exchange of concepts characterizes the new age coming. In the twenty-first century, institutions increasingly trade in ideas, and people, in turn, increasingly buy access to those ideas and the physical embodiments in which they are contained. The ability to control and sell thoughts is the ultimate expression of the new commercial prowess.

The accounting sheets tell the story. Physical property is becoming less important and less valued. Intellectual property, on the other hand, is the new ethereal gold. It is mind over matter in the new era. Lighter products, miniaturization, shrinking real estate, just-in-time inventories, leasing, and outsourcing all are evidence of the devaluation of the material worldview with its emphasis on physicality. That's not to suggest, however, that selfishness, greed, and commercial exploitation are shrinking as well. In truth, the Age of Access is likely to be far more exploitative. Controlling ideas, in today's world, is more powerful than controlling space and physical capital. The financial community's willingness to invest in pure intellectual capital, to the tune of hundreds of billions of dollars, is testimony to the changing sensibilities of a capitalist system whose very identity has been bound up in physical capital for so long.

The growing importance of ideas in the commercial sphere conjures a troubling specter. When human thought becomes such an important commodity, what happens to ideas that, while important, may not be commercially attractive? Is there any room left for noncommercial views, opinions, notions, and concepts in a civilization where people rely increasingly on the commercial sphere for ideas by which to live their lives? In a society in which all kinds of ideas are locked up in the form of intellectual property controlled by megacorporations, what is likely to be the effect on our collective consciousness and the future of social discourse?

Chapter Four

Monopolizing
Ideas

It is one of those strange twists of history that the capitalist system, whose very modus operandi was to expand markets and facilitate the exchange of property between sellers and buyers, is systematically going about the task of deconstructing its core principles and institutional foundations. Capitalism is reinventing itself in the form of networks and beginning to leave markets behind. In the process, new forms of institutional power are developing that are more formidable and potentially more dangerous than anything society experienced during the long reign of the market era. To understand why, we need to keep in mind how different networks are from markets.

Recall that in a network economy, property of all kinds continues to exist but is less likely to be exchanged. Sellers and buyers give way to suppliers and users. The act of alienation of property—negotiated exchange between seller and buyer—which is the heart of what a market system is all about, is less frequent. Enjoying short-term access is more important than purchase and long-term ownership. Commodifying a relationship between parties to access and share both tangible and intangible property is the heart of a network-based approach to commercial life.

While all forms of property are more likely to be accessed than purchased in a network economy, it bears repeating that tangible property is becoming increasingly marginal to the exercise of economic power, and intangible property is fast becoming the defining force in an access-based era. Ideas in the form of patents, copyrights, trademarks, trade secrets, and relationships—are being used to forge a new kind of economic power composed of megasuppliers in control of expanded networks of users.

These supplier-user networks concentrate economic power in the hands of fewer institutions even more effectively than was the case during the propertied era of seller-buyer markets. Being able to control the ideas of commerce, rather than just the tools, operating processes, and products, gives the new genre of global corporate suppliers an advantage unmatched in previous economic history. Having a monopoly over ideas in each commercial field allows a few firms to grab hold of the workings of an entire industry. To ensure success, industry leaders create vast supplier-user networks, making former competitors, as well as clients and other suppliers, wholly dependent on their ideas to survive.

The relatively new field of business format franchising and the even newer life-science field are two cases in point. The first uses intellectual property in the form of business formulas to exercise control over large retail networks. The second uses gene patents to establish captive networks of users ranging from farmers to researchers and health professionals. Both practices are good examples of the new power dynamics unfolding in the emerging network economy.

Franchising Access

The changing character of capitalism is reflected in the phenomenal growth of franchising over the past thirty years. Franchising combines virtually every element of the new network way of doing business. While product franchising has been part of the commercial landscape for more than a century, the radical new idea of business format franchising is of a very different character and operates by a set of assumptions that are more compatible with an Age of Access than with an older propertied era.

Product franchises began in the late nineteenth century when companies like Singer and McCormick needed to expand their market reach for sewing machines and farm equipment but were unable to generate sufficient capital to maintain their own retail outlets. By contracting with small independent businesses scattered across the country, the manufacturers were able to secure exclusive outlets and licensing agreements for their products. Local businesses put up the capital to finance retail operations in return for exclusive rights of distributorship. Today, automobile distributorships are the best known and most visible examples of traditional franchises.

Business format franchising, in contrast, is a relatively new invention. Here, what is being franchised is a business concept itself. Parent companies have realized that their intangible assets—the concepts and brand names—are of far greater value than the franchisees' tangible assets—the plant, facilities, machinery, and raw resources. McDonald's, for example, discovered that there is more money to be made "selling hamburger stands than in selling hamburgers."[1] Service companies in particular have started packaging their formulas for doing business, as well as their brand names, to local businesspeople in return for royalties on the volume of sales generated. The idea is to mass-produce concepts rather than merely products.

Each local outlet operates like a clone of the original business—in effect, re-creating the image and operating format of the parent company in every geographic market. In a typical franchise arrangement, the franchisee pays the parent company a licensing fee, usually ranging from $12,000 to $100,000. For an additional fee, the company provides the franchisee with equipment, training, and the right to use its brand image and trademark. The franchisee is responsible for financing the day-to-day business operations, including leasing property and facilities, paying insurance and utilities, and meeting payroll. The franchisee also pays the parent company a percentage of the gross sales, generally between 5 and 12 percent of revenue.[2]

Franchising is regarded by many as a win-win business proposition. The franchisor gains access to local markets without having to invest in expensive equipment and overhead costs and without having to oversee and run the actual business itself. The franchisee, in return, gains access to an operating formula, brand name, and marketing scheme that have proven track records for success.

Modern franchising has fundamentally changed the relationships between large and small businesses in every country. Until recently, small businesses were only loosely tied to big companies. Each operated more or less in its own sphere, filling separate and sometimes overlapping commercial niches. With franchising, big businesses began creating small businesses to act as their local surrogates. Small businesses become subcontractors for large companies, tied together in a rigidly defined network of mutually agreed-upon contractual arrangements. Local businesses give up their autonomy in return for gaining access to the economies of scale that normally give larger companies a competitive advantage.

Virtually every product and service imaginable is being franchised. There are franchises for house renovation and repair, lawn and garden care, maid services, pet-care products, health-care services, custom breweries, bird watching, travel agencies, hair salons, children's products, photographic services, fast foods, automotive services, job training, assisted-living facilities, hotel chains, car-rental agencies, cosmetics, driving schools, veterinarians, storage services, take-home food services, temporary employment services, home security, day-care centers, sports camps, tutorial services, interior-design services, furniture repair, funeral homes, legal services, and accounting and tax services.[3]

In just a few short decades, franchising has risen to become the most important new form of business organization since the advent of the modern corporation at the beginning of the twentieth century. Franchises currently account for more than 35 percent of all retail sales in the U.S., with gross revenues of $800 billion. Sales are expected to top $1 trillion by the end of the year 2000. There are more than 550,000 franchised businesses employing more than 7.2 million people in sixty industries.[4] A new franchise opens its doors every eight minutes, and the franchise industry itself is growing six times faster than the economy as a whole.[5] There are more than 2,000 franchised systems. Astonishingly, the majority of these franchise chains did not even exist twenty-five years ago.[6]

The franchising phenomenon is spreading quickly around the world, replacing traditional independently owned single businesses in every geographic region. Malaysia boasts 102 business franchises, nearly 80 of which are foreign-based. Indonesia also has a developed franchise market, as do Hong Kong and Singapore. Franchising is already well established in Western Europe and, for the first time, is making significant inroads into Eastern Europe and Russia. The opening up of the first McDonald's in Moscow several years ago was a watershed event in the history of the franchising movement. Poland, the Czech Republic, and even Yugoslavia and Bulgaria have franchised operations. In the Middle East, Egypt, Kuwait, Saudi Arabia, and Israel are leading the region in franchising operations. In Latin America, Brazil, Uruguay, Chile, and Argentina all have franchise systems.[7]

The franchise industry touts these local enterprises as the new entrepreneurs of the coming century, and at first glance, franchises do appear to look like small semi-independent businesses. A person contracts for the license; invests in capital equipment, plant, and property; hires workers; produces a product or service; and makes a profit—all distinguishing features of an owned business. But the franchisee does not actually own the business—namely, the idea, the concept, the operating formula, the brand identification, all the things that make a business a business. So, in reality, these enterprises are not independently owned businesses in the conventional sense of the term. As sociologist E. O. Wright has pointed out:

> The owners of fast food . . . franchises could be seen as occupying a contradictory location between the petty bourgeoisie or small employers and managers. While they maintain some of the characteristics of self-employed independent producers, they also become much more like functionaries for large capitalist corporations.[8]

The fact that the franchisee owns the physical capital, employs the labor, and produces the product or service is not as important as the fact that the intangible aspects that define the essence of the business remain the property of the franchisor.

Most people continue to harbor the belief that small-business ownership—one of the pillars of a market era—is alive and well in the new guise of the franchise. This is a gross misreading of the new dynamic unfolding in the capitalist system. The American Management Association understands the importance of the distinction between ownership and access even if the franchising industry continues to promote the misguided idea of "owning your own business." "Contrary to popular belief, a franchisor cannot 'sell' a franchise to a candidate," write Jan Kirkham and Timothy McGowan in *The Franchising Handbook,* a publication of the association.[9] This misunderstanding is not a mere question of semantics, say Kirkham and McGowan. A franchise is an agreement by a company to allow a second party access to its business concept, operations, and brand for a limited period of time, subject to renewal. The franchisee does not *buy* the business but rather is granted short-term access to use it under conditions established by the supplier. The relationship is not one of seller-buyer but rather supplier-user. It is the negotiation of access, not the transfer of ownership, that is at the core of the franchising agreement. This is a new kind of capitalism.

Thousands of new, small commercial enterprises are being established each year, and many people are risking their financial capital in the process, but again, what they are buying is access and the right to limited use rather than ownership of a business. Kirkham and McGowan hammer away on just this distinction, pointing out that the franchisee does not enjoy any of the rights that go with ownership of property. He or she cannot incorporate using the franchisor's name, because the franchisee doesn't own the name. The license can be sold only by the approval of the franchisor. The franchisee can merely sell the physical assets that he or she has purchased in order to run the business. And remember, the franchisee has to continually renew the franchising license. If the franchisee truly owned the license, he or she would never need to renegotiate renewal agreements.[10] "The use of the words *sell, buy,* and *owner* sends a message that is contrary to the real purpose of the franchise relationship," argue Kirkham and McGowan.[11] They remind us that "if I sell you something, you have bought it. If you have bought it, you own it. If you own it, you can do what you want with it."[12] None of these assumptions is operative under franchise licensing arrangements.

The franchising relationship provides a mirror into the new organizational features of a network economy. Its operating premises—its very center of gravity—pulls the commercial agenda steadily away from broadly distributed ownership of independent businesses and toward a regime made up of wholly dependent lessees sharing access to networks of powerful suppliers. This is a radical new commercial landscape where the traditional markers for business ownership are few and far between. For example, while franchisors retain tight control over the intangible assets, which are the most important since they define the essence of the business, they also often exercise varying degrees of control over much of the tangible assets as well. In many retail franchises, the franchisor owns the head lease for the franchisee's property and negotiates a sublease with him or her. In the United States, franchisors often own the land on which outlets are built. McDonald's founder Ray Kroc believed that ownership of the franchisee's building and land is the only way to guarantee near total control over his or her business. He wrote:

> I have finally found the way that will put every single McDonald's we open under our complete control . . . . It [the franchisee's sublease] says that if at any time McDonald's System Inc. notifies Franchise Realty Corporation that the operation does not conform in every way to the McDonald's standards of quality and service, this lease will be cancelled [sic] on thirty-day notice. Now we have a club over them, and by God, there will be no more pampering or fiddling with them. We will do the ordering instead of going around and begging them to cooperate.[13]

Dunkin' Donuts controls ⅔ of the real estate its outlets are on, either through direct ownership or by holding a head lease. In the United Kingdom, franchisors control 17 percent of the land and property of the franchisee.[14]

Many franchise agreements also stipulate that the franchisee lease his or her equipment from the franchisor, giving the parent company additional control over the operation of the business. Two-thirds of the franchise agreements give the franchisor control over the franchisee's telephone lines, either by direct ownership (46 percent) or by provisions in the contract that require the transfer of the telephone number back to the franchisor upon termination of the licensing agreement (41 percent).[15]

The franchisor also controls the day-to-day operations of the franchisee. The franchisor's manual describes, often in excruciating detail, how the operation is to be managed and run. McDonald's operating manual is more than 600 pages long. It prescribes cooking methods, the amount of food portions, cleaning requirements, and even the appropriate demeanor of McDonald's employees when waiting on customers.[16]

Franchisors have the right to inspect their franchisees' operations, often without notice, and interview customers as part of their evaluation process. KFC employs "mystery shoppers" who surreptitiously make purchases in its many outlets and draw up detailed reports on their experiences.[17]

Half of all franchise agreements specify the hours the business must be open. Eighty-three percent of the agreements give the franchisor the right to withhold permission from the franchisee who wants to be involved in other business ventures while also managing the franchise outlet. Many of the agreements even specify the maximum number of vacation days the franchisee can take each year. Finally, many franchisors also control pricing, long considered the undisputed right of the owner. Some franchisors set upper and lower limits on prices; others impose a ceiling or fixed price.[18]

According to University of Leicester researcher Alan Felstead, who has conducted an exhaustive study of franchise agreements, the result of all of these elaborate provisions built into the licensing agreements is that "despite investing large sums of money, often their life savings and/or funds raised by taking out a second mortgage on their homes, franchisees have virtually no ownership rights in the intangible business assets and only restricted rights in the more tangible ones."[19]

Much of the confusion, then, over whether a franchisee is an owner in the traditional sense or merely a glorified employee or agent of the parent company has to do with what he or she owns. In the Industrial Age, owning the physical capital, machines, property, and land; employing the workers; managing the production processes; and distributing the goods or services was sufficient to define ownership. In a network economy, in which intangible assets matter more than tangible ones, real ownership resides with those who possess the know-how, the concepts, the idea, the brand, and the operating formulas. "In the case of franchising," says Felstead, "economic power is exercised not by *directly* owning and controlling the physical assets of doing business, but by controlling the use to which the intangible assets, such as the trademark/idea/format, are put."[20]

The franchise, which is fast becoming the dominant form of local enterprise in the U.S.—and in other countries around the world—is as different from the conventional notion of an autonomous, individually owned and operated business as the latter is from craft shops operating under the restrictions imposed by guilds in the late Medieval Age. These new commercial institutions are a hybrid enterprise, a transitional form of business that lies somewhere along the road between a propertied era and the Age of Access.

Problems notwithstanding, a growing number of small, independently owned and operated businesses in the U.S. and other nations will likely disappear over the next twenty years, replaced, in large part, by franchises. In this new organizational scheme of things, where sellers and buyers give way to suppliers and users, where intangible assets count for more than physical assets, and where the individual investor purchases the right of access to use the business concept rather than the business itself, the nature of commerce becomes fundamentally reconfigured along new lines. Small, independently owned businesses, the backbone of the capitalist system, are rapidly being eclipsed and left behind by the system itself. The new enterprises replacing them bear all of the earmarks of a new capitalist ethos based increasingly on access to powerful supplier networks.

Leasing DNA

An equally significant shift from seller-buyer markets to supplier-user networks is occurring in the life-science industry. Our materials base is shifting from fossil fuels, metals, and minerals—the raw resources of the industrial revolution—to genes—the raw resources of the biotech century. Forty years of genetic research and development have paved the way for a gene revolution that is making its way into the marketplace, affecting virtually every industry and field. Genes are being used to create new types of genetically engineered supercrops, new pharmaceutical products, new kinds of fiber and construction material, and even new forms of energy. Government, universities, and life-science companies are in the midst of the most ambitious scientific project in all of history—deciphering the genetic code of many of the microorganisms, plants, and animals, including our own species, that make up the biology of life on earth. In less than a decade, virtually all 140,000 or so genes that make up the evolutionary blueprint of the human race will be located and identified.

The speed of the transition from fossil fuels to genes is extraordinary. For example, in the past three years, four of the giants of the petrochemical revolution—Monsanto, Novartis, DuPont, and Aventis—have made the decision to shed or sell some or all of their chemical divisions to concentrate almost exclusively on genetic research and genetic-based technologies and products. While chemical products are not likely to disappear in the foreseeable future, they are increasingly moving to the backwaters of commerce, making room for the genetic market.

In the Industrial Age, nonrenewable resources—fossil fuels, chemicals, metals, and minerals—were transformed into pure commodities. They were exhumed, extracted, processed, and sold by weight and grade in the commodities market. They were treated, from beginning to end, as negotiable property whose ownership could be transferred from sellers to buyers at each step of the economic process. Genes are not, however, treated the same way. They are not sold but only licensed out; not bought, only leased. Genes remain the possession of the suppliers in the form of patents and are loaned to users for short durations.

Like nonrenewables, genes exist in nature and must be extracted, distilled, purified, and processed. Life-science companies are bioprospecting the four corners of the planet, looking for rare genes in microorganisms, plants, animals, and humans that may be of commercial value in developing a new food crop, creating a new drug, producing new fibers or sources of energy.

When genes with potential commercial values are located, they are patented and become, in the eyes of the law, inventions. This critical distinction separates the way chemical resources were used in the industrial era from the way genes are being used in the biotech century. When chemists discovered new chemical elements in nature in the last century, they were allowed to patent the processes they invented to extract and purify the substances but were not allowed to patent the chemical elements themselves—patent laws in the United States and in other countries prohibit "discoveries of nature" from being considered inventions.

No reasonable person would suggest that a scientist who isolated, classified, and described the properties of hydrogen, helium, or aluminum ought to be granted the exclusive right, for twenty years, to claim the substances as a human invention. In fact, in 1928, claimants sought a patent on tungsten and were denied their claim by the U.S. Patent and Trademark Office (PTO). The federal courts subsequently upheld the PTO's ruling, saying that while the claimant was the first to discover tungsten and did successfully purify it, the substance itself had always existed in nature and therefore was merely a discovery and could not therefore be considered an "invention."[21]

In 1987, however, in apparent violation of its own statutes governing patents on discoveries of nature, the PTO issued a sweeping policy decree declaring that the components of living creatures—genes, chromosomes, cells, and tissues—are patentable and can be treated as the intellectual property of whoever first isolates their properties, describes their functions, and finds useful applications for them in the marketplace.

Human genes and cells, as well as the genes and cells of other creatures, already have been patented, and industry watchers predict that in less than twenty-five years, much of the genetic commons—the legacy of millions of years of biological evolution—will have been isolated, identified, and enclosed in the form of intellectual property, controlled, for the most part, by a handful of giant transnational life-science companies.

Patenting the raw resources of the new economy fundamentally changes the way those resources are treated in commerce. Sellers and buyers of raw resources are replaced by suppliers and users. In the coming era, biological resources, the most basic of all resources and the critical material of the new economy, will be accessed but not sold.

Already the repercussions of moving from seller-buyer to supplier-user relationships are being felt, particularly in agriculture. The transnational life-science companies have been quietly buying up the remaining independently owned seed companies in recent years, giving them vast control over the germ plasm upon which all of agricultural production depends. The companies then slightly modify the seeds or strip out individual genetic traits, or recombine new genes into the seeds and secure patent protection over their "inventions." The goal is to control, in the form of intellectual property, the entire seed stock of the planet.

Ten life-science companies now own 32 percent of the $23 billion commercial seed trade. Three life-science companies, DuPont, Monsanto, and Novartis, have combined seed revenues of $4.5 billion a year.[22] Monsanto alone has spent more than $8 billion in acquiring seed and agricultural biotech companies in recent years, making it an industry leader. In 1998, Monsanto added to its seed collection by purchasing two of the world's top-ten seed companies: DeKalb Genetics and Cargill's international seed business.[23] Monsanto is also seeking to buy Delta and Pine Land Co., the world's largest cottonseed company, and has already purchased Plant Breeding International, a U.K.-based company formerly owned by Unilever. Monsanto, once a chemical company, now a life-science company, is the world's second largest seed company.[24] The life-science giant controls 33 percent of the soybean market, 15 percent of the maize seed market, and with the acquisition of Delta and Pine Land, 85 percent of the cottonseed market in the United States.[25]

Other life-science companies holding major portions of the world's seed stock include Groupe Limagrain of France; AgriBiotech, Inc., a U.S. firm; Astra Zeneca of the U.K. and Sweden; Sakata, of Japan; and KWS AG, of Germany.[26] The market for genetically engineered seeds is expected to top $2 billion by the end of the year 2000, and $20 billion by the year 2010, according to the International Seed Trade Federation.[27]

To understand the historic significance of both controlling and patenting the world's seed germ plasm, we need to bear in mind that from the beginning of the Neolithic revolution in agriculture until now, farmers have owned their own seeds. For thousands of years, farmers have saved seeds from their harvests to be used in later growing seasons. Seeds also have been shared with extended family members and neighbors and occasionally have been bartered for other things.

Now, this fundamental relationship between farmers and their seeds has been broken for the first time. Patented seeds are never sold, in the conventional sense of the term. Rather, patented seeds are leased to farmers for their one-time use over a single growing season. The new seeds collected during the harvest belong to the patent holder and therefore cannot be used by the farmer the next growing season. Thus the farmer is granted only short-term access to someone else's intellectual property. The seeds are never technically sold or legally purchased, only rented.

Monsanto and the other life-science companies have made it known that they will prosecute any farmer who saves and replants any of their patented seeds. Penalties may include criminal charges and fines exceeding $1,000,000 for each violation. Monsanto has even hired Pinkerton investigators to monitor farms and interview seed cleaners, farm-supply dealers, seed-company salesmen, and others in search of potential violators. According to Progressive Farmer, a trade journal, Monsanto has already brought legal action against hundreds of farmers for patent infringement.[28]

By patenting the world's remaining seed stock, life-science companies are effectively gaining control over much of the agricultural production of the planet. They are the suppliers, and every farmer in the world becomes a user, buying access to the seeds of life each new growing season.

Anxious to make sure that farmers will not violate company patents by illegally using harvested seeds, and aware that it is impossible to police every farmer in the world to see if they're adhering to the terms of the seed-borrowing agreements, the life-science industry has created a technological solution to ensure 100 percent compliance. Delta and Pine Land and the U.S. Department of Agriculture (USDA) have received a patent on a seed-sterilizing technology that prevents farmers from replanting seeds. According to Harry Collins, vice president of transfer technology for Delta and Pine Land, new genes are inserted into tobacco plants—and soon other plants as well—that, when sprayed with a chemical compound, turn off a "blocker" switch that allows the patented seeds to be fertile. When the plant produces the seed, it won't germinate because the blocker gene won't work. Dubbed "Terminator technology" by Rural Advancement Foundation International (RAFI), a civil society organization that has drawn public attention to the new technology, the process already has been used effectively on cotton as well as tobacco.[29]

Melvin Oliver, the USDA scientist responsible for creating the Terminator technology, said, "The need was there to come up with a system that allowed you to self-police your technology, rather than trying to put on laws and legal barriers to farmers saving seed, and to try and stop foreign interests from stealing the technology."[30] Critics, however, argue that farmers should not have to seek "access" each year to seeds that used to be reproduced and used over and over again after an initial purchase.

Opposition to the Terminator technology among farm organizations, international agricultural bodies, and even countries quickly mounted. In October 1998, the Consultative Group on International Agricultural Research, the world's largest agricultural research body—funded by the U.N. and World Bank—recommended that its sixteen member institutions prohibit the use of the Terminator technology in their research programs. India, the world's second most populated country, has banned the Terminator technology.[31] In October 1999, in response to worldwide condemnation of the Terminator technology, Monsanto announced that it would not employ it. The company said, however, that it was exploring other options to protect its intellectual property, including techniques that would allow the company to activate specific genes in the plants only after farmers pay additional access fees for the right to use the new traits.

For the millions of farmers around the world whose survival depends on saving seeds and exchanging them with their neighbors over the fence, having to access seeds each year from one of a handful of transnational life-science companies could tip the scales toward insolvency. Lawrence Busch, a sociologist at Michigan State University who has been tracking the debate, speaks for the growing chorus of critics when he warns, "Wars and civil disturbances and catastrophes of a natural variety occur. Those are the kinds of things that can wipe out seed supplies. If farmers can't plant the stuff that they harvest, and become totally dependent on this, you are really raising the ante on the possibility of mass starvation."[32]

The elimination of widespread ownership of the seeds of life and their concentration in the hands of a few companies mark a turning point in the history of agriculture. Like other commercial fields, agricultural commerce is moving from a seller-buyer to a supplier-user relationship. For millions of farmers, the propertied era is fast giving way to an Age of Access. Ownership of seeds by farmers, long regarded as one of the most basic forms of property, is becoming an anachronism in the emerging biotech century.

Life patents also are being extended to other commercial arenas where traditional notions of property and the transfer of ownership between sellers and buyers have long been the custom. For example, farmers and scientists who purchased animals in the past have always been able to claim their offspring as their property. That's no longer the case. Technically, the supplier of patented animals owns all the offspring of the same genotype. Therefore if an animal is cloned and patented, the cloned copies are considered the intellectual property of the patent holder, and a royalty must be paid for each birth. This is going to become increasingly important in the years ahead as cloned, patented animals are used in food production, as a source of xenotransplants, as chemical factories to secrete useful drugs in their milk, and as models in medical research. Instead of owning animals, farmers, researchers, and others will purchase access to the use of patented, cloned animals and will continue to pay access fees in the form of royalties on any cloned offspring produced.

It might surprise most people to learn that they no longer have property in themselves—that even their DNA and cells are no longer theirs to dispose of as they see fit. Recall, it was John Locke, the Enlightenment political philosopher, who argued that every person enjoys property in themselves—their bodies, labor, and mental abilities. In the Age of Access, this conventional idea of property in oneself is being challenged.

An extraordinary court case in California several years ago established a new legal precedent for what can and can't be claimed as property in oneself. An Alaska businessman, John Moore, discovered that his own body parts had been patented without his knowledge or consent. Moore had been diagnosed with a rare cancer and was undergoing treatment at UCLA. At the time, an attending physician and researcher discovered that Moore's spleen tissue produced a blood protein that facilitates the growth of white blood cells that are valuable anticancer agents. The university created a cell line from Moore's spleen tissue and received a patent on their "invention" in 1984. The cell line is estimated to be worth more than $3 billion. Moore subsequently sued the University of California, claiming a property right over his own tissue.

In 1990, the California Supreme Court ruled against Moore, holding that he had no property right over his own body tissues. Still, the court upheld the primary claim of the university that the cell line itself, while not the physical property of Moore, could justifiably be claimed as the intellectual property of UCLA.

This case reflects the biases of a new era: Tangible property in one's tissue is discounted, while intangible property in the form of a patent on the cell line from that same body is elevated and guaranteed legal protection. If any of Moore's family and direct descendants were to need his cell line in the future for their own medical treatments, they would have to pay a fee to UCLA to secure access to it.[33]

Patents on human genes and cells are becoming commonplace. Today, if patients want to be screened to see if they have a gene or genetic predisposition for certain diseases like breast cancer, Canavan, and cystic fibrosis, they first have to pay a fee that may include a royalty assessment to the company that holds the patent on that particular gene. While conventional genetic screening tests cost less than $100, genetic tests involving patented genes can cost as much as $2,500. Increasingly, people in search of genetic information, for whatever purposes, will have to pay exorbitant access fees every time they use the gene in question.

By monopolizing the gene pool, in the form of patents, a handful of life-science companies could seriously undermine the future of health-care services and even threaten the viability of the health-care system itself. In the course of the next two decades, people will be able to be screened for tens of thousands of genes and genetic predispositions. Many people may wish to take advantage of these genetic screening tests either as part of their normal preventive care or for diagnosing the onset of illnesses. Doctors and HMOs, however, probably will balk at providing broad genetic screening tests because the cost per patient could run into the tens or even hundreds of thousands of dollars. Life-science firms, for their part, are likely to keep the costs of their genetic screenings high because they enjoy a monopoly over a patented gene, thus assuring windfall profits for their companies. On the other hand, if a patient becomes ill or is misdiagnosed because the doctor refused to screen for a particular gene, he is likely to sue his health-care provider. Growing litigation could lead to escalating costs of providing health-care for millions of people. Either way, patents on genes may result in greatly increased costs of providing health care.

In 1998, researchers at Johns Hopkins University and the University of Wisconsin, under licensing agreements with the Geron Corporation, a California-based biotech company, announced that they had succeeded in isolating and perpetuating human stem cells, the primordial cells from which each individual develops into a human being. Patent applications are pending at the PTO. If the patent is granted, Geron will control the basic cell of human life for twenty years, giving the company unprecedented power to dictate the terms of future medical research and even the future evolutionary direction of the human race. Researchers hope to use the human stem cell to find ways to turn on and off the various genetic switches that govern human development. They say such research will lead to new ways to produce human proteins, cells, tissues, and organs. In the future, anyone who might need to avail him- or herself of medical therapies arising from the stem cell research would have to pay for access to the procedures.

In Iceland, the government signed a $200 million agreement in 1999 with a Swiss pharmaceutical company, Roche Holding AG, to screen the genes of all 270,000 Icelanders in the hope of finding useful genes and genetic predispositions that might prove helpful in research and be commercially valuable in the creation of new gene products. In the future, if Icelanders want to use either the genetic information or products that result from the research, they will have to pay a fee to the company for the right to access their own genetic heritage.[34]

Control over intangible assets and various forms of intellectual property gives transnational companies the edge to create powerful supplier-user networks and concentrate even greater economic power in wholly new ways. The shift from seller-buyer markets to supplier-user networks and from broadly distributed ownership to short-term access to capital, goods, and services raises a number of disturbing economic and social questions. To begin with, antitrust laws are designed, by their very nature, to protect markets from being destroyed, and markets, recall, are places where sellers and buyers come together to sell and buy goods and services. Networks, however, are by their very nature designed to eliminate markets made up of sellers and buyers and replace them with supplier-user chains. If networks continue to eliminate markets, are they inherently in violation of antitrust statutes whose sole purpose is to protect conventional markets? If not, how do nations fashion new legal restrictions to prevent companies from using their power over ideas and intellectual capital to monopolize and control networks? Seth Shulman, in his book *Owning the Future,* makes the point that "we have yet to establish a clear sense of what anti-trust means in the knowledge economy." Like a growing number of observers, Shulman suggests that "we need to revitalize our notion of anti-trust law to explicitly restrict monopolies over the infostructure—monopolies that represent some of the most dangerous concentrations of power we have seen yet."[35]

We have barely begun to discuss the new challenges posed by network ways of doing business and how they should be addressed in public policy. As the global economy continues its metamorphosis from ownership to access, however, these questions will inevitably come to the fore in every country.

Chapter Five

Everything
Is a Service

How might the world be today if Henry Ford had thought of the automobile more as a service than a product and had decided to lease his cars rather than sell them? The twentieth century could have turned out very differently. As it is, the automobile became the ultimate litmus test for measuring personal success in the propertied age.

Buying an automobile, for most people, represents a baptism into the adult world of property relationships. It is a signal of our willingness to accept the responsibilities that go along with being a member of the propertied class. In contemporary society, where rites of passage are few, owning an automobile remains the one constant bridge from adolescence to adulthood.

Moreover, in a culture obsessed with the notions of autonomy and mobility, the automobile is, perhaps, the ultimate technological expression of these cardinal values. Especially among the young, car ownership is a way of claiming personal identity and a stake in society. It is a statement that one exists and is to be taken seriously. For men in particular, an automobile is the most personal of all possessions and thought of as an extension of who they are and how they would like others to perceive them.

It's no wonder that car ownership has been so highly regarded. But now, like so many other valued products in society, the automobile is being transformed from a good to a service. In an era where the automobile has been central to our way of life, our economy, and our sense of personal identity, its metamorphosis from something people own to something they lease is a sign of the dramatic changes taking place in the organizing of economic relationships.

In less than eighteen years, noncommercial auto leasing has risen from obscurity to encompass one out of every three automobiles and trucks on the U.S. roads.[1] One-third of the new vehicles being driven remain the property of the automakers or dealers, who lease them to their customers. Half of the luxury cars on the road today are leased. More than 90 percent of Jaguar's XJ model are leased. In upscale areas like California's Marin County, more than 60 percent of all the automobiles are leased.[2] The auto- and truck-leasing trend is catching up in Europe and other parts of the world as well. In Germany, 20 percent of cars are currently leased, but mostly by companies.[3]

There are a number of reasons for the shift from ownership to leasing. With sticker prices of new automobiles rising, many prospective customers simply cannot afford the expensive down payments and financing charges. A decade ago, customers spent twenty-two weeks' worth of their wages on the purchase of a new car. By the mid-1990s, twenty-six weeks' worth of wages were required to buy a comparable new vehicle. Leasing generally requires only one month's security deposit. Because interest on car loans is no longer deductible, leasing has become even more attractive as a financing mechanism. Leasing also allows customers to "notch up" and drive a more expensive car that would be out of their reach if they had to finance its purchase. Still more important, when customers lease, they pay only for the portion of a car's value they actually use.[4]

Ford pioneered the leasing concept in the 1980s and remains the industry leader, accounting for 26 percent of all leases written in the first two months of 1998.[5] Among the foreign exports, Mitsubishi is number one, leasing more than half of its vehicles.[6] Even Rolls-Royce leases its famed Silver Dawn. Many wealthy patrons prefer a $1,699 monthly lease payment to a purchase fee of between $139,000 and $149,000.[7]

Leasing first caught on among wealthier buyers who preferred not to have lots of funds tied up in ownership. That's still the case. Upper-income men and women, according to the market surveys, are more likely to lease.[8] Already comfortable with the idea of substituting access for ownership in their commercial and business dealings, and more disposed to think of a car as a service rather than a product, high-end customers have been won over to leasing in just a few short years.

In a society characterized by shorter product life cycles and continuous innovation, an increasing number of drivers view leasing as a more convenient way to stay current. Studies show that people who buy automobiles keep them for about three and a half years, while those who lease exchange automobiles every two to three years.[9] The auto dealers, for their part, know in advance when the customers' leases run out and can anticipate getting to them at just the right time to renegotiate the leases.

For automobile dealers, leasing is a way of commodifying a long-term relationship with a customer. Rather than treat each purchase as a discrete transaction, as has been the custom with a conventional sale, auto dealers now focus on the servicing of a relationship over time. Ford Motor Company says that nearly 50 percent of its lessees come back for another Ford, twice the rate of conventional buyers.[10]

Mercedes-Benz has taken the idea of leasing a step further with its "variations" leasing program in the United Kingdom. Under the terms of the lease, a customer can lease whatever car he wants within a given price range covered by the lease agreement, and exchange his automobile for another model whenever he chooses. Pool leasing transforms the automobile from an owned property to a pure service experience. Access, not ownership, becomes the heart of the commercial relationship. Says Helmut Werner, CEO of Mercedes-Benz, "[We] don't want to just sell another car, but rather offer a complete package of transportation services."[11]

Even more advanced is the European Car Sharing Network—a car-leasing service that provides members with twenty-four-hour access to automobiles in more than 300 cities and towns throughout Europe. The "share cars" are leased through the CityCarClub. Each member pays a deposit and receives a personal key and booklet showing the cars available in his town. Reservations for a car can be made by phone immediately in advance of picking up the car. The cars are located at special reserved parking lots throughout the city. Each location has a lockable store containing the car keys. The member takes the car he's booked and at the end of the trip returns it to the place he picked it up. He fills in a receipt, shows his mileage, and returns the receipt and keys to the locker. The club handles all maintenance and servicing as well as insurance, and bills the member at the end of the month.[12]

CityCarClubs now exist in Germany, Switzerland, Australia, Ireland, Norway, Sweden, Denmark, and the Netherlands. Their promotional brochure quotes Aristotle: "On the whole, you find wealth much more in use than in ownership," and many people seem to agree—currently there are 38,000 members, and the annual growth rate in membership is 50 to 60 percent.[13]

The change in the basic way we think about our relationship to the automobile, from a product we buy to a service we access, is part of the vast restructuring going on in the capitalist system as it makes the transformation from a goods-producing to a service-performing and experience-generating economy. Our long attachment to ownership is beginning to weaken. The new temporal realities of a hypercapitalist society are forcing a reevaluation of the idea of market exchange of property, just as was the case at the dawn of the Industrial Age, when the new fast-paced, more highly mobile world occasioned by the invention of the print press, the mechanical clock, the compass, and steam power forced a similar change. In the years ahead, we will come to think of our economic life more in terms of access to services and experiences and less in terms of ownership of things, marking the end of the propertied era and the beginning of the Age of Access.

The Rise and Fall of Propertied Goods

The importance of private property in the modern world is unquestionable. Harvard sociologist Daniel Bell identifies private property as the "axial institution" of capitalist society.[14] Anxious to justify a private-property regime, economists have spent nearly three centuries in a vain search to find some inextricable law of nature that binds the notion of private property to a larger metaphysics. Nineteenth-century sociologist Paul Lafargue humorously noted that in their zeal to show the universal nature of private property, economists ascribed the convention to the lowly ant, who, they argued, is known to hoard provisions. Lafargue quipped, "It is a pity that they should not have gone a step farther and affirmed that, if the ant lays up stores, she does so with a view to sell the same and realize a profit from the circulation of her capital."[15]

English jurist Sir William Blackstone defined property as "that sole and despotic dominion which one man claims and exercises over the external things of the world, in total exclusion of the right of any other individual in the universe."[16] Property, then, is a social convention for negotiating individual spheres of influence in the modern world. The concept of "mine and thine" allows us to make distinctions and establish relationships with one another in a social context. Every day, in large and small ways, we are faced with property questions and, for the most part, maintain our complex social relationships using agreed-upon notions of who owns what. As long as human relationships remain anchored in geography, some form of property regime must exist.

Still, property is an elusive concept. On the one hand, it seems so easy to identify in all of its various forms. Even the most uneducated of souls recognizes property when he sees it and understands viscerally what is meant by the term. On the other hand, few concepts have proven more difficult to pin down.

Philosophers and kings, theologians and politicians have grappled with the notion of property from time immemorial and have yet to come up with a satisfactory explanation of what exactly it is. That's probably because our ideas about property keep changing over the course of history, which suggests that property, like other social inventions, is not an idea cast in stone but rather a fluid concept subject to the whims and caprices of the particular time and place in which it is being applied. The notion of property, for example, meant something very different in the Medieval Age from what it does now in the modern world.

Feudal society was conceived as being part of a "great chain of being," a hierarchically structured natural and social world that stretched from the lowliest creatures to the princes of the Church. The entire chain was

God's Creation and was organized in such a way as to ensure that each creature performed his role as God had prescribed it, which included serving those above and below according to his station.

Since God is the owner of His Creation, all things in the earthly world ultimately belong to Him. God grants human beings the right to use His property so long as they are righteous and fulfill their obligations of homage and fealty both to Him and to every other person on the social ladder in the way He has preordained. In reality, the Church and nobility acted as God's surrogates. They decided, by force of arms, the terms by which God's earthly estate was to be divided up, administered, and used.

Private property, then, was a complex phenomenon in feudal society and was tightly bound to the idea of proprietary relationships. Things were not owned outright or exclusively by anyone but rather shared in various ways under the conditions established by a stringent code of mutual obligations. When the king granted land to a lord or vassal, "his rights over the land still remained, except for the particular interest he had parted with."[17] The result, says historian Richard Schlatter, is that "no one could be said to own the land; everyone from the king down through the tenants and sub-tenants to the peasants who tilled it had a certain dominion over it, but no one had an absolute lordship over it."[18]

The "Great Transformation," as economic historian Karl Polanyi once referred to the revolution in social relations that ushered in the modern era of property relations and market capitalism, began with the enclosure decrees in Tudor England in the 1500s. For centuries in England and on the European continent, people belonged to the land. The enclosure acts introduced, for the first time, the idea that the land could belong to people in the form of real estate. The Parliamentary acts and decrees mandating enclosure were designed to break up the landed estates into individual pieces of property that could be bought and sold—that is, exchanged in the marketplace. Land became private property, and proprietary relationships, which had governed the conduct of human beings in the Christian hierarchy, gave way to property relationships.

Imagine the wholesale change in socialization that must have accompanied the radical shift in the way people related to their ancestral grounds. Recall that in English law, proprietary rights were sacrosanct. Although the everyday life for serfs was more often than not a precarious and nasty affair, English covenants guaranteed every serf a right to belong to the land of his or her ancestors. Even the most capricious of landlords could not, under penalty of law, expel his serfs from the land they were born onto. By enclosing the land commons and transforming it into private property that could be exchanged in the marketplace, English politics succeeded in freeing millions of peasants from their fixed obligations but also severed their traditional birth rights of attachment to place. Owning land in the form of real estate became the foundation for the restructuring of all human relationships along private property lines. Uprooted and set loose from their ancestral lands, former serfs began contracting and selling their labor power for wages in the fledgling urban and industrial markets that were beginning to spring up in England and, shortly thereafter, on the European continent.

The philosophical rationale for the modern notion of ownership was taken up first in the seventeenth century by the political philosopher John Locke. His theory of property was published in 1690. *Of Civil Government* quickly became the secular bible for a middle class that was beginning to flex its muscle on the English political stage. Locke's writings served as a rallying cry for the Glorious Revolution and parliamentary reforms in England and later provided the philosophical foundation for the French and American revolutions.

Locke believed that private property is a *natural right* and not something that Church or state authority grants as a privilege, conditional on performance of agreed-upon social obligations. The Enlightenment philosopher argued that each man creates his own property by adding his labor to the raw stuff of nature, transforming it into things of value. While Locke acknowledged that the earth and all of its creatures are common to all human beings in the state of nature, he was quick to add that each man, in turn, "has a *Property* in his own *Person*. This no Body has any Right to but himself." Locke went on to assert that "the *Labour* of his Body, and the Work of his hands . . . are properly his." That being so, Locke concluded, "Whatsoever, then, he removes out of the state that Nature hath provided and left it in, he hath mixed his labour with it, and joined to it something that is his own, and thereby makes it his property." As to the question of how much property a person might legitimately claim for himself, Locke said, "As much land as a man tills, plants, improves, cultivates, and can use the product of, so much is his property."[19]

Locke's natural-rights theory of property was wildly popular with the new generation of independent farmers, merchants, shopkeepers, and small capitalists who were transforming English life and ridding the country of the last vestiges of feudal privilege. But his treatises offered more than a mere explanation of the natural-rights theory of property. He elevated human labor and glorified acquisition as the crowning achievement of human existence. Unlike medieval churchmen, who thought of human labor as a set of necessary obligations to fulfill, Locke saw in it opportunities for which every man ought to strive. Property, in turn, became a visible sign of each man's personal triumph in the world. The shift from proprietary to property relations changed the very nature of human relationships and gave rise to modern sensibilities, including the new sense of self and the creation of the private realm and new institutions like the nation-state and the constitutional form of government.

While Locke was concerned with how human beings create property, the Scottish economist Adam Smith was more interested in how property comes to be exchanged in the marketplace. Smith divided history into a progression of stages—hunting, pasturage, agriculture, and commerce— and traced the evolution of property that accompanied each era. Smith argued that in the hunting stage, simple possession existed and was ritualized, but the idea of a property regime did not yet exist. The pasturage stage, said Smith, introduced the idea of animals as property and established, for the first time, settled laws or agreements concerning property.[20] In the agricultural era, land was slowly transformed into property relations. It was in this period, said Smith, that land and other forms of fixed and mobile property became transferable after death—by the enactment of wills—signaling a significant turning point in the nature of property relations. Inheritance introduced the idea of alienation or exchangeability of property between successive generations and began to make of it a form of power that could be used to create and maintain class distinctions. The fourth stage of property, the commercial stage, is characterized by trade and the widespread exchange and diffusion of property in the marketplace.[21]

Smith focused most of his attention on the economics of exchanging property. He argued that an invisible hand ruled over the marketplace, overseeing the details of economic life. The invisible hand was likened to the mechanical pendulum of a clock, meticulously regulating supply and demand, labor, energy, and capital, automatically assuring the proper balance between production and consumption of the earth's resources. If left relatively unfettered by government interference, the invisible hand would provide an efficient mechanism for the continuous exchange of property between sellers and buyers.

In modern times, then, property has come to mean the exclusive right to possess, use, and dispose of things in the marketplace. Something is said to qualify as property if one can occupy or hold it and exclude others from having it; if one can use it in any way one chooses as long as the use doesn't harm anyone else; and if one can dispose of it by transferring or selling it to another party. Of the three criteria, the last is the most important from the perspective of the market. The ability to alienate—to make property fungible in the marketplace—is the heart of a capitalist economy.

In the first stage of industrial capitalism, goods, which had been made in the home or by local craftsmen for barter and only occasionally for market exchange, were gradually taken out of the house and produced en masse in factories. Furniture, cloth and later clothes, utensils, soap, and countless other homemade items were now made cheaper, better, and in greater volume in the commercial sphere. Long accustomed to making these goods for their own use, millions of working people began, for the first time, to use their new factory wages to purchase factory-made items in the marketplace. The house itself was transformed from a place of production to a place of consumption.

We often forget that for thousands of years the home was the primary site for virtually all economic activity. The very term *economy* is derived from the Greek word *oikos,* which means managing the household economy. As late as 1900, labor historian Harry Braverman reminds us, much of production was still centered in the home, even in the dense urban areas and sprawling cities of America. Families living in the highly industrial regions, like the coal and steel communities of Pennsylvania, were still producing most of their food at home—more than half the families raised their own poultry, livestock, and vegetables, and purchased only potatoes at the market.[22] According to the U.S. Census Bureau, between 1889 and 1892, more than half of the families surveyed were still baking their own bread. While men's clothes were generally store-bought, women's and children's clothes were still stitched and tailored at home— first by hand, then with the Singer sewing machine.[23]

The struggle between homemade and factory-made often became the critical generational battleground between immigrants to the new world and their more Americanized children during the early years of industrial production. First-generation Americans, anxious to become part of the American dream, coveted store-bought goods and were embarrassed about their parents' insistence on producing goods at home. The lines were clearly drawn. One was either "old-fashioned" or "modern." Modernity triumphed, and physical goods of all kinds became commodities produced in factories and purchased in the marketplace in the form of private property.

Mass-produced material goods dominated the capitalist economy in the United States from the beginning of batch-and-flow production processes in the 1880s until well into the middle decades of the twentieth century. In an era in which the amassing of physical capital defined the terms of commerce, and consumer goods determined the status and well-being of millions of consumers, property rights reigned supreme. The world, it seemed, was suddenly awash in physical capital and consumer goods, and all of society was swimming in a sea of private property. The push into the suburbs and the opening up of the highway culture in the 1950s and 1960s, and the near fetish of consumption that accompanied it, was the high-water mark of the era of property relationships, a time when to have, hold, and exclude was the raison d'être of human existence in the non-Communist world.

The Birth of the Service Economy

Even as the production, exchange, and accumulation of property—in the form of both capital and consumer goods—was becoming a national pastime, other forces were at work in the evolving capitalist market that would eventually undermine private-property relations and the elaborate social system that had grown up around it.

The increasing complexity of large-scale business operations, more discretionary family income, and the entrance of large numbers of women into the workforce led to the introduction of business services and then later consumer services into the capitalist mix. At first, business services were an adjunct to the production and distribution of goods. Railroads, utilities, and other large-scale manufacturing concerns required ever more complex forms of coordination and organization. Business services, including accounting, financial planning, transportation, and communications, began to play an increasingly prominent role in the production and distribution of goods. At the same time, an affluent middle class began to spend more of its discretionary income on services of all kinds. The process accelerated as more and more women entered the workforce. Activities that women normally provided in the home, including child care, senior care, preparation of meals, health care, haircuts, and the like, were moved to the marketplace as paid commercial services. Between 1899 and 1939, the amount of flour consumed by commercial bakeries rose from 1/7 to 2/5 of the total produced. The production of canned vegetables increased fivefold; canned fruits twelvefold.[24] Braverman observes that "the source of status is no longer the ability to make things but simply the ability to purchase them."[25] Entertainment and leisure-time activities, which had been, for the most part, family affairs or public activities, also began to migrate to the marketplace, where they were made into commercial services of various sorts. Braverman summarizes the impact of this change in the structure of human relations in the first decades of the twentieth century this way:

> *Thus the population no longer relies upon social organization in the form of family, friends, neighbors, community, elders, children, but with few exceptions must go to market, and only to market, not only for food, clothing, and shelter, but also for recreation, amusement, security, for the care of the young, the old, the sick, the handicapped. In time not only the material and service needs but even the emotional patterns of life are channeled through the market.*[26]

By the time Daniel Bell wrote his book *The Coming of Post-Industrial Society* in 1973, the performance of services had eclipsed the production of goods and become the driving engine of capitalism in both North America and Europe. Although "services" is a bit of a mercurial, catchall category and open to widely differing interpretations, it generally includes economic activities that are not products or construction, are transitory, are consumed at the time they are produced, and provide an intangible value. *The Economist,* partially in jest, once suggested that services are "anything sold in trade that could not be dropped on your foot."[27] They include professional work (legal, accounting, and consulting), the wholesale and retail trades, transportation, communications, health care, child care, senior care, entertainment and paid leisure activity, and government social programs.

In 1973, sixty-five out of every hundred workers were already engaged in services. In the European community, 47.6 percent of workers were in the service sector in the early 1970s.[28] Today, the service industries employ more than 77 percent of the U.S. workforce and account for 75 percent of the value added in the U.S. economy and more than half of the value added in the global economy.[29] Percy Barnevik, the former CEO of Asea Brown Boveri Ltd., predicts that by the year 2010, services will make up more than 90 percent of the U.S. economy, and manufacturing activities less than 10 percent.[30]

The shift in primary commerce from goods to services makes property far less important in both business and personal life. In the Age of Access, we are more likely to measure economic activity in "MTBH—the mean time between haircuts" than by the number of widgets produced and sold, writes Peter Martin in the *Financial Times*.[31] Daniel Bell captured, at least in part, the significance of the transformation taking place in capitalist commerce when he observed that "if an industrial society is defined by the quantity of goods as marking a standard of living, the post-industrial society is defined by the quality of life as measured by the services and amenities—health, education, recreation, and the arts—which are now deemed desirable."[32]

Of course, what has been left unsaid in all of the discussions about the transition to a service economy, and what bears repeating, is that services do not qualify as property. They are immaterial and intangible. They are performed, not produced. They exist only at the moment they are rendered. They cannot be held, accumulated, or inherited. While products are bought, services are made available. In a service economy, it is human time that is being commodified, not places or things. Services always invoke a relationship between human beings as opposed to a relationship between a human being and a thing. Access to one another, as social beings, becomes increasingly mediated by pecuniary relationships.

The metamorphosis in the organization of human relations from the production and commercial exchange of propertied goods to access to commodified service relationships is transforming in nature. Yet our society continues to act as if property relations are fundamental when, in reality, economic forces are making physical property, at least, less relevant. Perhaps we have been reluctant to come to grips with a world in which the production and exchange of property is no longer the sole reference point for measuring economic activity because we are afraid of losing our moorings. Our codes of conduct, our civic values, indeed our deepest sense of who we are in relationship to the people, the institutional forces, and the world around us have for so long been mediated by property relations that the thought of being cast adrift in a new, less material, less boundaried, more intangible and ephemeral world of commodified services is unsettling. We'd have to rethink the social contract from beginning to end if we were to wrestle seriously with the impacts of a world based more on access than on ownership.

That day of reckoning, however, may be near because of two changes that Daniel Bell and other forecasters could not have anticipated. First, even goods themselves—the bulwark of a private property regime—are becoming transformed into pure services, signaling the end of property as a defining concept of social life. Second, the nature of services is changing. Traditionally, services have been treated more like goods and negotiated as discrete market transactions, each one separated in time and space. Now, with the advent of electronic commerce and sophisticated data feedback mechanisms, services are being reinvented as long-term multifaceted relationships between servers and clients.

The Evolution of Goods into Services

As goods become more information-intensive and interactive and are continually upgraded, they change character. They lose their status as products and metamorphose into evolving services. Their value lies less in the physical scaffolding or container they come in and more in the access to services they provide. Taichi Sakaiya, the director-general of the Economic Planning Agency of Japan, understood the change taking place in the way we perceive of goods when he wrote, "The significance of material goods [will be] as containers or vehicles for knowledge-value."[33]

Companies are revolutionizing product designs to reflect the new emphasis on services. Instead of thinking of products as fixed items with set features and a one-time sales value, companies now think of them as "platforms" for all sorts of upgrades and value-added services. In the new manufacturing schema it is the services and upgrades that count. The platform is merely the vessel to which these services are added. In a sense, the product becomes more of a cost of doing business than a sale item in and of itself. The idea is to use the platform as a beachhead, as a way of establishing a physical presence in the customer's place of business or domicile. That presence allows the vendor to begin a long-term service relationship with the customer. For this reason, the platforms often are sold at cost in the expectation of selling more lucrative services to the customer over the lifetime of the product.

The toy maker Lego Group AS of Denmark is selling a new toy that combines a computer brain with Lego building blocks so that children can build robotic toys. The product can be plugged into a PC, and new commands that expand the number of things the toy can do can be downloaded from a central Web site.[34] Similarly, emWare, Inc., in Salt Lake City, has created a lawn-sprinkler system linked to the Internet. The sprinkler itself is really a platform for a range of upgraded services that can be integrated into it. For a service fee, the sprinkler can be programmed to automatically contact the National Weather Service Web site to check on weather conditions and forecasts and turn the spray on and off accordingly.[35]

Now, even the telephone itself is becoming a disposable service. In 1999, a new kind of telephone was patented that is so cheap, it is sold for a "fixed amount of air time" and then thrown away once the air time is used up. Its inventor, Randice Lisa Altschul, says the disposable phone will likely be used by harried mothers, children, and travelers who don't want to worry about losing a telephone. The same disposable technology could be used for a range of electronic devices, including hand-held electronic games. The point is, the physical container becomes secondary to the unique services contained in it. What the customer is really purchasing is access to time rather than ownership of a material good.[36]

Encyclopaedia Britannica is a good case study of how economic conditions are hastening the metamorphosis of conventional goods into pure services. Until very recently, a hardback set of the thirty-two volumes of *Encyclopaedia Britannica* cost $1,600 and was considered a major financial investment for most American homes. In the early 1990s, Bill Gates approached Encyclopaedia Britannica with the idea of creating a digital version of its product that could be delivered at a much cheaper retail price on CD-ROM. Worried that the cheap digital version would undermine sales of its printed volumes, Encyclopaedia Britannica declined the offer. Gates then bought Funk and Wagnalls and combined its contents with audio and visual material readily available in the public domain to create a digital encyclopedia called Encarta. The electronic form of the encyclopedia was put on a CD-ROM and sold for $49.95.[37] Besides selling for a fraction of the cost, Microsoft's Encarta was continuously upgraded and updated. As a result, within less than a year and a half it became the best-selling encyclopedia in the world.[38] Quickly losing market share, Britannica was forced to respond with its own online version. Subscribers could pay $85.00 for an entire year of "unlimited access to Britannica Online's vast resources."[39] The company then went a step further, providing free ongoing access to its entire database. The company's revenue now comes from advertisers, who place tailor-made ads at specific Encyclopaedia Britannica entry sites. *Encyclopaedia Britannica* has literally dematerialized into a pure service.

In recent years, a debate has been raging in the library world about the question of ownership of books and collections versus access to online publications. Librarians Eleanor A. Goshen and Suzanne Irving of the State University of New York at Albany note that "within the past decade in academic libraries, economic realities have caused a paradigm shift away from an emphasis on acquiring comprehensive research collections to an emphasis on developing effective methods for maintaining access . . . to research materials that are infrequently used in a particular institution."[40] Insofar as research libraries are concerned, much of the information can be accessed more readily from the Internet and other electronic data highways and at lower cost than purchasing the journals and books and holding them in inventory in large library facilities.[41]

Already, textbooks are being put online. John Wiley and Sons put two standard research reference books, the Kirk-Othmer *Encyclopedia of Chemical Technology* and the *Encyclopedia of Electrical and Electronics Engineering*, online in 1999. These books, which in the past were purchased and owned in the form of physical copies, are now accessible for a fee.[42]

While the demise of print has been forecasted for years, it appears that electronic-based access to material is finally becoming a reality for the first generation of young people who grew up with computers and feel more comfortable accessing information from a screen than viewing it on a printed page. Jeff Rothenberg, a senior computer scientist at the Rand

Corporation, believes that the day is not far off when books printed on paper will be seen "more as objets d'art than things we use all the time."[43]

Books are not the only products dematerializing into electronic services in the new cyberspace economy. The same process is unfolding in diverse commercial fields. For example, the seven regional Bell telephone companies and other giant telecommunications companies now provide voice mail services. Rather than maintaining home answering machines, customers can access voice storage and retrieval systems. In this case, as in countless others, a product is being replaced by a service, and ownership is being eclipsed by access. Writing in the *Harvard Business Review,* Jeffrey Rayport and John J. Sviokla point out that the shift from a marketplace transaction to a marketspace service is occurring with increasing frequency as consumers come to feel more comfortable with access over ownership in their daily lives. They write, "If access can be acquired without the answering machine itself, the customer gains the benefits of the software-defined services without the nuisance of acquiring and maintaining the hardware-defined product."[44]

Robert B. Shapiro, chairman and CEO of Monsanto, is among the new breed of corporate entrepreneurs who are beginning to shift the focus of their business operations from sales to use, emphasizing access over ownership in their marketing strategy. In a 1997 interview, Shapiro observed that consumers don't buy things for themselves but rather for what they do, and gave an example of Monsanto's line of nylon fiber that is made into carpets. "Nobody really wants to own carpet," said Shapiro, "they just want to walk on it. . . . What would happen if Monsanto or the carpet manufacturer owned that carpet and promised to come in and remove it when it required replacing?"[45] Shapiro mentioned in the interview that his company is "starting to look at all our products and ask, what is it people really need to buy? Do they need the stuff or just its function? What would be the economic impact of our selling a carpet service instead of a carpet?"[46]

In some instances, the transformation from selling goods to providing access to services is resulting in significant resource savings, reduction in manufacturing emissions and waste, and less environmental harm. Carrier, the largest manufacturer of air-conditioning equipment, now offers coolth services. Instead of selling an air conditioner, it provides air-conditioning service to its clients. Carrier installs its equipment on a client's premises and charges a service fee for maintaining an agreed-upon level of comfort. Unlike traditional product-based sales, in which a company attempts to sell the largest capacity piece of air-conditioning equipment it can—which means using up more energy than necessary—in a service relationship based on access, the idea is to find ways to minimize the use of energy in order to save on the cost of the service. Carrier provides ancillary services, including lighting retrofits and installation of super windows, so that the client will use less energy flow-through to maintain the necessary comfort level. The cost savings increases the bottom line for the company while cutting down on the wasteful use of energy resources and the emission of greenhouse gases.

Companies in the chemical supply industry also have taken the leap from selling the product to providing a service. An innovative new approach to doing business between chemical suppliers and automobile companies, called "shared savings," was pioneered in the mid-1980s and is fast becoming a prototype for the new commerce based on service and access rather than on sale and ownership.

Chemical supply companies traditionally have sold chemicals to automobile companies for their various production processes, and the customers have paid per drum (or kg, liter, etc.) used. The relationship was between seller and buyer and involved discrete market transactions in which property—in this case, chemicals—was sold. The supplier's incentive was to sell as much of its chemicals as possible while minimizing its up-front costs of production, handling, and transport. Of course, the supplier's desire to sell as much chemicals as it can conflicts with the customer's desire to buy and use as little chemicals as are needed to get the job done and assure appropriate quality controls. Often, the differing objectives of sellers and buyers create conflict. In the conventional seller-buyer model, the seller may reduce the quality of its chemical blends. Because the seller is not responsible for the environmental costs associated with the final use and disposal of its products, it has little or no incentive to invest in costly research to develop less toxic chemical compounds.

In a shared savings arrangement, the automobile company never buys the chemicals. Rather, the chemicals remain the property of the chemical supplier. The supplier enters into a performance contract in which it is responsible for both the management and the application of the chemicals at the customer's site of operations. Instead of buying the products, the automobile company buys access to a service. Once again, the seller-buyer relationship is transformed into a server-client one.

The chemical performance contracts are designed to create incentives between the parties that will result in cost and waste reductions and increased profit margins. In the typical performance contract, the supplier is expected to maintain an agreed-upon level of quality control in return for a fixed monthly fee. The supplier can increase profits by reducing chemical use and overall chemical costs and thus improve both the product and delivery system.

Chrysler has a shared savings arrangement with PPG Industries at its Belvedere, Illinois, plant. PPG is responsible for all chemicals relating to the cleaning, treating, and coating of Chrysler vehicle autobodies. Chrysler never buys the paint from PPG but rather pays the supplier a fixed service fee per quality vehicle produced. In other words, PPG is no longer selling paint but rather servicing its client by managing the painting process itself. Chrysler, in turn, enters into a performance agreement with PPG to secure access to state-of-the-art expertise in paint management with a world-class supplier.[47] The shared savings strategy has saved the company more than $1 million a year.

In gain-sharing arrangements, the parties take the performance contract a step further. If, for example, the supplier can introduce innovations that reduce hazardous waste generation, the automobile company, which is responsible for these costs, agrees to share the cost savings with the supplier, giving the supplier further incentive to introduce processes that will lead to additional cost savings for the automobile company.

PPG/Chemfil and Ford Motor Company's gain-sharing arrangement at the automobile company's Taurus assembly plant in Chicago has resulted in significant environmental remediation. Ford's introduction of aluminum body panels threatened to increase sludge from wastewater treatment to legally hazardous levels. PPG/Chemfil was able to modify the wastewater treatment plant process and reduce sludge generation by 27 percent, saving Ford the additional expense that would have been involved in waste management.[48] Ford shared the savings with PPG/Chemfil.

This new approach to doing business, based on access to services rather than the sale of products, has the potential to make environmental savings an intimate part of the commercial mix in many industries. Environmentalists Paul Hawken and Amory and Hunter Lovins go even further, suggesting that "mere product-sellers will become suspect" in the coming Age of Access. "Why—a prospective buyer may ask—if your product delivers its service with all of the operational advantages you claim, don't you want to capture those advantages for yourself by owning the product and just providing me with its service?" The inference to be drawn, they say, is that "if you want to sell it to me and leave me to pay its operating costs, there must be something wrong with it!"[49]

The End of Sales

Gain sharing is becoming popular in a wide number of fields for the simple reason that in some industries there is little or no money to be made any longer in pure sales. With material and production costs moving toward zero and transaction costs following suit, there's less margin in sales. The problem is compounded by there being too many suppliers in a given industry all competing for the attention of a limited number of customers, further depressing prices and margins. How, then, does a company successfully win market share when the quality of its goods is virtually indistinguishable from its competitors' and everyone's making too much of the same product? The answer, say a growing number of companies, is to abandon sales altogether.

In a buyer's market, getting in the customer's door means letting go of the idea of selling a good or service, as radical as that might seem. The supplier has to represent zero cost to the customer. But without sales, how does the vendor make money? By comanaging the customer's operations, improving its performance and profit, and sharing in the gains. The point that needs to be emphasized is that the supplier sells nothing to the customer. Instead he lends his know-how and expertise to help run the customer's business. The customer, in effect, becomes a client and partner.

Baxter Healthcare Corporation has a gain-sharing arrangement with Duke University Medical Center. Baxter manages the entire cost of Duke's surgical supplies and guarantees an annual ceiling on Duke's expenditures in return for a comanager's fee. If Duke's costs exceed the ceiling, Baxter pays the difference. If, however, Duke's costs are lower than the ceiling, Baxter receives a part of the savings.[50]

The health-care industry is particularly open to gain-sharing arrangements as a way to cut runaway medical costs. Several drug companies have begun to introduce the idea of "disease management" and have entered into gain-sharing arrangements with a growing number of HMOs. The drug companies agree to take responsibility for the total treatment of a patient, including disease prevention, patient care, and the administration of drugs. Eli Lilly has singled out five major diseases: diabetes, heart disease, central nervous system disorders, cancer, and infectious diseases for disease management. By shifting focus from selling drugs to servicing patients, companies like Lilly hope to move up the value chain. The drug companies help reduce HMO and hospital costs by using effective disease management, and the HMOs and hospitals, in turn, share the savings with them.[51]

The New Service Providers

Many of the larger companies in the information-technology business, who just a few years ago made their profits selling hardware and software, have begun to make the transition to becoming service providers. Companies like IBM, General Electric, Xerox, and Hewlett-Packard are realizing that physical products provide little margin for profits. With the containers or platforms becoming so cheap to produce, and quality controls indistinguishable, the only area where opportunities exist to make money is in delivering expertise to customers in the form of services. While gross margins in manufacturing today are generally less than 30 percent, gross margins in service-related activities often exceed 50 percent.[52]

Xerox and Pitney-Bowes operate mailrooms and copy centers, and distribute electronically-generated documents. Honeywell designs and operates whole data systems. Clients lease the systems rather than purchasing them outright. Again, for Honeywell's customers, the name of the game is access to expert services.

Nearly $20 billion of IBM's $70 billion in revenue in 1995 was generated from business services. Lloyd G. Waterhouse, a general manager of IBM's global services, says that services continue to grow faster than revenue generated by selling hardware and software.[53] Waterhouse points out that IBM manages systems that include more than half a million non-IBM computers and that IBM global services often will recommend a competitor's product if it's the best match for the client's need. According to Data Quest, a leading market research firm, global information-technology services alone exceeded $234 billion in 1996 and are expected to reach $400 billion by the year 2000.[54]

General Electric expects its service-generated revenue to reach $15 billion by the end of the year 2000. GE's chairman, John F. Welch, put his finger on the new pulse that is moving mainstream business from selling things to customers to supplying services to clients. He notes, "I can expand a lot faster by upgrading or maintaining the equipment I have installed than by trying to sell more units."[55] Welch says that the proof lies with the company's bottom line, which shows that product-related services are growing at "two to three times the rate of products themselves."[56]

Giving Away the Goods, and Charging for the Services

Perhaps the best evidence of the changing relationship between a product and the services that accompany it lies in the market value of each in relation to the other. Until recently, a service warranty was tacked on to a product, sometimes for a minimum additional charge, or, more often than not, provided free as an incentive to purchase the item. Now that relationship is being turned around. As noted earlier, a growing number of companies are giving away their products for free to attract customers, and then charging their clients for managing, upgrading, and otherwise servicing the products.

When Motorola introduced its Micro-Tac cellular phone in 1989, it retailed for $2,500. Just five years later, the same phone was priced at $100. Today, cellular telephone companies often give the Motorola phone away to new subscribers for free as an inducement to use their telecommunications services.[57]

In 1993, Computer Associates International, Inc., launched its new software accounting program, Simple Money, and priced it at zero. The company was banking on the belief that word of mouth about its generous offer would encourage widespread use and that it would recoup its initial offering by selling its new clients ongoing upgrades and services. (The cost of actually producing each additional diskette, with its software program on it, was so low as to be inconsequential.)[58]

In the information-technology industries, the race to give away products is gaining momentum and becoming standard commercial practice. Netscape gives away its Web browser. Microsoft gives away its Internet Explorer Web browser. Sun Microsystems distributes Java for free.[59] In the case of the software companies, the cost of producing and delivering each additional product approaches zero. At the same time, if the company can convince enough end users to switch to its programs, the firm can set an industry standard and in the process sell upgrades and services to its clients at significant margins.

Giving away software programs is a particularly effective strategy for information-technology firms because the more people who are linked together through a company's programs, the greater the benefits are to each participant and the more valuable the enterprise's potential services become. In the industry, this phenomenon is known as the "network effect." The larger the network, the greater the links, the more valuable the network becomes to those who are part of it. Giving away software helps build networks and is increasingly seen as a cost of doing business.

Again, the question is, how does a company make money when the costs of manufacturing products are declining toward zero in many fields, leaving little room for profit? How does one even price an item whose production cost is negligible? The answer is to give away the product and charge customers for the sophisticated services that accompany it.

Business Week glimpsed the far-reaching significance of this basic change in the relationship between products and services in an article appropriately entitled "The Technology Paradox." Its reporters wrote:

> *The new rules require more than ingenuity, agility, and speed. They call for redefining value in an economy where the cost of raw technology is plummeting toward zero. Sooner or later, this plunge will obliterate the worth of almost any specific piece of hardware or software. Then, value will be in establishing a long-term relationship with a customer—even if it means giving the first generation of a product away.*[60]

In the network economy, characterized by shorter product life cycles and an ever expanding flow of goods and services, it is human attention rather than physical resources that becomes scarce. Giving away products will increasingly be used as a marketing strategy to capture the attention of potential customers. Holding their attention will depend on the ability of companies to deliver effective services and create lasting relationships.

When virtually everything becomes a service, capitalism is transformed from a system based on exchanging goods to one based on accessing segments of experience. If, for example, one contracts for an air-conditioning service rather than buying the air conditioner itself, one pays for the experience of having air conditioning. The new capitalism, then, is far more temporal than material. Instead of commodifying places and things and exchanging them in the market, we now secure access to one another's time and expertise and borrow what we need, treating each thing as an activity or event that we purchase for a limited period of time. Capitalism is shedding its material origins and increasingly becoming a temporal affair.

Chapter Six

Commodifying
Human
Relationships

One person's idea of utopia is often another's dystopian nightmare. Think of waking up one day only to find out that every aspect of your being has become a purchased affair, that your life itself has become the ultimate shopping experience.

The distinguishing characteristic of modern capitalism is the expropriation of various facets of life into commercial relationships. Land, human labor, production tasks, and social activities that once took place in the home all have been absorbed into the market and made into commodities. Still, as long as commerce was bound to discrete transactions between sellers and buyers, the commodification process itself was limited in time and space to either the negotiation and transfer of goods or the time elapsed in the performance of services. All other time still was free of the market and not beholden to market consideration. In the emerging cyberspace economy, network forces pull all remaining free time into the commercial orbit, making each institution and individual a captive of an all-pervasive "commerciality."

The Age of Access is defined, above all else, by the increasing commodification of all human experience. Commercial networks of every shape and kind weave a web around the totality of human life, reducing every moment of lived experience to a commodified status. In the propertied era of capitalism, the emphasis was on selling goods and services. In the cyberspace economy, the commodification of goods and services becomes secondary to the commodification of human relationships. Holding clients' and customers' attention in the new fast-paced, ever changing network economy means controlling as much of their time as possible. By shifting from discrete market transactions that are limited in time and space to commodification of relationships that extend open-endedly over time, the new commercial sphere assures that more and more of daily life is held hostage to the bottom line.

One need only open up the pages of any of the countless books being churned out by marketing and management consultants, economists, forecasters, and futurists to learn that success in the new era will belong to those who are able to make the transition from a production to a marketing perspective and from the notion of making sales to establishing relationships. In their book *Blur: The Speed of Change in the Connected Economy,* Stan Davis and Christopher Meyer point out that in the old economy, "the idea is to inspire repeat purchases, as a string of discrete transactions." In the new economy, however, the goal of every company is "to establish ongoing relationships between themselves and their customers."[1] In *The One to One Future,* marketing consultants Don Peppers and Martha Rogers write that "no matter how creative and innovative your firm is, the only software genuinely worth having is the *customer relationship.*"[2] Peppers and Rogers add, "all your products are ephemeral. Only your customers are real."[3]

The Customer Is the Market

In the industrial economy, with its emphasis on mass production and the sale of goods, securing a share of the market was utmost in the minds of every entrepreneur. In the Age of Access, with its emphasis on selling specialized services and providing access to expertise of all kinds, the role played by suppliers changes markedly, says Wim Roelandts of Hewlett-Packard. "We are shifting from being box sellers," says Roelandts, "to becoming trusted advisors."[4]

The new idea in marketing is to concentrate on share of customer rather than share of market. Peppers and Rogers argue that in the network economy, "you will not be trying to sell a single product to as many customers as possible. Instead, you'll be trying to sell a single customer as many products as possible—over a long period of time, and across different product lines."[5]

When businesses talk about letting go of the idea of selling products one at a time to as many customers as possible and, rather, concentrating on establishing a long-term relationship with each individual customer, what they're really focusing on is the potential of commodifying a person's entire lifetime of experiences. Marketing specialists use the phrase "lifetime value" (LTV) to emphasize the advantages of shifting from a product-oriented to an access-oriented environment where negotiating discrete market transactions is less important than securing and commodifying lifetime relationships with clients. Automobile dealer Carl Sewell estimates, for example, that each new customer that comes through the door of a Cadillac dealership represents a potential lifetime value of more than $322,000. The figure is a projection of the number of automobiles the customer is likely to purchase over his or her lifetime as well as the services those automobiles will require over their lifetimes. Mark Grainer, chairman of the Technical Assistance Research Programs Institute (TARP), estimates that the average "loyal" customer of a supermarket is worth more than $3,800 a year.[6] The key is to find the appropriate mechanism to hold on to the customer for life.

To calculate the LTV of a customer, a firm projects the present value of all future purchases against the marketing and customer-service costs of securing and maintaining a long-term relationship. Credit card companies, magazines, and mail-order catalogs, which rely on subscriptions and memberships, have long used LTV cost-accounting projections. Now the rest of the economy is beginning to follow suit.

The commercial potential of capturing a share of customer is directly proportional to the projected duration of his or her consumer lifetime.

For that reason, many companies make every effort to capture customers at a very early age to optimize their potential LTV. Hyatt Hotels features its Camp Hyatt and a special newsletter aimed at its youngest LTV customers. A&P provides children's shopping carts to accustom youngsters to making their own selections in the store. Delta Airlines has its Fantastic Flyer club for kids.[7]

Peppers and Rogers offer a good hypothetical example of how relationship marketing based on LTV might work in practice. Suppose a diaper service were to provide you with all of the disposable diapers you need for your baby for a subscription fee. Rather than purchasing each diaper as a discrete transaction in the store, you will be getting unlimited access to diapers for as long as the baby requires them. Such companies already exist around the United States. But relationship marketing doesn't stop there. The same firm that contracts with you to provide disposable diapers might also contract, on a subscription basis, to provide you with toys, baby food, formula, and baby clothes. And why stop there? Once establishing a comprehensive service relationship, why not extend it through adolescence and into the teenage years—in other words, why not maximize LTV? Say Peppers and Rogers:

> To the extent that you can maintain that relationship and nurture it over time, you could, over the years, sell toys for older children, school clothing and school supplies, family vacations, video games, compact discs, and even financial services to a family planning ahead for college expenses.[8]

Determining a person's LTV is made possible with the new information and telecommunications technologies of the network economy. Electronic feedback loops and barcodes allow companies to receive continuously updated information on clients' purchases, giving them detailed profiles on customers' lifestyles—their dietary choices, wardrobes, states of health, recreational pursuits, and travel patterns. With appropriate computer modeling techniques, it is possible to use this mass of raw data on each individual to anticipate future desires and needs and map out targeted marketing campaigns to lure customers into long-term commercial relationships.

Many in the information sciences are suggesting even that the new technologies be thought of as relationship technologies, or R-technologies, rather than information technologies. "We need to turn away from the notion of technology managing information and toward the idea of technology as a medium of relationships," says Michael Schrage of the MIT Sloan School's Center for Coordination Science.[9] French economist Albert Bressand says that R-technology is an appropriate way to describe the new technologies because "relations rather than material products are what is processed in these machines."[10]

What is becoming clear to management and marketing experts, and a growing number of economists, is that the new computer software and telecommunications technologies allow for the establishment of rich webs of interconnections and relationships between suppliers and users, creating the opportunity to quantify and commodify every aspect of a person's lived experience in the form of a long-term commercial relationship. Says Bressand, "The time has come to shift from the engineering approach of information technology, which was totally warranted at the beginning, to the human and relationship approach."[11]

In marketing circles, using R-technologies to commodify long-term commercial relationships is called "controlling the customer." Continuous cybernetic feedback allows firms to anticipate and service customers' needs on an ongoing open-ended basis. By turning goods into services and advising clients on upgrades, innovations, and new applications, suppliers become an all-pervasive and indispensable part of the experiential routines of customers. To borrow a Hollywood term, companies serve as "agents," performing a range of services. The goal is to become so embedded in the life of the customer as to become a ubiquitous presence, an appendage of the customer's very being, operating on his behalf in the commercial sphere.

Agents in the new schema are "systems integrators," a phrase coined by Robert C. Blattberg, professor of retailing at the Kellogg Graduate School of Management, and Rashi Glazer. They coordinate an increasing share of the commercial life of their clients.[12] In a sense, agents serve as go-betweens. They manage the continuous flow of information between the global economy and the end-use clients. Their function is a marketing one—to find the most effective way of establishing, maintaining, and enhancing relationships with clients.

Of course, the kinds of relationships these technologies conjure up are, by their very nature, one-sided. Despite the fact that the Internet and cyberspace give a modicum of counter-surveillance power back to the individual consumer and allow for interactivity, the company knows far more about the customer than he or she will ever glean about the company. The algebra of the new electronic marketplace still favors the corporate players.

Firefly, a start-up company now owned by Microsoft, is a cyberspace music vendor that uses software initially designed at the MIT media lab. Its 3 million registered users rank their preferences among hundreds of musical groups and composers. Firefly then makes recommendations of what other music the users might like based on the rankings of other customers with similar musical interests. In this instance, the participants willingly provide data about themselves in return for access to information of value to them. However, the great bulk of information generated each day about the buying patterns and lifestyles of millions of customers is collected and often sold to third parties for solicitation purposes without any consensual agreement by those whose information is being expropriated.

Critics of the indiscriminate use of R-technology argue that potential customers ought to be compensated by any firm using personal data about them for commercial purposes. James Rule, a sociologist at the State University of New York at Stony Brook, proposes that each person has a right to

> withhold, sell or give away rights to commercial sale or exchange of information about himself or herself. . . . Everyone consenting to any release of personal information would retain a data rights agent, who would establish a computerized account for each client. Every time an organization sold or traded its mailing list, it would be legally obliged to collect royalties for the individuals concerned.[13]

In the old industrial economy, each person's own labor power was considered a form of property that could be sold in the marketplace. In the new network economy, selling access to one's day-to-day living patterns and life experiences, as reflected in purchasing decisions, becomes equally coveted and a much sought-after intangible asset.

The Shift from a Production
to a Marketing Perspective

The shift in emphasis from manufacturing and selling products to establishing and maintaining long-term commercial relationships brings the marketing perspective to the forefront of commercial life. The production imperative, which reigned supreme in the industrial era, is increasingly viewed as a back-office function of marketing. When even goods become platforms for managing services, and services become the primary engine driving global commerce, then establishing relationships with end users is critical. Marketing in the new network economy becomes the central framework, and controlling the customer becomes the goal of commercial activity.

Controlling the customer is the final stage in a long commercial journey marked by the increasing wresting away of both ownership and control of economic life from the hands of the masses and into the arms of corporate institutions. Recall that in the early stages of a production-oriented capitalism, economic tasks in the home and craft shops were spirited away and placed in factories by capitalist entrepreneurs. By assuming ownership and control over the tools of production, the capitalists were able to make previously self-sufficient families and artisans dependent on a wage system to secure their livelihoods and survival. Workers were further stripped of any last vestige of control over the production function with the introduction of division of labor and the assembly line in the early decades of the twentieth century. Frederic Taylor introduced his principles of scientific management to the factory floor and front office, revolutionizing the organization of production. Using a stopwatch, Taylor timed every movement of the workers with an eye toward improving their efficiency. The goal was to gain near total control over the worker in the production process.

Today, as the marketing perspective gains ascendancy and commodifying relationships with consumers becomes the essential business of business, controlling the customer takes on the same kind of import and urgency as controlling the worker did when the manufacturing perspective prevailed. If the stopwatch and assembly line provided the technological means to control the worker, cybernetic feedback loops and barcodes provide the technical means to control the customer. In the new century, organizing consumption becomes as important as organizing production was in the last century. The idea is to make the totality of one's experience dependent on commercial agents. Although the end user is engaged in the process, he or she becomes ever more reliant on intermediaries who serve his or her needs. Controlling the customer means exactly that—being able to hold and direct his or her attention and manage the minuscule details of each person's life experiences. The commercial agents assume the role of caretaker.

In the industrial economy, discrete market transactions and the transfer of property between seller and buyer afforded the customer a high degree of control over each consumption decision. In the Age of Access, however, customers risk slowly losing control over the process as short-term market decisions give way to long-term commercial relationships with trusted intermediaries, and the purchase of goods gives way to the contracting of a range of services that extend to virtually every aspect of one's lived experience. The customer becomes mobilized and embedded within a dense web of ongoing commercial relationships and may become totally dependent on commercial forces that he or she little understands and over which he or she has less and less control. In some ways, the new commercial dependency shares much in common with the kind of social dependency that arose under the welfare regimes of the post–World War II era. As democratic governments entered into expanding social service relationships with their citizenry, the democratic impulse that gave rise to these social compacts soon got lost in the growing dependency of large numbers of people on the very government services they had supported.

For example, consider financial planning. Many investment companies have begun to make the transition from simply trading stocks and bonds and managing customer portfolios to becoming a full-service provider—a systems integrator. Clients are looking to companies like Merrill Lynch to help them create customized investment packages for their specific needs and goals. Some financial institutions are becoming customer agents, providing complete financial planning services that include yearly business plans, personal budgeting plans, retirement income plans, estate planning, tax and accounting services, legal assistance, and other services. The idea is to bring the client into an all-encompassing relationship with an agent. The financial institution handles every aspect of the client's financial dealings for a lifetime and beyond. The client gains access to specialized expertise and trusted advisors who act on his behalf, often as his agent, surrogate, or advocate.

In the Age of Access, while the clients make the ultimate choice to enter into or leave these long-term, multifaceted relationships, the complexity of the services rendered and the expertise needed to perform those services can become difficult to understand and even baffling after a while—especially if the customer cedes those tasks over to a third party early on. Not ever having to be personally engaged in the details of these services, the client often remains untutored and ignorant of the forces at work and may become increasingly dependent on the "expert" agents over time to manage his or her affairs. The agents, in turn, become the gatekeepers—a concept we will explore further in chapter 9—controlling the many channels of supply and distribution that connect each consumer to the global marketplace and the outside world.

It's no wonder that so many firms are making the leap from manufacturer and producer to agent and distributor. Once again, we see that in the Age of Access, controlling the customer is far more important than controlling the product. The product, after all, is just part of the services that make up the relationship with the client.

Medco Containment Services is a good example of a company whose sole mission is gaining access to and control over the customer. Medco is the largest mail-order drug distributor in the United States. The company has successfully positioned itself between the major pharmaceutical companies and the nation's leading health maintenance organizations (HMOs). Medco offers one-stop shopping for all pharmaceutical products and purchases and distributes drugs from all the leading pharmaceutical companies. Its buyers search for the best prices and guarantee their customers dollar-specific savings. In return for the savings, customers agree to let Medco "have a say in how customers manage their diagnosis, treatment, and home-health aftercare of each drug's patients," virtually ensuring that more drugs will get sold.[14] Medco has become, for all intents and purposes, the gatekeeper between the end users—HMOs—and the nation's pharmaceutical companies by virtue of the access it enjoys with the customers.

The drug companies found themselves increasingly at the mercy of Medco in recent years because of the control it exercised over customers' preferred drug lists. Merck decided that the best way to fend off the threat was to acquire Medco, which it did. Even after the acquisition, Medco continues to require Merck to discount its prices if it wants to have its products distributed through Medco channels. By the end of the year 2000, Merck estimates that 80 percent of its drug business will be through Medco. "When that happens," says sales consultant Mack Hannan, "Merck's 5,500 sales representatives at the time of Medco's acquisition will no longer be needed to call on individual practice physicians, doctors' groups, and hospitals."[15] Merck's sales force will likely disappear. The drug company will become what Hannan calls a tier-two supplier, and Medco, because it controls the gateway to the customer, will triumph.

Like Amazon.com and Nike, Medco is a pure marketing mechanism, freed up from the burdens of owning factories and having to invest in expensive and time-consuming research and development. Virtually propertyless, its prime asset is access to customers and its ability to forge long-term commercial relationships with end users. That's all it needs in a network economy, where the marketing perspective takes precedence over the manufacturing mode.

The evolution of marketing has as much to do with saturated consumer demand as with the new information and communications technologies that make possible a seamless one-to-one relationship between firms and customers. Innovations in manufacturing processes, especially in the post–World War II era, greatly expanded the flow of new goods into the marketplace. In the early years after the war, pent-up demand was sufficient to absorb virtually every item that came off the assembly line. The Great Depression and war years had slowed the production stream to a trickle. Anxious to make up for lost time and the years of going without the necessities and luxuries of life, the GI generation went on a buying spree. The migration to the suburbs, the creation of the highway culture, and the proliferation of shopping malls all became magnets for consumption. In the 1950s it was a seller's market. Manufacturing was king, and the corporate eye was fixed almost exclusively on the costs of production and distribution. With consumers buying as fast as the products could be made, there was little need to worry about developing long-term relationships with customers. Cash registers were ringing away. Discrete market transactions appeared sufficient, and repeat business seemed assured.

By the 1960s, however, consumer markets were becoming overrun with goods. Most families had two automobiles parked in their garages, washers and dryers humming away in their laundry rooms, and color televisions blaring in virtually all the rooms of their houses. Companies began to face a new reality: overproduction against falling consumer demand. The question was no longer how to produce fast enough to keep up with the consumer market but rather how to capture and hold the attention of the consumer long enough to make him or her a loyal, long-term customer.

One of the first to catch the significance of the shift from a production to a marketing prospective was Peter Drucker, the father of modern business management practices. He wrote:

> *The customer is the foundation of a business and keeps it in existence. He alone gives employment. And it is to supply the customer that society entrusts wealth-producing resources to the business enterprise. . . . Because it is its purpose to create a customer, any business enterprise has two— and only these two—basic functions: marketing and innovation. . . . Marketing is the distinguishing, the unique function of the business. . . . It is the whole business seen from the point of view of the final result, that is, from the customer's point of view. Concern and responsibility for marketing must therefore permeate all areas of the enterprise.[16]*

Business consultants began to urge their corporate clients to spend less time focusing on production and more on marketing if they wanted to capture market share. In a landmark article entitled "Marketing Myopia," Theodore Levitt, professor emeritus at the Harvard Business School, argued that companies are too concerned with the products they produce and not concerned enough with the customers they serve. He argued that businesses should develop their business plans from the customer end backward rather than the production end forward. The goal of business, he suggested, is to capture customers, not simply produce goods and services.[17] All of the new voices in marketing and management share a common sentiment—that the emphasis on building long-term customer relationships is far more important to a company's success than the more narrow objective of making discrete sales transactions.

While the shift from a seller's to a buyer's market hastened the transition from a production to a marketing orientation and the new information technologies of the network economy made possible the commodification of an ongoing lifetime relationship with customers, it was technological change in the production process in the 1980s and 1990s that guaranteed the ultimate ascendancy of the marketing perspective and the relegation of production to a function of the marketing process.

The new ability to customize production to the needs of each customer made it necessary for business operations to begin at the customer end and work backward toward the factory floor in the commercial process. Instead of suppliers mass-producing products and then creating markets to distribute them, consumers increasingly inform suppliers of their unique individual needs, which are then produced to their specifications.

The change from mass production to mass customization began in earnest in the 1980s. With consumer markets saturated, many suppliers of mass-produced goods found themselves with too much excess capacity and bloated inventories. Because so many suppliers were in each field and there was so little to differentiate the products of one company from another, the only way to stay ahead of the competition was to slash prices and lower profit margins. The steady decline in sales volume and profits convinced some companies that they had to radically change their direction if they were to survive. By differentiating their product offerings from their competitors', these companies hoped they could secure a larger share of the market and stay competitive. They began experimenting with new ways of organizing production in an effort to customize goods to each buyer. Production processes were revolutionized with the introduction of modular equipment, giving manufacturers the ability to tailor products to the customized needs of each client.

Motorola was one of the leaders in the new field of mass customization. Motorola was suffering declining sales in the face of intense competition from Japanese manufacturers. Hardest hit was Motorola's pager division. Japanese firms were selling high-quality pagers on the global market at half the price of the U.S. product. With other American manufacturers of pagers rapidly going out of business, Motorola decided that the only way to stay in the market would be to differentiate its product line and provide customers with the opportunity to customize their purchases. The company introduced its new line of pagers with hardware and software features that could be arranged in more than 29 million combinations. Any of the combinations could be produced with zero setup time and in lots of one. Meanwhile, manufacturing time was cut from more than five hours to less than twenty minutes. To capture and hold the customers, Motorola revamped its ordering process with the introduction of time- and cost-saving information technology. An order that used to take a month to process was reduced to an hour and a half.[18]

Bally Engineered Structures, a Pennsylvania-based company that specializes in manufacturing walk-in coolers, freezers, and cold-storage buildings, went through a similar conversion. Like Motorola, Bally was faced with market saturation and stiff competition, forcing it to drive down prices and lower profit margins. Bally retooled its manufacturing facilities in the 1980s by introducing modularized panels and accessories that could be customized to the design requirements of each of its customers. The new processes are so efficient that Bally can manufacture and deliver customized products four times faster than its competitors produce the older standardized products.[19]

Being able to customize goods to each customer's needs and desires gives firms a tremendous advantage over the competition. Because the new commercial process begins with the customer and works its way back to the production process, the structuring of the relationship between the firm and the consumer—the marketing function—is the critical factor. It determines the nature of the production. At the same time, the codesign of products creates a relationship between the company and end user that's more like that between a server and client than a seller and buyer. In short, customization comes to be regarded more as the contracting of a service.

New Kinds of Communities

R-technologies reach out to encompass the whole of a person's life experiences. The power of these marketing tools lies in the ability to create a comprehensive environment for organizing personal life and restructuring social discourse. Because they increasingly become a primary means by which people communicate with one another, R-technologies can be used to reconfigure the most fundamental categories of social existence. Already, in marketing circles the talk runs to ways of using R-technologies to create new kinds of communities made up of like-minded people who come together because of their shared interest in a particular commercial endeavor, activity, or pursuit. There's a growing awareness among management and marketing experts alike that establishing so-called "communities of interest" is the most effective way to capture and hold customer attention and create lifetime relationships. The companies become the gatekeepers to these newly defined communities and, for a price, grant customers access to these coveted new social arenas.

Marketing consultants Richard Cross and Janet Smith list several critical stages in the creation of communities of interest. Stage one is awareness bonding. The idea is to make the customer aware of your firm's product or service with the expectation of negotiating a first sale. Stage two is identity bonding. The customer begins to identify with your firm's product or service and incorporates it into his sense of self. It becomes one of the many ways he differentiates himself in the world. For example, driving a Cadillac or a VW Beetle serves as a social statement as much as a means of transportation. Stage three is relationship bonding, which we've explored above. The firm and the customer move from an arm's-length relationship to an interactive one. This is where R-technologies begin to play an important role. They help create what marketers call "customer intimacy." Hallmark's reminder service, for example, keeps a list in their electronic files of the important birthdays and anniversaries in your family and e-mails you a timely reminder along with suggestions of appropriate cards to send.[20]

Stage four is community bonding. The company brings its customers into relationships with one another based on their shared interest in the firm's products and services. The company's task is to create communities for the purpose of establishing long-term commercial relationships and optimizing the lifetime value of each customer. "This bond is extremely durable," say Cross and Smith. "To break it, competitors must actually disregard social ties among friends, colleagues, or family."[21]

The key to creating communities of interest is to plan events, gatherings, and other activities that bring customers together to share their common interest in your company's brand. Holiday Inn's Priority Club brings together between 500 and 1,000 of its most frequent guests, twice a year, at one of its resorts for a weekend of entertainment and recreation, peppered with several roundtable discussions with hotel management. The outings for Priority Club members include professional sports clinics, celebrity speakers, and special tours. The idea is to provide a time and place for club members to meet and form bonds of intimacy with one another and Holiday Inn executives. Members are encouraged to participate in focus-group discussions and "to share feelings and ideas with us," says Ken

Pierce, vice president of frequency marketing for Holiday Inn.[22] Some of its 3.8 million members also are invited to become members of the company's many regional advisory boards. Priority Club members have proven to be loyal customers, spending, on average, 60 percent of their nights on the road at Holiday Inns.[23]

Backroads is an upscale tourist company that organizes bicycle and walking tours through some of the most scenic areas of the world. The company provides tents, prepares the food, and shuttles the guests to the various sites by van. The true value of the Backroads service, says authors Larry Downes and Chunka Mui in their book, *Unleashing the Killer App*, lies in "the quality of its network of customers, who pay, in part, for the opportunity to interact with and be entertained by *each other*. . . . We take such trips because we know that the company attracts like-minded individuals and we know that we'll make some new friends by the end of the trip."[24] Backroads, say Downes and Mui, is about "creating communities of value by valuing community."[25] Companies like Backroads will increasingly rely on R-technologies in the future to search out prospective customers based on their consumer profiles, lifestyles, and spending patterns. As software profiling becomes even more sophisticated, it will be possible to match the very specific lifestyle interests of prospective customers with particular trips, ensuring a more meaningful experience and the likelihood of creating effective community bonding among the guests.

Burger King Kids Club brings children together in a "community of interest." The club's 4 million members receive discounts on meals and a number of perks, including three age-directed magazines. A pen-pal club matches up Burger King Kids Club members. The company supplies the children with special Burger King stationery and pens. By 1994, the club was operating in more than twenty-five countries. The company is outspoken about the purpose of its Kids Club. Burger King's Michael Evans says, "We want to capture the hearts and minds of kids and keep them until they're 60."[26] In the meantime, sales of Burger King Kids Meals have tripled since the club was established in 1990.

The recreational vehicle (RV) industry boasts more than thirty manufacturer-sponsored RV clubs. Members are drawn together into a like-minded community by owning the same kind of RV. "It's a whole psychological study in customer bonding," says Warren MacKenzie of Foretravel, Inc.[27] MacKenzie adds that "our whole motivation in supporting the club is to develop a continuing loyalty to the product and the company." MacKenzie says, "We can almost pinpoint the percentage of sales that can be credited towards the club and the support of the club."[28]

Many of the RV clubs maintain their own park grounds or have reserved designated areas for their members in campgrounds. The Winnebago-Itasca Travelers Club, with its 14,000 members and 250 chapters, holds frequent rallies throughout the U.S. and Canada. Members receive a monthly magazine and perks, including road service, trip routing advice, insurance, product discounts, and even mail-forwarding service when they are on the road. The club accounts for more than 20 percent of the company's annual motor home sales.[29]

The transformation in the nature of commerce from selling things to commodifying relationships and creating communities marks a turning point in the way commerce is conducted. The commercial sphere is broadening its reach and deepening its penetration into virtually every aspect of human existence. In the twenty-first century, the economy becomes the arena where human beings live out much of their day-to-day experiences. In this new world, ownership of things, while important, is less important than securing commercial access to networks of mutual interests, webs of relationships, and shared communities. To belong, in the new era, is to be connected to the many networks that make up the new global economy. Being a subscriber, member, or client becomes as important as being propertied. It is, in other words, access rather than mere ownership that increasingly determines one's status in the coming age.

While there has been considerable public rift in recent years over the deregulation of government services and activities and their subsequent absorption into the commercial sphere, far less attention has been focused on the absorption of the personal sphere into the marketplace. The commodification of human relationships is a heady venture. Assigning lifetime values (LTVs) to people with the expectation of transforming the totality of their lived experience into commercial fare represents the final stage of capitalist market relations. What happens to the essential nature of human existence when it is sucked into an all-encompassing web of commercial relationships?

The growing shift from the commodification of space and goods to the commodification of human time and lived experience is everywhere around us. Every spare moment of our time is being filled with some form of commercial connection, making time itself the most scarce of all resources. Our fax machines, e-mail, voice mail, and cellular phones, our twenty-four-hour trading markets, instant around-the-clock ATM and online banking services, all-night e-commerce and research services, twenty-four-hour television news and entertainment, twenty-four-hour food services, pharmaceutical services, and maintenance services, all holler out for our attention. They worm their way into our consciousness, take up much of our waking time, and occupy much of our thoughts, leaving little respite.

When every endeavor is transformed into a commercial service, we run the risk of falling into a kind of temporal Malthusian trap. Although a day is limited and fixed to twenty-four hours, new kinds of commercial services and relationships are limited only by the entrepreneur's ability to imagine new ways of commodifying time. Already, even in the early stage of the transition to the Age of Access, the commodification of time is becoming saturated. Every institution and human being is being courted and connected to some form of commodified service or relationship. And while we have created every kind of labor- and time-saving device and activity to service one another's needs and desires in the commercial sphere, we are beginning to feel like we have less time available to us than any other humans in history. That is because the great proliferation of labor- and time-saving services only increase the diversity, pace, and flow of commodified activity around us.

The network-based economy does indeed increase the speed of connections, shorten durations, improve efficiency, and make life more convenient by turning everything imaginable into a service. But when most relationships become commercial relationships and every individual's life is commodified twenty-four hours a day, what is left for relationships of a noncommercial nature—relationships based on kinship, neighborliness, shared cultural interests, religious affiliation, ethnic identification, and fraternal and civic involvement? When time itself is bought and sold and one's life becomes little more than an ongoing series of commercial transactions held together by contracts and financial instruments, what happens to the kinds of traditional reciprocal relationships that are born of affection, love, and devotion? The fact that marketing professionals and corporations are seriously engaged in developing what they call long-term "customer intimacy" and are actively experimenting with a host of vehicles and venues for establishing deep "community bonding" is disturbing enough. What is more worrisome is that these large-scale efforts to create a surrogate social sphere tucked inside a commercial wrap are, for the most part, going unnoticed and uncritiqued, despite the broad and far-reaching potential consequences for society. When virtually every aspect of our being becomes a paid-for activity, human life itself becomes the ultimate commercial product, and the commercial sphere becomes the final arbiter of our personal and collective existence.

Chapter Seven

Access

as a Way

of Life

We are readying a new stage of capitalism that is, in many ways, unlike anything we've experienced before. All the familiar economic totems seem to be dissolving one by one. Emerging in their place are new commercial icons for a new age in history.

The birth of a network economy, the steady dematerialization of goods, the declining relevance of physical capital, the ascendance of intangible assets, the metamorphosis of goods into pure services, the shift in first-tier commerce from a production to a marketing perspective, and the commodification of relationships and experiences all are elements in the radical restructuring going on in the high-tech global economy as part of humanity begins to leave markets and property exchange behind on its journey into the Age of Access.

Everywhere we look today, access is becoming the measure of social relations. Our transportation, our neighborhood businesses, our personal health, even the seeds of life and biological processes are being restructured to accommodate a new world defined by access relations. Unlike the earlier notion of private property, whose merits and shortcomings were taken up among philosophers and made the subject of great social debate, access has slipped into the body politic and nettled its way into virtually every nook and cranny of private and public life with little discussion.

The shift from ownership to access is often a piecemeal affair. The transformation is sometimes so nuanced that it goes virtually unnoticed and becomes transparent only in hindsight. The change in housing arrangements over the past twenty-five years is a good example of the kind of subtle transition taking place in countless industries and fields as the economy and society make the slow changeover from ownership to access relationships.

Housing in the United States—and in other countries as well—is being conceptually revamped. Its new configuration is beginning to reflect the sensibilities of an Age of Access. While the final metamorphosis to "access living arrangements" may still be a generation or more away, the gestation process is far enough along to reveal the outline of a new kind of home environment tailored for a new economy.

Gated Communities

Residential communities called "common-interest developments" (CIDs) have been popping up across the American landscape. Many are walled, fenced, and gated and designed specifically to restrict access. Gatekeepers—security guards—are positioned at guardhouses at the front entrances to make sure only residents, their guests, and authorized visitors and vendors are allowed into the community. While these types of communities were an oddity thirty years ago, they are quickly becoming the norm in most new housing developments. More than 30 million Americans, or 12 percent of the U.S. population, currently reside in some 150,000 common-interest developments.[1]

Common-interest developments share a number of features that distinguish them from other kinds of housing, including common ownership of some property and mandatory membership in a home-owners association. Residents of CIDs own their own units and share ownership of "common areas," including parks, lawns, roads, parking lots, swimming pools, tennis courts, and recreation centers. If the CIDs are composed of condominiums or co-ops, then the residents collectively own the entire building and each individual owns only the "air space" within each unit. Every home owner belongs to a membership association and is required to pay monthly or annual dues for the management and maintenance of the community. Again, as is increasingly becoming the case with other commercial activities, membership and dues are critical components of this new kind of living arrangement based on gatekeeping and access relationships.

New common-interest development associations are being established at a rate of 4,000 to 5,000 per year.[2] If the current rate of growth continues—and every indication is that it will increase even more rapidly over the next two decades—common-interest developments could gradually rival existing municipal governments, notes Robert H. Nelson, an economist at the U.S. Department of the Interior.[3] Were CIDs to become the prevailing way of organizing living arrangements, the new institution, says Nelson, "could be as important as the adoption in the United States of the private corporate form of business ownership."[4]

Unlike conventional communities, which are made up of a hodgepodge of privately owned homes and businesses and publicly owned and maintained resources and amenities, CIDs are totally commodified living spaces.[5] Public spaces and public property do not exist. And unlike in traditional communities, which allow for the free flow of people, goods, and services, in CIDs access is tightly circumscribed and a principal reason why people choose to live there.

CIDs are about selling a way of life as opposed to selling merely a house. The homes themselves are embedded in a network of services that make up a unique living experience and bear a strong resemblance to other goods or forms of property that have become containers or platforms for the services and experiences that accompany them.

Walt Disney's planned community in Florida—Celebration—is in many ways a prototype of the new genre of real-estate developments— communities where buying a house is merely the ticket for gaining access to a prepackaged lifestyle.

The $2.5 billion community is being built just outside Disney's World Theme Park in Orlando.[6] The Celebration sales brochure devotes much more copy to emphasizing the way of life residents will experience than the features of the houses that will be constructed, giving the clear impression that Celebration is more a celebration of lifestyle than living quarters. As stated in the Celebration brochure:

> *There once was a place were neighbors greeted neighbors in the quiet of summer twilight. Where children chased fireflies. And porch swings provided easy refuge from the cares of the day. The movie house showed cartoons on Saturday. The grocery store delivered. And there was always that one teacher who always knew you had that special something. Remember that place? Perhaps from your childhood. Or maybe just from stories. It held a magic all of its own. The special magic of an American home town.*[7]

Disney architect Joe Barnes strikes the central theme of what planners hope will be the Celebration experience. "If you're building a house at Celebration," says Barnes, "you're building more than just an individual house on an individual lot; you're creating community."[8]

The Disney community, however, is of a very different sort. It is not an organic creation, built painstakingly over many years by a combination of trial and error, the wrangling of competing interests, and human beings coming together in shared civic engagement. Rather it is a predesigned construction from beginning to end, a carefully planned commercial venture, part living space, part theater, for those who are willing to pay the admission fee. Purchasing a home and becoming a member of the Celebration home-owners association is the gateway to the Disney experience.

Commercial real-estate developers like Disney create CIDs to appeal to a whole range of lifestyle groups, including singles, empty-nesters, retirees, and working couples. The three most popular lifestyle CIDs are retirement communities, golf and leisure communities, and suburban new towns. CIDs are particularly appealing to the aging baby boomer population that is edging toward retirement and more interested in leisure-time activities.

Prestige communities are still another form of CID. The wealthiest members of society often choose to live among those of similar means, and they welcome the kind of controlled security and access restrictions that come with living in CIDs.

New towns are large developments that create a total community all at once. New towns like Reston, Virginia, and Columbia, Maryland, boast schools, commercial offices, shopping centers, parks, and other amenities one might find in a traditional town or city—except here, the entire town is a commodified experience. Relationships are commercially structured. There is no public life in the sense that we have come to know it. While there is governance and even voting rights, the franchise is based on commercial ties, not citizenship.

CIDs have their roots at the turn of the twentieth century. An English court stenographer, Ebenezer Howard, envisioned a new kind of town that would incorporate the best features of city and country life. He called his vision "garden cities." Howard looked askance at what he regarded as the rather disorganized patterns of development found in traditional towns. He advocated the radical notion of creating a whole town at once, designed in minute detail, in advance, by engineers, architects, and other professionals. "It is essential," wrote Howard, "that there should be unity of design and purpose—that the town should be planned as a whole, and not left to grow up in a chaotic manner as has been the case with all English towns, and more or less so with the towns of all countries."[9] He dreamed of grand circular cities crossed by wide boulevards and peppered with parks, gardens, and arcades. The outside perimeter would house factories and be surrounded by an agricultural belt, making the whole venture a self-contained human enterprise. The government would be a democratically controlled corporate technocracy, administered with all of the efficiency of professional managers and engineers, unimpeded by the traditional jousting that comes with partisan politics and the pleading of parochial interests. His corporate structure of government anticipated by several decades what would become the organizational format for common-interest developments.

CIDs enjoyed a limited existence during the first half of the twentieth century. In 1928, Charles Stern Ascher built the first planned community in America: Radburn, New Jersey. It was administered by private government, responsible to a home-owners association.[10] In 1962, there were fewer than 500 such entities in the U.S.[11] The idea didn't take off on a grand scale until the late 1960s, when land was becoming more scarce and costlier, especially near major metropolitan areas, forcing commercial real-estate investors to rethink space requirements. CIDs fit the bill. By spacing homes closer together and providing common areas—parks, gardens, swimming pools, tennis courts—developers were able to cut costs and still provide home owners with amenities they had come to expect in suburbia. Buyers were willing to give up their expansive lawns and acreage in return for shared common spaces where residents could enjoy their recreational pursuits. With the help and financial underwriting of the Federal Housing Administration, CIDs blossomed. Industry forecasters predict that by the end of the year 2000, there will be more than 225,000 CIDs, with more than 48 million members.[12]

Many people choose to live in CIDs because of the conveniences and services they provide. However, people's living experiences are commodified often at the expense of their ownership rights. The governing assumptions and contractual arrangements that accompany CID living subtly strip away ownership and property rights and steadily reorient residents toward the advantages and pitfalls that come with access living arrangements. Because a home is, for many people, the single most important form of property they will ever own, it's instructive to examine how the CID way of life is beginning to undermine the traditional property perspective and, in the process, laying the philosophical and legal foundations for an age in which owning a home becomes less important than experiencing a lifestyle.

To begin with, the statutes and covenants governing the CIDs give residents less ownership rights over their own property than traditional home owners enjoy. The CIDs, which often are thought of as private governments or quasi-governments, are established by the commercial real-estate developer. He or she draws up the constitution and writes the bylaws and covenants. The declaration of covenants, conditions, and restrictions "describes all easements within the development, imposes a system of architectural or design review, imposes private restrictions on the use and enjoyment of property and sets forth a regulatory scheme to ensure that the restrictions are observed by future owners."[13] Because the developer retains ownership of unsold lots and enjoys enhanced voting rights, he or she has effective control over all association decisions until well into the development of the community. For example, the developer staffs all board positions with his employees and generally retains three votes for every unsold unit, giving him undisputed control until the entire project is sold. Even then, the developer presides over the CID during a transition period until the elected residents take over all the board-of-directors positions. Says Evan McKenzie in his book *Privatopia,* "The developer's idea of how people should live is, to a large extent, cast in concrete."[14]

Even with voting rights, the will of the majority is often thwarted. Only property owners are allowed to vote, and then it's on the basis of one vote for each unit owned. If several adults are living in the same unit—for example, husband, wife, and grandparents—only one viewpoint can be expressed. The rest are left out of the process, leaving many residents without a voice in governance. Moreover, many owners rent their units out as investments. In California, for example, approximately 20 percent of all units are rented. While the tenants live in the community and are subject to its statutes and covenants, they have no vote and no say in decisions made that affect their living conditions and arrangements.[15]

Restricted access to the governing process has its consequences. CID boards exercise vast powers over the private lives of their members and, as a result, often undermine the rights of property owners to exclusive control over their own property. Among other things, says McKenzie, "most CID boards have the right to enter individual homes as they deem appropriate and necessary to protect everyone's investment."[16] Equally egregious, CID boards can impose restrictions on residents' behavior or how their homes can be used, and even how their guests are to be treated.

The legal restrictions governing how a private home can be used are called "servitudes." Some of the CID restrictions are so invasive and encompassing as to corrupt the very idea that one is king or queen of his or her castle. In Rancho Bernardo, a CID of some 33,000 residents just north of San Diego, the list of servitudes is long and sometimes absurd. In his book *America II,* Richard Louv describes some of the restrictions governing behavior.

> *Even vegetable gardens are frowned upon . . . Fences, hedges, or walls . . . may not be more than three feet tall. Signs, other than for-sale signs, are prohibited. Trees must be kept trimmed and may not grow above the level of the roof, which must be covered with red tiles. Residents are not allowed to park recreational vehicles or boats in their driveway; a special communal parking area is set aside for them. One village, designed for seniors, prohibits grandchildren from using the recreational center, and home visitation by children is strictly limited.*[17]

Rancho Bernardo is not alone in its restriction policies. Similar rules exist in CIDs across the country. McKenzie cites a number of examples. In Ashland, Massachusetts, a Vietnam veteran was prohibited from displaying the American flag on Flag Day. In Monroe, New Jersey, a CID board sued a home owner because his wife, who was forty-five at the time, was three years younger than the association's age minimum for establishing residency. The court upheld the CID board decision, ordering the man to sell or rent his unit or live there without his wife. In Fort Lauderdale, Florida, a condominium manager ordered a couple to stop entering and leaving their house through the back door because they were wearing a path into the lawn. In Boca Raton, Florida, an association took a resident to court because her dog exceeded the thirty-pound weight limit.[18]

Some CIDs have rules even on what kinds of furnishings can be placed near windows and what color residents can paint their rooms. Others set time limits for how long guests can visit, and impose curfews on socializing with neighbors outside after a certain hour.[19] Most residents of CIDs say they are willing to give up some of their individual property rights in return for enjoying access to a network of like-minded people who share common values, sensibilities, and lifestyles. Membership in a CID, after all, brings with it benefits that are not available to the solitary home owner. One gives up the autonomy that goes with a strict private-property regime for the interdependence that goes with purchasing a commodified relationship with others.

While CID covenants chip away at the rights that accompany private ownership of homes, developers argue that residents have a choice not to live in a CID community or to sell and move if they're unhappy. The problem, says McKenzie, is that "it is increasingly difficult to find non-CID housing in many parts of the country."[20]

Constitutional scholars worry that CIDs are undermining more than private-property rights. By restricting community access CIDs, it is argued, are violating the basic right of every American to move freely, congregate, and express him- or herself in public. Access is central to the new CID living arrangements, as it is in managed health care (HMOs) and all of the other commercial endeavors built on "memberships" in commodified communities. In the case of CIDs, where every square foot of living space is part of a commercial arrangement, what happens to the notion of public space and the basic First Amendment rights of freedom of assembly and speech? For example, security guards often have to make subjective decisions about who should be let through the gates and who should be excluded. For the most part, the gatekeeping decisions reflect the prevailing biases in society at large. One planning consultant put it in stark terms: "[A] black person who shows up in one of these places is likely to get busted."[21] Because CIDs are private domains, their boards of directors argue that they are free to dispense with First Amendment rights that guarantee free access. Since CIDs have no "public space," they do not have to open their communities to the public.

Anxious not to appear overtly biased, some CIDs charge an admission fee for entrance into their communities, which has the effect of excluding the poor. Sea Pines Plantation in Hilton Head, South Carolina, charges nonmembers a three-dollar fee for the right to walk on its streets.[22]

Members of a CID association may have agreed to restrictive covenants that limit access to their lives, neighborhoods, and communities, but nonmembers have not. The question of the rights of nonmembers to freely circulate, solicit, petition, and distribute materials inside CIDs has led to a growing number of lawsuits. The California Court of Appeals ruled that the Leisure World development could not prohibit nonmembers from distributing their material in the community simply because it was not a Leisure World in-house publication. Commenting on the court's decision in the *Yale Law Journal,* attorney David J. Kennedy observed that "Leisure World's restriction on speech by nonmembers dramatically illustrates the ability of developers to create a captive audience, access to which may then be auctioned off to the highest bidder." Kennedy goes on to say that "where such communities are the dominant forms of residential living, less well-financed or less popular viewpoints run the risk of being heard rarely if at all."[23]

Although private property has been the foundation of the modern era, it has been accompanied all along the way by a public property regime and the attendant rights that go with participation in the public square. The point is, private property has been treated as sacrosanct but not hegemonic. There always have been spaces left for public discourse and engagement. As we have seen, CIDs eliminate those public spaces and the First Amendment rights that accompany them. Whole communities become commercial domains, and herein lies the rub. In CIDs, not only are the rights that go with participation in the public sphere eliminated, but so are all notions of public space itself. In the final analysis, says McKenzie, "residency in CIDs requires home buyers to become part of a corporation and live according to its rules. . . . In this sense, CIDs represent a tendency toward universalization of corporate values."[24]

The phenomenal growth of CIDs in the past quarter of a century speaks volumes to the change in thinking that has brought commercial values to the fore and shunted civic values to the periphery of human life. For an increasing number of Americans, writes Bettina Drew in the *Yale Law Review,* the fact that "community is now a product we can purchase rather than something we create for ourselves suggests how deeply the values of the marketplace have penetrated into American domestic life."[25]

In the growing discussion over the economic and social significance of CIDs, it needs to be emphasized that millions of Americans purchase homes in common-interest developments expressly to protect their property rights. Part of the appeal of gated communities is the belief that by living with others who share common values and enjoy comparable incomes, and by being able to shut out others who might threaten real estate values, one's investment in home and property can be secured. Still, as mentioned above, people's decisions to relocate to CIDs are heavily influenced also by their desire to buy into a way of life, to secure access to a network of people, services, and amenities that will allow them to live out a particular lifestyle. CIDs promote the idea of commodifying one's living experience as much, if not more, than securing one's property. In this sense, CIDs are transitional residential communities. They are halfway stations for millions of families who find themselves caught between two worlds and ways of life—an older one based on the primacy of ownership and property relations, and a new one based on the primacy of commodified relationships and access to shared lifestyle experiences.

Renting a Lifestyle

Although CIDs are the most visible manifestation of the changing sensibilities in housing, other forces also are helping to redefine the nature of the "home experience." While home ownership is at its highest level in American history—66.7 percent of American households own their homes—analysts note a counter trend that may portend a fundamental rethinking of the notion of ownership, especially among a growing number of wealthier Americans and those in the younger generation.[26]

The apartment rental market, which has long been the domain of lower-income families, single people, and young married couples not yet able to afford their first home, is changing character and increasingly catering to the new interests of an upwardly mobile generation who put more value on short-term access to services, amenities, and experiences and who are less willing to be weighed down by the responsibilities that go along with traditional home ownership.

The Villas at Beaver Creek in the wealthy suburb of Las Colinas, near Dallas, is a good example of the new wave in apartment rentals. In return for rental payments that range from $645 to $1,365 a month, tenants enjoy access to one- to three-bedroom apartments with "homelike" amenities, including gas fireplaces, large kitchens with modern appliances, walk-in closets, and garages. The complex is gated, offering additional security, and is equipped with a clubhouse, fitness and business centers, two swimming pools, a steam room, a hot tub, and a sauna. Robyn Muller, who with her husband rents a three-bedroom, two-bath apartment in the complex, says, "It's like a big house, but we have conveniences we need and don't have to deal with the yard."[27]

The Mullers are among the nation's 34.7 million household renters. All together, renters account for 33 percent of all U.S. households.[28] What's different about the "new renters" is that unlike traditional renters who would prefer home ownership but can't afford it, this upwardly mobile group has chosen rental to ownership as a lifestyle decision.

Apartment developers have targeted the "lifestylers" and begun to construct apartment units with cathedral ceilings, crown moldings, and other features meant to offer the feel of a house without the inconveniences that come with ownership. Because the emphasis is on renting a total experience, these new apartment complexes concentrate on the services as much as, if not more than, the living space. Renting these upscale units often means gaining access to business centers, media facilities, libraries, and fully equipped fitness centers with personal trainers. Some even provide a concierge, the morning newspaper, and continental breakfast free of charge.

For many Americans, part of the lure of home ownership has been its value as an investment. From the end of World War II until the early 1980s, home values continued to appreciate. Since then they have appreciated at a much slower rate, leveled off, or even declined in some areas of the country, making homes far less attractive long-term investments.

Now a growing number of affluent Americans find themselves less concerned with the investment value of a home and more concerned with the amount of time they consume in maintaining it. A recent study prepared by Coates and Jarratt, Inc., a Washington, D.C., consulting firm, for the National Multi Housing Council and the National Apartment Association, argues that time considerations are critical to winning over the wealthy and the younger generation, and recommends a number of services and amenities to make apartment living more convenient— including food delivery services, "smart" appliances, pet-sitting, on-site child-care services, and state-of-the-art computer and telecommunications facilities. The report concludes:

> *Time is the universally most limited commodity. . . . Two-income households and single-parent households are stressed to accomplish traditional domestic duties in the face of constrained budgets and constrained time. The great need, therefore, is for processes, products, and services that give higher value added to time or that save time or eliminate time-consuming activities.*[29]

The study acknowledges that the biggest obstacle to renting is the conventional belief that owning a detached single-family home with a yard is the epitome of the American dream, but suggests that the "increasing pressure of available time may help shrink that belief."[30] Just as time scarcity is predisposing businesses to concentrate their efforts on short-term access over long-term ownership in commercial dealings, a similar consideration is beginning to tilt the real-estate market away from ownership and toward rental among some in the younger and more wealthy segments of the population.

Time considerations are not the only factor driving the change in attitudes. The changing nature of employment also is having an impact on the decision to own versus to rent. Companies continue to reengineer and downsize their workforces, pushing more and more workers into just-in-time employment. Having a steady job with a single employer over a lifetime has been replaced by being leased out on temporary assignment for the duration of a given project. Workers from upper management to the factory floor have had to become used to the idea of an increasingly volatile labor market and be prepared to adjust to continuous changes in their employment and even in their livelihoods and careers. Holding on to a house for an extended period of time makes less sense in a network world in which short life cycles extend not only to products and services but to employment as well.

Additionally, home ownership involves expensive entry and exit costs. Down payments and sales commissions are factors to reckon with. If the duration of tenure for a typical home owner continues to shorten because of employment changes, the home has less time to appreciate in value. For many home owners that means the appreciation may not rise high enough to cover the 6 to 7 percent selling cost of the home, leaving the home owner with a net loss.

The issue was taken up in the journal *Real Estate Issues* in the summer of 1998. John R. Knight and Cynthia Fiery Eakin make the point that since a home is the largest investment in property most families ever make, prospective home owners are likely to think twice before committing their financial resources to ownership, especially if they are concerned about short-term job tenure and continuous employment relocation. The authors observe that

> *recent trends in labor markets affect both the expected length of tenure and the uncertainty with which length of tenure can be assessed. Increased mobility implies that the decision point for renting or buying will be reached by families more frequently, and the underlying cause for increased mobility, shorter and less secure labor arrangements, implies that the decision, when reached, will more likely be to rent than to buy.*[31]

While home ownership still holds sway, the future is likely to see a slow, steady shift toward rentals as more and more younger Americans bring their living arrangements in line with forces that are moving the rest of society to an Age of Access.

Time-Share Communities

Both CIDs and upscale rentals reflect the growing interest in access ways of living. They are, however, merely the beginning of a reform in the way human beings relate to residency. On a deeper level, people's sense of home, which always has been grounded in geography and spatial identification, is giving way to a new sense of living arrangement as a short-term temporal affair.

Time-shares are revolutionizing the very concept of real estate around the world. Having access to a time-share is an alternative to buying a second home or vacation home and is particularly attractive to highly mobile professionals who like to vacation regularly but do not want to be burdened with maintaining a second residence or tying up their financial capital in a house. Global companies like Hyatt, Marriott, Disney, Inter-Continental, Embassy Suites, Hilton, and Radisson all have entered the time-share market in the belief that in the future, wealthier consumers in every country will be far more likely to buy access to second homes and vacation homes than to buy the homes themselves.

Time-sharing is a way to subdivide the use of a condominium. Recall that with a condominium, one purchases the air space in his or her unit as well as a share of the common space, which is the physical building itself and the grounds. With time-shares, one buys access to the use of a home for a specific amount of time each year. The access price also includes fees for upkeep and maintaining the building's common areas.

The idea behind time-shares began in the 1960s in the ski resorts of the Alps. Anxious to make sure skiers would return to the slopes each year, but knowing they would not be likely to buy chalets, local developers hit on the time-share scheme. The concept spread to the U.S. in the 1970s in the wake of the energy crisis. Developers found themselves with too many unsold condominiums in places like Florida and California. By selling access to the condominiums, they were able to fill their units.

The time-share industry is growing at 15 percent per year, or faster than the overall travel industry. Time-share sales, which were only $490 million in 1980, have risen steadily to more than $5 billion.[32] The number of people with time-shares is expected to grow from 4 million to 11 million by the year 2010. While Americans are the largest single investors in time-shares, with 52 percent of the global market, Europeans account for 21 percent of the worldwide market.[33]

The time-share developers' biggest challenge, says the *Wall Street Journal,* is "convincing the affluent that buying a resort share is preferable to owning a second home, a traditional status symbol."[34] Like CIDs the solution lies in the services and amenities that accompany the time-share, say marketing specialists in the time-share business.

The Franz Klammer Lodge in Telluride, Colorado, is a time-share "private residence club" for skiers. Members pay between $118,000 and $154,000 in return for five or more weeks of access to the luxury resort each year. To make each member feel like the time-share is more of a home than a hotel, the club keeps its members' private belongings in storage throughout the year. When members arrive, they find their ski clothes, family photos, and other personal items already in place and the refrigerator stocked with their favorite foods and beverages. "Call it the illusion of ownership," writes Mitchell Pacelle in the *Wall Street Journal*.[35]

Hotel chains are drawn to time-shares because the profit margins are higher than for hotels. High-end time-shares can provide a 25 percent or more margin, more than double that of most hotels. Time-shares also are cheaper to build and operate than hotels, and cheaper to finance. With time-shares, the time is sold before construction, providing much of the operating funds to finance the development. Also, year-round occupancy rates exceed 80 percent, compared to 60 percent in the hotel industry.[36]

The early time-share market suffered from the customers' inability to exchange time for access to other locations. Realizing that, especially among young professionals, mobility and new experiences are as important as time scarcity, companies like Resort Condominiums International (RIC) and Interval International began the practice of establishing a worldwide time-share exchange business. Networks allow holders of time-shares to exchange vacations with other holders in different parts of the world. One might exchange one's time-share in a resort condominium in Vail, Colorado, for a week in a Tuscany time-share villa. RCI currently has more than 2 million members in its exchange club. Interval has nearly 700,000 members.[37] Disney, Marriott, and Hilton have their own exchange clubs.

Some companies are taking the next step, selling points—a form of time-share currency—rather than selling time-shares in a particular property. Converting units of time into fungible currency represents the ultimate passage to an era based on time rather than resource scarcity and on access rather than ownership. Customers buy points—each point represents a unit of time—which can be exchanged for a range of travel and leisure services, including lodging, air travel, cruises, golf green fees, rental cars, and anything else of value in the travel, leisure, and entertainment industries.[38]

Renting, purchasing time-shares, and buying points all are ways of "temporizing" commerce. Instead of buying a property, one buys access to a property—the right to use an apartment, condominium, villa, or other facility for a designated length of time. Again, as is increasingly the case in other areas of the emerging network economy, the seller-buyer relationship is slowly being replaced by the supplier-user or server-client relationship, marking the passage of a propertied era and the rise of the Age of Access.

Real-Estates vs. Temporal-Estates

We are indeed coming to borrow more and more of our existence in the form of rentals, leases, memberships, and the like. But does the change from ownership to access make much of a real difference in the grand scheme of things? On the one hand, borrowing virtually all of one's needs in small, accessible, short-term time segments can make life seem more liberating. There is an ancient adage that "the more we possess, the more we are possessed by our possessions." Freeing ourselves from ownership, then, can free us from the near obsession that often accompanies possession. On the other hand, might not the shift from ownership to access potentially undermine the sense of personal responsibility that goes with possession? Ownership brings with it a deep sense of obligation and commitment that is not present in a borrowing culture. It's a well-accepted fact of life that someone who owns his or her own home is far more likely to be concerned with its upkeep and maintenance than one who rents living quarters. Taking care of one's possessions—and even the surrounding environment—in a propertied society becomes as important as taking care of one's own life. That's because we come to think of our possessions as extensions of ourselves.

Georg Friedrich Hegel, the German philosopher, was among the first to recognize the power of property to act as an appendage of our being. Hegel believed that each individual expresses his or her sense of personality by imprinting it onto possessions. It is by way of fixing one's will onto objects in the external world that each person projects his or her being and creates a presence among fellow human beings. Work, in Hegel's cosmology, is a creative expression rather than an exercise of labor, and the product of that work represents an expropriation of the world and its incorporation into the projected personality of the owner. He writes:

Personality is that which struggles to . . . give itself reality, or in other words to claim that external world as its own.[39]

As one's personality is always present in the owned object, property becomes an extension of one's personality. Others, in turn, come to know and recognize one's personality through the objects one owns. Hegel, then, viewed property as more than just a way to satisfy needs. On a more profound level, property is an expression of personal freedom. By surrounding oneself with property, a person inflates his or her personality in time and space, creating a sphere of personal influence. In short, he or she creates an expanded presence in the world.[40] No wonder "pride of ownership" is such a defining feature and core value of a propertied era.

In a society where virtually everything is accessed, however, what happens to the personal pride, obligation, and commitment that go with ownership? And what of self-sufficiency? Being propertied goes hand in hand with being independent. Property is the means by which we gain a sense of personal autonomy in the world. When we access the means of our existence, we become far more reliant on others. While we become more connected and interdependent, do we risk at the same time becoming less self-sufficient and more vulnerable?

The shift in the structuring of human relationships from ownership to access appears to invite a trade-off of sorts whose outcome is far from certain. Will we liberate ourselves from our possessions, only to lose a sense of obligation to the things we fashion and use? Will we become more embedded in networks of relationships, only to become more dependent on powerful networks of corporate suppliers?

These questions become even more important when it comes to the temporizing of living arrangements. Again, in the Age of Access, space gives way to time, and human attention becomes more scarce and coveted than physical location. Place, which for so long provided context and helped characterize a person's very being in the world, is less relevant in today's high-speed, highly mobile society.

Another German philosopher, Martin Heidegger, reminds us that the word *human* comes from *humus,* which is Latin for a nourishing and fertile ground. In Hebraic mythology, God is said to have fashioned Adam from the clay of the earth. Our long attachment to the soil, which has been fixed in property relationships and ownership rights and has helped shape and define the essence of who we are, is loosening. The electronic media revolution has played a significant role in the temporizing of life by annihilating distances and bringing people together in "real" time, irrespective of spacial divides. The telephone, radio, and television have made location less of a constant in the fashioning of social relationships.

Recalling his own childhood before the automobile, the poet Siegfried Sassoon noted that anyone living more than ten miles away was beyond calling distance: "Dumborough Park was twelve miles from where my aunt lived . . . My aunt was fully two miles beyond the radius of Lady Dumborough's 'round of calls.'"[41] Today, virtually everyone in the world is only a phone call away.

Media historian and critic Joshua Meyrowitz argues that the electronic media fundamentally disorients our sense of "historical geography." "Where we are physically no longer determines who and where we are socially," says Meyrowitz.[42] Nowhere is this notion more true than in the new world of cyberspace, where increasing numbers of people spend more and more of their time embedded in relationships that have no geographic frame of reference whatsoever. Millions of people now conduct business and carry on active social lives independent of spatial referencing. Virtual addresses are fast replacing geographic addresses for people around the world. The ease with which people have been willing to suspend geographic referencing altogether in their commercial and social undertakings is remarkable and a further testimonial to the waning significance of place in people's lives.

While a large part of our conscious life has already journeyed into the more temporal world of access relationships with seeming indifference, a more primordial part of our nature resists and remains rooted to the soil and the notion of territoriality. The ground remains our most basic connection, even in a world of electronic connectivity. Our very physical being is borrowed from the earth around us. The great twentieth-century physicist Erwin Schrodinger captured the essence of our being. He wrote:

> Thus you can throw yourself flat on the ground, stretched out upon Mother Earth, with the certain conviction that you are one with her and she with you. You are firmly established, as invulnerable as she . . . As surely as she will endow you tomorrow, so surely will she bring you forth anew to new striving and suffering.[43]

Our more ancient nature is embedded as much in geography as in temporality. We are connected to the earth as well as to time. Territory, then, is more than just a social convention. It is also a state of being. That's probably why home ownership is so pervasive. Home ownership allows us to experience the ancient feeling of rootedness to place, to territory, to our origins.

Still, for many of the millions of people who choose to live in the new CID developments, even ownership of home and land becomes secondary to access to amenities, services, and commodified experiences. CIDs lack the kind of rooted history of traditional communities. They are wholesale fabrications, designed by specification and plopped down onto a cleared space without historical referencing. They are ahistorical communities. People do not so much think of their CIDs as "where they come from." If there is a geographic reference, it is usually only to fix the duration and direction of their daily commute. Few people feel a deep kinship to their CIDs as a place in the same way people have felt toward more traditional communities. In this sense, the deep value of owning one's place as a sign of one's rootedness to geography already has been lost for growing numbers of people. In its stead is the more facile temporal value of securing commercial access to a social network of shared lifestyle experiences.

Of course, it could be argued with equal passion that rootedness to geography and the distinctions of mine and thine that go with home ownership and landed property ought to be left to wither and die. After all, the human odyssey is littered with the blood of countless human beings sacrificed in the struggle to usurp or protect territory. While ownership of home and land connects people to the roots of their earthly existence, it also creates schisms and promotes xenophobism. Conflict, suffering, and war are the dark side of the "territorial imperative." Some would argue that by steadily reducing the significance of place and elevating the value of relationships and experiences, we may slowly advance the human agenda to a higher plane. Others, however, might counter that in the new Age of Access, where questions of mine and thine begin to recede to the background, we risk losing our moorings and a sense of deep communion with the physical and biological ground to which we owe our very existence and being in the world.

The questions, then, are: Can embeddedness in temporal networks be a sufficient and meaningful surrogate for rootedness in place? Is geography an indivisible context, or merely a marginal remnant of a bygone era?

Is it a reference point and constraint, or only one of many considerations to be taken into account? While the yearning for place still remains strong for some people, the desire to annihilate space and temporalize our existence is becoming an equally powerful force for others. The extent to which we transform our living arrangements from ownership to access will be a test of the struggle between two very different sensibilities about who we are and what we choose to be in the world of the twenty-first century.

Enclosing

the Cultural

Commons

Chapter Eight

The New
Culture of
Capitalism

The big changes in history, the ones that fundamentally alter how we think and act, have a way of creeping up on society until one day everything we know is suddenly passé and we realize we are in a whole new world. It wasn't until the late nineteenth century, for example, that the British historian Arnold Toynbee coined the term *Industrial Age*, nearly a hundred years after it first arrived on the world scene.[1]

Similarly, for the better part of the twentieth century, a new form of capitalism has been slowly gestating and is only now about to overtake industrial capitalism. After hundreds of years of converting physical resources into propertied goods, we are now increasingly transforming cultural resources into paid-for personal experiences and entertainments.

In the new age of cultural capitalism, access becomes far more relevant and property far less so in the ordering of commercial life. Property relations are compatible with a world in which the primary task of economic life is the processing, manufacturing, and distribution of physical goods. Inert objects are easily measurable, and because hard goods can be quantified, they're amenable to price. They are solid and therefore exchangeable between parties. They can be possessed by only one party at a time and fit the requisite of exclusivity. They are both autonomous and, for the most part, mobile—with the exception of real estate. They lend themselves to the rather simple notions that underlie property relationships.

But in the new cultural economy, the organization of commercial life is not so simple. It is a world of symbols, webs and feedback loops, connectivity and interactivity, in which borders and boundaries become murky and everything that is solid begins to melt.

We are entering a new era of digital communications technologies and cultural commerce. In fact, the two together create a powerful new economic paradigm. More and more of our daily lives is already mediated by the new digital channels of human expression. And because communication is the means by which human beings find common meaning and share the world they create, commodifying all forms of digital communications goes hand in hand with commodifying the many relationships that make up the lived experience—the cultural life—of the individual and the community.

After thousands of years of existing in a semi-independent realm, occasionally touched by the market but never absorbed by it, culture—shared human experience—is now being drawn into the economic realm, thanks to the hold the new communications technologies are beginning to enjoy over day-to-day life. In a global economy increasingly dominated by a commercial electronic communications grid and every kind of cultural production and commodity, securing access to one's own lived experiences becomes as important as being propertied was in an era dominated by the production of industrial goods.

Communication and Culture

Even many of the most ardent supporters of the new communications revolution have yet to fully grasp the close relationship that exists between communications and culture. If culture is, in the words of anthropologist Clifford Geertz, "the webs of significance" human beings spin around themselves, then communications—language, art, music, dance, written text, film, recordings, software—are the tools we human beings use to interpret, reproduce, maintain, and transform these webs of meaning.[2] "To be human," notes media theorist Lee Thayer, "is to be *in* communications in *some* human culture and to be in some human culture is to see and know the world—to communicate—in a way which daily recreates that particular culture."[3] Anthropologist Edward T. Hall reminds us that "communication constitutes the core of culture and indeed of life itself."[4] There is an inseparable link, then, between communications and culture. "Culture communicates," said the late anthropologist Edmund Leach.[5]

Information specialists and engineers tend to view communications more narrowly as the transmission of messages. Their focus is on how senders and receivers encode and decode and use channels effectively with the least amount of noise. This process approach to communications, which dates back to the pioneering work of Norbert Wiener and other cyberneticians in the late 1940s and early 1950s, is concerned with how one person uses communication to affect the behavior or state of mind of another person.

The anthropological school, in contrast, sees communication as the generation of social meaning through the transmission of texts. Semiotics, a field pioneered by Swiss linguist Ferdinand de Saussure and American philosopher Charles Saunders Pierce, is concerned with how communications establish meaning, reproduce common values, and bind people together in social relationships. Structuralists are interested in how language, myth, and other symbolic systems are used to make sense of shared social experiences.[6] This is the sense in which communications and culture each become an expression of the other.

It's no accident, then, that communication and community stem from a common root. Communities exist by sharing common meanings and common forms of communications. While this relationship seems obvious, it's often overlooked in discussions of communications, the implicit assumption being that communication is a phenomenon in and of itself, independent of the social context it interprets and reproduces. Anthropologists argue that communications cannot be divorced from community and culture. Neither can exist without the other. That being the case, when all forms of communication become commodities, then culture, the stuff of communications, inevitably becomes a commodity as well. And that is what's happening. Culture—the shared experiences that give meaning to human life—is being pulled inexorably into the media marketplace, where it is being revamped along commercial lines. When marketing experts and cyberspace pundits talk about using the new information and communications technologies as relationship tools and preach a commercial gospel based on selling personal experiences, commodifying long-term relationships with customers, and establishing communities of interest, what they have in mind, be it conscious or not, is the commercial enclosure and commodification of the shared cultural commons.

Herbert Schiller, professor emeritus of communications at the University of California at San Diego, poignantly observes that "speech, dance, drama, ritual, music, and the visual and plastic arts have been vital, indeed necessary, features of human experience from earliest times." What is different, says Schiller, is "the relentless and successful efforts to separate these elemental expressions of human creativity from their group and community origins for the purpose of *selling them* to those who can pay for them."[7]

The evidence is everywhere. The culture industries—a term coined by German sociologists Theodore Adorno and Max Horkheimer in the 1930s—are the fastest growing sector of the global economy. Film, radio, television, the recording industry, global tourism, shopping malls, destination entertainment centers, themed cities, theme parks, fashion, cuisine, professional sports and games, gambling, wellness, and the simulated worlds and virtual realities of cyberspace are the front line commercial fields in an Age of Access.

Cultural life, because it is a shared experience between people, always focuses on questions of access and inclusion. One either is a member of a community and culture and therefore enjoys access to its shared networks of meaning and experience, or one is excluded. As more and more of the shared culture deconstructs into fragmented commercial experiences in a network economy, access rights will similarly continue to migrate from the social to the commercial realm. Access will no longer be based on intrinsic criteria—traditions, rights of passage, family and kinship relations, ethnicity, religion, or gender—but rather on affordability in the commercial arena.

The Rise of Cultural Production

The transformations from industrial to cultural capitalism and from property rights to access rights have been slow. The roots of the change can be traced back to the latter part of the nineteenth century. Several social forces emerged during the late Victorian era whose full impacts are only now being felt as the global economy makes the final shift to cultural production as the dominant form of commercial activity.

Daniel Bell divides modern civilization into three distinct but interacting spheres: the economy, the polity, and the culture. The essential principle in the economic sphere, he argues, is the economizing of resources. In the political sphere, participation is the prime value. In the cultural sphere, the value is fulfillment and enhancement of self.[8] Over the course of the past century, the values of the political and cultural spheres have increasingly been commodified and drawn into the economic sphere.

The notions of democratic participation and individual rights found their way to the marketplace, where they were reborn in the guise of consumer sovereignty and consumer rights. For millions of Americans, the rights to buy and own have become far more significant expressions of personal freedom than the exercise of the franchise at the ballot box. We need recall that consumption, up until the early 1900s, had only a negative connotation. To consume meant to lay waste, to pillage, to exhaust and deplete. At the turn of the nineteenth century, when a person had tuberculosis, it was popularly referred to as "consumption." The introduction and widespread use of store-bought, brand-name products and the rise of mass advertising and marketing campaigns all served to glorify the act of consumption. For the waves of immigrants anxious to claim a part of the American Dream, the ideal of civic participation, although honored in the classroom and in official celebrations, was less coveted than the array of choices available in the beckoning department store palaces. "Participation" fell from its lofty perch in the political realm and metamorphosed into the idea of unlimited consumer choice in the commercial realm.

Culture, on the other hand, continued, for a time, to be the refuge of those critics who warned of the pervasive presence of material values. Romantics and later Bohemians searched for self-fulfillment in nature and in the arts, hoping to find a nonmaterialist road to progress. "Man," they argued, "does not live by bread alone." They evangelized for the uplifting of the human spirit and viewed the arts and aesthetic experience as liberating tonics to a life of relentless toil and constant material accumulation.

The social critics longed for personal transformation rather than mere material wealth. Their desire for self-fulfillment, however, was also gradually pulled into the commercial arena, as had occurred with the uprooting of participation as a civic value in the political sphere and its subsequent reimplantation as a consumer value in the marketplace.

The story of how the consumption ethic and the self-fulfillment ethic, initially at odds, began to find common ground in the capitalist marketplace in the twentieth century is one of the most important and interesting chapters in commercial history. The force that brought together these two seemingly irreconcilable values was the arts, the prime communicator of cultural norms.

The arts are the most sophisticated mediums of human expression. They are honed to the task of communicating the deepest meanings of culture. The arts organize and communicate social experience in a way that penetrates to a deeper recess of the human spirit than economic and political forms of communication. The lasting effects of rock music and new forms of art and dance on the social psyche of the baby boom generation in the 1960s and 1970s is testimony to the power of the arts to convey social meaning and create a sense of shared values.

It was during the romantic period of the eighteenth and nineteenth centuries that artists came to be associated with oppositional values. They expressed the feelings and desires that had been repressed by the philosophy of the Enlightenment and the demands imposed by the industrial marketplace. In a world organized around efficiency, utility, objectivity, detachment, and a fixation on material values and property accumulation, the artists communicated the other side of human experience—the side anxious to burst out of the confines of an industrial way of life. The artists became the Janus face of modernity. They substituted subjectivity for objectivity, and creativity for industriousness. The artists communicated the feelings of abandon and ecstasy, of liberation from the drone of a puritanical way of life that yoked people to workbenches and machines. The artists spoke to each individual's desire to find personal self-expression and fulfillment in a world awash in mass production and lost in a mass anonymity.

The oppositional stance of the arts was taken up by a new generation of Bohemian artists and intellectuals in the 1920s in places like New York City's Greenwich Village. They found themselves at odds with the older Protestant ethic that continued to promote the ascetic values of self-sacrifice, hard work, and the sublimation of bodily and emotional pleasures. The new artists, observes Mike Featherstone, professor of social theory at Nottingham Trent University in the United Kingdom, "celebrated living for the moment, hedonism, self-expression, the body beautiful, paganism, freedom from social obligations, the exotica of far-away places, the cultivation of style and the stylization of life."[9] As fate would have it, their sensibilities, although meant to be oppositional to the prevailing capitalist system, became the ideal stimulant for an economy in the throes of a transition from a production to a consumption mode.

For the first hundred or so years of capitalist development, the emphasis was on savings, capital formation, organization of the modes of production, and disciplining workforces. Capitalism's success, however, created a new challenge by the early decades of the twentieth century—how to get rid of the accumulated inventories of goods streaming off assembly lines and conveyer belts in factories around the country. Entrepreneurs found their solution in harnessing the very oppositional values that had been used by artists to critique the capitalist way of life.

If the older production-oriented capitalism had repressed creativity, self-fulfillment, and the desire for pleasure and play, the new consumer-oriented capitalism would release these pent-up psychological needs by using the arts to help create a vast consumer culture. The new consumer-oriented marketplace drew the arts from the cultural realm, where they were the primary communicator of the shared values of the community, to the marketplace, where they were made the hostage of advertising firms and marketing consultants and used to sell a "way of life."

In the 1920s one began to hear the phrase "consumer culture" for the first time. Advertisers purloined the best young writers, artists, and intellectuals of the day and put them to the task of attaching cultural significance to commercial products. Creativity, self-fulfillment, a sense of community, and spiritual elevation—all things normally sought after in the cultural realm—were fast becoming purchasable in the marketplace in the form of culturally ascribed products and services. In the process, the utility value of goods and services became tangential to their psychological value.

Advertisers successfully used a host of mediums, including chromolithography, the electric light, film, print, and radio, to draw the psychic energy of the public away from the cultural sphere and to the commercial marketplace. The new communications technologies and artistic mediums gave the capitalist market a powerful advantage over traditional cultural mediums like paintings, dance, song, theater, pageantry, parades, festivals, sports and games, and civic involvement, all of which relied heavily on intimate face-to-face engagement to reproduce shared experiences. Culture now could be harnessed in bits and pieces to electronic mediums and spread quickly over great distances, bringing the masses of people together in simulated kinds of shared cultural experiences that, while less intimate, were often more seductive and entertaining. Locally reproduced art and culture were hard pressed to compete with electronically generated art forms like film and radio.

Because the arts—and the artists—were appropriateed for the marketplace, the culture was left without a strong voice to interpret, reproduce, and build on its own shared meanings. The significance of this capitulation didn't become obvious, however, until the 1960s. By the time Andy Warhol unveiled his reproductions of Campbell's soup cans and other products as works of art, the transition from traditional culture to consumer culture was far along. Art, once an adversary to the values of the marketplace, was now its primary apostle and the main communicator of its values.

Today, however, capitalism faces a new challenge. Video artist Nam June Paik put it best when he remarked that "there is nothing more to buy."[10] For the wealthy nations, and in particular the top 20 percent of the world's population who continue to enjoy the many fruits dished up by the capitalist way of life, the consumption of goods is reaching the point of near satiation. There is only so much psychic value one can get out of having two or three automobiles, a half dozen televisions, and appliances of every sort servicing every possible need and desire.

It is at this juncture that capitalism is making its final transition into full-blown cultural capitalism, appropriating not only the signifiers of cultural life and the artistic forms of communication that interpret those signifiers but lived experience as well. Alvin Toffler is one of a growing number of futurists who envision the companies of tomorrow planning out and managing whole parts of people's lives. "Eventually," says Toffler, "the experience-makers will form a basic—if not the basic—sector of the economy." When that happens, says Toffler, "we shall become the first culture in history to employ high technology to manufacture that most transient, yet lasting of products: the human experience."[11]

Norman Denzin, professor of sociology at the University of Illinois, echoing the sentiments of the French postmodernist Guy Debord, is more critical in describing the monumental change in human relationships brought on by the forces of cultural capitalism. He writes: "Lived experience is the last stage of commodity reification. Put another way, lived experience . . . has become the final commodity in the circulation of capital."[12]

In the Age of Access, one buys access to lived experience itself. Economic forecasters and consultants talk about the new experience industries and the experience economy, phrases that did not exist even a few years ago. Experience industries, which include the whole range of cultural activities from travel to entertainment, are coming to dominate the new global economy. Futurist James Ogilvey observes that "the growth of the experience industry represents a satiation with the *stuff* that the industrial revolution produced." Ogilvey says that "today's consumers don't ask themselves as often, 'What do I want to *have* that I don't have already'; they are asking instead, 'What do I want to *experience* that I have not experienced yet?'"[13]

Ogilvey, like other analysts of capitalist trends, is beginning to sense the significance of the transition from an industrial economy to an experience economy. He makes the point that "the experience industry is all about trading in what makes the heart beat faster."[14] Although he acknowledges that critics will "object to the commodification of passion," he argues that "passion is so much safer" when confined to the market than "when it erupts through the sublimations of religion and politics."[15]

Management consultants B. Joseph Pine and James Gilmore advise their corporate clients that "in the emerging Experience Economy, companies must realize they make *memories,* not goods."[16] They suggest that manufacturers, for example, "experientialize" their goods. Automakers, they argue, should focus on enhancing the "driving experience," furniture producers the "sitting experience," appliance manufacturers the "washing experience and cooking experience," apparel manufacturers the "wearing experience."[17]

Pine and Gilmore report that employment in the experiential industries is growing nearly twice as fast as in the service sector as a whole.[18] The birth of the experience industry is the next stage of evolution of the capitalist system that began with the commodification of land (the enclosure movement) and led to the commodification of home and craft production and then family and community functions. Now the totality of our existence is being commodified: the foods we eat, the goods we produce, the services we perform for one another, and the cultural experiences we share.

The Oldest Cultural Industry

Companies in every country are engaged in the business of packaging cultural experiences. The most visible and powerful expression of the new experience economy is global tourism—a form of cultural production that emerged from the margins of economic life just a half century ago to become one of the largest industries in the world. Tourism is nothing more than the commodification of cultural experience.

Travel for pleasure is now the third largest household expense after food and housing.[19] According to the World Travel and Tourism Council (WTTC), the industry represents more than 11 percent of the world's gross domestic product (GDP) and is projected to double to more than 20 percent of world GDP by the year 2008.[20] World travel and tourism has leaped from $1.9 trillion in economic activity in 1987 to $3.7 trillion in 1998 and is expected to top $7.5 trillion by 2008.[21] Travel and tourism now accounts for 7.5 percent of all the capital investment made in the world and is the largest commodity in world trade for many countries. In 1998, more than $779 billion was expended in new capital investment, and that figure is expected to jump to $1.8 trillion in the global economy by the year 2010.[22]

Currently more than 230 million people around the world—10 percent of the total global workforce—are employed in jobs generated by the travel and tourism industry.[23] In Australia, Canada, France, Germany, Italy, Japan, the United States, the United Kingdom, and Brazil, the travel and tourism industry is the top employer.[24] In North America, 20.8 million people work in this sector; in the European union, more than 22 million people; in Northeast Asia, 77.6 million people; in Southeast Asia, 33.7 million people; in Eastern Europe, 15.2 million people; in Latin America, 9.9 million people.[25] The industry is expected to generate an additional 100 million new jobs over the next ten years and account for 11.4 percent of all taxes, or $1.8 trillion worldwide, by the year 2010.[26]

Twenty years ago, some 287 million people took international trips. In 1996, more than 595 million people traveled abroad. The World Tourism Organization forecasts that by the year 2020, more than 1.6 billion of the expected world population of 7.8 billion people will take a foreign trip.[27] The G-7 countries—the United States, Japan, Germany, the United Kingdom, Italy, France, and Canada—account for 30 percent of the world's tourists.[28] While economists continue to think of the global economy in terms of industrial production, traditional services, and information goods, tourism is fast challenging these traditional categories.

The term *tourist* appears to have been used for the first time in the early nineteenth century to refer to young British aristocrats for whom it became customary to take a lengthy three-year tour of Europe to round out their cultural educations before embarking on careers.[29] By the 1840s, the advent of the railway brought travel and tourism within the reach of middle- and even working-class families. British trains, for example, would ferry people out from Birmingham and other large cities to the sea for weekend excursions.[30]

Tourism turned into a formal business at the hands of Thomas Cook, regarded by many as the father of the modern travel and tourism industry. Cook was the first to package tours and transform travel into a paid experience. He began, modestly, by organizing a packaged cut-rate rail excursion for hundreds of Temperance society members traveling from the midland cities of Derby and Nottingham to a mass rally to be held in Leicester.[31]

Cook drew a new class of customers into travel. Many were hardworking professionals—teachers, clergy, lawyers, accountants—anxious to broaden their personal education. Cook brought the cultural experience of travel and tourism within their grasp, launching a commercial revolution whose full potential is only just now beginning to be felt in the global economy.

It should be emphasized that Cook's success in packaging cultural experience would not have been possible without sweeping developments in transportation and communications technology. The railroad and steamship shattered distances traveled, making it possible for large numbers of people to take overnight, weekend, and even longer excursions. The telegraph, and later the telephone, made it possible to coordinate tours from home offices and ensure safe and dependable service and passage. Steam power and electricity compressed time and space and transformed travel from "travail" to pleasure. Cultures once separated by geography and time suddenly became accessible and objects of commodification.

In 1856, Cook launched his first "grand tour" of Europe, followed several years later by tours to the United States and the Holy Land.[32] His first round-the-world tour set sail in 1872. By 1880, Cook's three sons had sixty foreign offices and were publishing a travel and tourist guide, *The Excursionist*, in five different languages.[33] Cook was also the first to use mass advertising and marketing campaigns and special promotions to build a clientele. The Cook agency became one of the first international companies to enjoy brand-name recognition.

Many, like the American writer Mark Twain, sang Cook's praises. Twain wrote:

> *Cook has made travel easy and a pleasure. He will sell you a ticket to any place on the globe . . . . It provides hotels for you everywhere . . . and you cannot be overcharged, for the coupons show just how much you must pay. Cook's servants at the great stations will attend to your baggage, get you a cab . . . procure guides for you . . . or anything else you want, and make life a comfort and satisfaction to you. Cook is your banker everywhere, and his establishment your shelter when you get caught out in the rain. . . . I recommend your Grace to travel on Cook's tickets; and I do this without embarrassment for I get no commission. I do not know Cook.*[34]

Cook made travel and tourism affordable for middle- and working-class people by standardizing and mass-producing it, just as Henry Ford would do with automobiles fifty years later. His organizing principles for producing cultural experiences laid the foundation for the travel and tourism industry and remain today the basis for organizing much of the rest of the experience industry.

Cook understood that commodifying experiences requires a different sensibility than selling products or simple services. He saw early on that being successful meant transforming the seller-buyer relationship to a supplier-user, or server-client, one. He eliminated the idea of dividing up travel and tourism into discrete market transactions between different sellers and buyers, and inaugurated an era of one-to-one customer bonding based on the principle of paid access for comprehensive service. For a set fee in advance, he provided everything for his clients while under his care, from transportation, food, and lodging to sightseeing and money exchange. His ideas anticipated HMOs and other contemporary ventures that provide unlimited care in return for fixed fees in advance. In this respect, he probably deserves to be regarded as the father also of cultural production and the first practitioner of experiential capitalism.

Cook's tours brought the marketplace to the culture. Today, however, it is the culture that is being brought to the marketplace. In recent years, tourism has become much more like staged commercial entertainment than cultural visitation. While often billed as learning experiences, tours are becoming far more theatrical in nature. The goal is to amuse and entertain as much as educate and enlighten, and if the local ambiance is bereft of sufficiently interesting and evocative experiences, then they often are manufactured to ensure a predictable and uniform experience for every customer.

Tourism and entertainment are fusing together into cultural productions that are more a simulation of experience than authentic experience itself. In his book *A Continent of Islands,* author Mark Kurlansky recounts the story of how a local foundation in Curaçao decided to expand its tourist sites of old churches and mansions to include peasant huts because the tourists were interested in mixing with the "locals." The foundation contracted with the eighty-year-old son of a slave, John Scoop, who was paid a subsidy to maintain his corn-thatched former slave house as a living museum.

> *Scoop would show people around his one-room house with traditional tools and a copy of the emancipation decree from 1868. . . . He had wanted to modernize but his mother wouldn't let him. Now he was being paid to keep things the way they were.*[35]

"Natural" and "historic" reconstructions have become increasingly popular with a public weaned on theme parks like Disney World. Williamsburg, Virginia, for example, is a tasteful, built-from-scratch reproduction of a Revolutionary-era Southern town, complete with local tradesmen and shopkeepers in historic garb with well-stocked shelves, welcoming droves of tourists to experience a bygone time. This staged authenticity is becoming the norm in many areas of the United States. Some American cities have rejuvenated their downtown areas with "themed" reconstructions, including New York City's South Street Seaport and Baltimore's Harbor Place. These tourist attractions, part fantasy, part reality, appeal to visitors seeking the unusual in a playful, dramatic, but safe setting.

While Cook's vision was to sell enlightenment, the new experience-based tourist organizations are as likely to sell fun, play, and adventure. In 1950, two young Europeans, Gerard Blitz and Gilbert Trigano, formed a company called Club Med. By 1990, Club Med owned or leased ninety-eight resort villages from Brazil to Malaysia. A Club Med vacation is meant to be part tourism and travel and part entertainment. The different resorts cater to different lifestyles and desires. There are family Club Meds, singles Club Meds, and sports-oriented Club Meds. In 1995, more than 1.4 million people traveled to Club Med resorts.[36]

Like Cook's tours, Club Med sets a fixed price in return for access to a complete lived experience. The "cashless trip" is designed to take care of the client's every whim and desire, to manage his or her entire experience while in Club Med's able hands. The resorts are like carefully constructed sets, designed to mirror the "authenticity" of each local environment. For example, its Playa Blanca resort on the Pacific Coast of Mexico is billed as an "authentic Mexican village." In his book *Tourists: How Our Fastest Growing Industry Is Changing the World,* author Larry Krotz observes that "few authentic Mexican villages offer air-conditioned rooms, tall drinks by the pool, and free Scuba certification."[37]

Natural and historic reconstructions, themed cities, and lifestyle vacations in "authentic" surroundings all are part of a burgeoning global travel and tourism industry that's bringing cultural production to the very center of economic life. All over the world, new spaces are being created—"touristic spaces"—for people to visit. "These [tourist] attractions," says Daniel J. Boorstin, "offer an elaborately contrived indirect experience, an artificial product to be consumed in the very places where the real product is as free as the air."[38] Dean MacCannell, in his book *The Tourist: A New Theory of the Leisure Class,* adds that these new artificial spaces allow tourists to sightsee without having to come into direct contact with foreign people. They are safe oases where one can view activity as one would on a television screen, comfortably and from a distance.[39]

Touristic spaces are a relatively new phenomenon. Public spaces of cultural significance are increasingly being cordoned off with security guards, gatekeepers, and entrance fees. These are intimate parts of a country's culture that are being transformed into "access zones," reserved for those who can afford to pay for the privilege of experiencing someone else's culture.

More and more of the global cultural sphere—its natural wonders, cathedrals, museums, palaces, parks, rituals, festivals—is being siphoned off into the marketplace, where it is being transformed into various forms of cultural production for the entertainment and edification of the world's wealthiest human beings. What was once the historical largesse of these cultures become mere props and stages—backdrops—for enacting paid-for cultural experiences.

Where an earlier industrial capitalism captured and exploited natural resources and local labor pools for the purpose of producing goods and services, the new cultural capitalism expropriates cultural resources for the purposes of cultural production. Although host communities and countries charge gatekeeping fees for the right of access to their cultural treasures and sacred places, ceremonies, and gatherings, the price of admission is generally low, no more than a token. In Costa Rica, for example, the access fee to the country is only $1.40. In Kenya, it's slightly more than $10.[40] Only Bhutan, the remote mountain kingdom wedged between Tibet, Nepal, and Bangladesh, charges a high entrance fee of $450, partly to discourage tourism and control the number of people coming into the country.[41]

The people whose culture is being transformed into a cultural commodity often share very little of the tourist dollar. Although tourism brings money and jobs to communities and countries around the world, studies show that little of the money spent filters down to the mass of people living there. *Leakage* is the term used to refer to money that goes in and then immediately out of the country. Most of the hotels, airlines, vacation clubs, tour companies, and chain restaurants are parts of international companies, many of whom are headquartered in a handful of world-class cities in the G-7 nations. Robert Burns, the former chairman of the WTTC, argues that leakage is less than 10 percent of expenditures. Others disagree. Third World tourism analyst Kreg Lindberg says that leakage, especially in developing countries, is much higher: 70 percent in Nepal, 45 percent in Costa Rica, and 60 percent in Thailand. Leakage for most Third World countries is generally around 55 percent according to Lindberg.[42]

Leakage notwithstanding, world travel and tourism is likely to continue to gain momentum in the twenty-first century as the top 20 percent of the world's population spend an increasing amount of their income on cultural consumption and lived experiences. The WTTC, the World Trade Organization, and lending institutions like the World Bank are devoting more research and resources to travel and tourism, realizing that the capitalist system is in the throes of an historic shift in primary commerce from industrial to cultural production. The WTTC has initiated a four-part program it calls the "Millennium Vision." The plan calls for making travel and tourism a strategic economic development and employment priority by encouraging open and competitive markets, promoting sustainable development, and eliminating barriers to growth.[43] Of particular interest to the WTTC is the development of infrastructure—airports, roads, rail, ports, and basic services such as utilities, telecommunications, hotels, restaurants, shops, and recreational facilities. "As the number of travelers inexorably increases," says the WTTC, "it is becoming clear that failure to expand and modernize infrastructure is perhaps the greatest single challenge to travel and tourism's achieving its wealth and job creation potential."[44] Convincing host communities and countries to finance the modernization of infrastructure ensures a built-in subsidy to the travel and tourist industry and is regarded as critical to its future growth and development.

The other essential priority for the tourist industry is sustainable development. Protecting wildlife, conserving biodiversity, maintaining local ecosystems and biological habitats, and establishing preserves and parks are considered as important as building infrastructure. The interest in preserving the natural as well as the cultural heritage of communities and countries is part and parcel of the new emphasis on access to lived experiences. After more than two centuries of exploiting natural resources for industrial production, countries are beginning to realize that the wealthy members of society, at least, are more interested now in experiencing rather than expropriating natural wonders. Their attention has shifted from making things out of nature to enjoying nature itself.

Typical of the trend is the planned construction of the Yellowstone Club in Pioneer Mountain, Montana. The club, like other resorts, vacation lodges, and planned communities in the West, caters to a new kind of transplanted Westerner who is willing to pay handsomely for access to the Big Sky country. At Yellowstone Club, potential members have to be worth at least $3 million to qualify for the 864 memberships being made available. The initiation fee for all new members is $250,000, and annual dues are an additional $16,000. In return, members can experience spectacular views of the Spanish Peaks north of Yellowstone National Park and enjoy access to amenities ranging from fishing and riding to golfing.[45]

The new pioneers, sometimes referred to as "amenity migrants," are changing the face of the Western plains and Rocky Mountain region. They are wealthy and willing to pay top dollar to experience what's left of the beauty and majesty of the Western landscape. Some, like J. Francis Stafford, the former Catholic archbishop of Denver, are worried about the changing demographics of the West. In a pastoral letter, Stafford warns that "what we risk creating with the new pattern of development is a theme park 'alternative reality' for those who have the money to purchase entrance." He contends that "around this Rocky Mountain theme park will sprawl a growing buffer zone of the working poor."[46] The archbishop concludes that the West is fast becoming a "leisure colony" for the more affluent members of American society.

Many of the new "settlers" are engaged in heated battles with local farmers, ranchers, miners, and loggers, whose propertied way of life depends on the continued expropriation of natural resources. The newcomers prefer to leave those same resources in their pristine states so they can experience the regions' unspoiled nature. For the affluent settlers, experiencing the land is far more important than harnessing it.

The question of ownership and use versus access and enjoyment is dividing people and businesses into warring camps all over the world. The travel and tourism industry will likely find itself increasingly embroiled in the politics of industrial versus cultural production as the world economy changes its first-tier economic priorities in the coming decades.

Mall Culture

While travel and tourism is steadily stripping away the cultural landscape, enclosing bits and pieces of it into commodified tourist areas, a similar process is occurring in the public square. For hundreds of years the public square has been regarded as a cultural commons, an open space where people congregate, communicate with one another, share their experiences, and engage in cultural exchanges of various kinds, including festivals, pageants, ceremonies, sports, entertainment, and civic involvement. Although commerce and trade traditionally take place in the public square, the market has always been a derivative activity. The primary activity has always been the creation and maintenance of social capital, not market capital. It has been the one place open to everyone, rich and poor. There are no gatekeepers or tolls. It is the agreed-upon arena where the culture, in all of its forms, reproduces itself and grows.

Now, in less than thirty years, the public square—the meeting ground for culture—has all but disappeared, swallowed up by a radical new concept in human aggregation steeped in commercial relations. After hundreds of years of market activity being peripheral to and a derivative of culture activity, the relationship has been reversed. Today, cultural activities in the public square have been absorbed into enclosed shopping malls and become a commodity for sale. The shopping mall has created a new architecture for human assembly, one immersed in a world of commerce in which culture exists in the form of commodified experiences. In this sense, the shopping mall shares much in common with the modern travel and tourism industry.

In fact, the International Council of Shopping Centers even publishes a tourist guide to shopping centers across the United States. It's no wonder. In Alabama, for example, Riverside Galleria is the state's number-one tourist attraction. In Arkansas, the McCane Mall is the state's leading tourist destination. In Illinois, Gurnee Mills is second only to the Lincoln Zoo in tourist visits. Virginia's Potomac Mills draws more tourists than any other site, in a state rich in landmarks and history. The Mall of America in Minneapolis—the largest mall in the United States—attracts more visitors every year than Disney World, Graceland, and the Grand Canyon combined. The U.S. Department of Commerce reports that 85 percent of international visitors listed shopping as their number-one tourist activity while in the United States.[47]

Shopping malls are becoming places where one can buy access to lived experiences of every kind. One can attend classes, take in a stage show, drop off a baby at a child-care center, take medical exams, eat, attend an art exhibit or concert, engage in sport, exercise and jog, attend religious services, stay overnight in a hotel, buy conveniences, watch a parade, visit a festival, meet a friend, and congregate with neighbors.

The mall culture is a creature of suburban development and the spread of the highway culture. Once confined to American soil, shopping centers now are found in virtually every country in the world. There are more than 43,000 shopping centers—including 1,800 enclosed malls—in the United States.[48] More than half of all retail sales are generated inside these establishments.[49] Even more important, these are the places where most people spend much of their leisure time. By the mid 1980s, American teenagers were spending more time inside shopping malls than anywhere except for home and school.[50] These are the new domains where people live out much of their social life—where they engage one another in discourse or just in passing. Whatever parts of the culture are reproduced are done so largely inside these walls, along the promenades, and under the lit-up atriums and arches.

Malls are sophisticated communication mediums designed to reproduce parts of the culture in simulated commercial forms. They rely on all of the most advanced electronic technologies to create an artificial cultural milieu. Carefully choreographed architectural motifs, automated climate-controlled environments, sophisticated lighting schemes, and computerized surveillance systems all work together to "communicate" a special cultural place, different from the shared cultural spaces that exist on the other side of the mall gates.

Of course, the most important difference is that shopping malls are private domains with rules and regulations governing access. While their walkways, benches, and tree-lined open spaces give malls the appearance of being public spheres, they are not. The cultural activity that takes place there is never an end in itself but always instrumental to the central mission, which is the commodification of lived experiences in the form of the purchase of goods and entertainment.

The first shopping center in the United States was developed by J. C. Nichols, in Kansas City in 1924. The Country Club Plaza became the prototype for the shopping centers that followed after World War II. With its Mediterranean architecture, tiled fountains, and wrought-iron balconies, it created an attractive fantasylike environment for consumers to browse in.[51]

The first enclosed mall—Southdale—was constructed in Edina, a suburb of Minneapolis, in 1956. By controlling the temperature year round, Victor Green, its designer, was able to create a near hermetically sealed simulated environment, a place where people could leave behind the outside world, with its noises, distractions, spontaneous eruptions, and surprises.[52]

Today, malls are theatrical spaces, elaborate stages where the drama of consumption is acted out. The developers borrow heavily from Hollywood in the construction of these environments. To begin with, the spaces are planned in a way that encourages visitors to suspend disbelief once inside, as one would in a movie theater. Malls are timeless—there are few or no clocks in malls. The inside ambiance is both exotic and comfortable, with running fountains, small sparkling pools with lily pads floating along the surface, palm trees offering shade from the overhead lights, store façades leading into cavernous interiors stocked with various treasures. Looking down over a second-level railing into the center court of a shopping mall called Greengate, William Kowinski, author of *The Malling of America*, says that he felt as if he were "standing on a balcony looking down on a stage, waiting for the show to begin."[53]

Behind the stage, the producers and directors of these elaborate cultural productions have developed a highly sophisticated game plan for ensuring that the theatrical experience leads to sales. Real estate developers, marketing analysts, economists, architects, engineers, space planners, marketing experts, landscape architects, interior designers, and public relations firms work together to create what they call the "retail drama"— the ideal commercial mix of tenants (the talent), stage settings, and performances to guarantee the optimum theatrical experience and maximum sales. The "mix" is the formula used to control which stores are allowed access to the mall. Owners "cast" for the best combination of stores—so many department stores, jewelers, sporting goods stores, video stores, bookstores, restaurants, boutiques, and novelty shops—to create the most appropriate buying environment. The mixes are tailored to the income levels, ethnic compositions, gender, and lifestyles of potential customers. Indexes, like the Value and Life Style (VALS) program created by the Stanford Research Institute, correlate age, income, and family makeup with data on leisure preferences and cultural backgrounds to anticipate the kinds of shopping experience the customers are likely to want. Shoppers are divided by lifestyle categories. The "achievers" ("hard-working, materialistic, highly educated traditional consumers; shopping leaders for luxury products") are likely to shop at Brooks Brothers, Bloomingdale's, or Neiman Marcus. The "emulators" ("younger, status-conscious, conspicuous consumers") are likely to shop at Ann Taylor or Ralph Lauren. "Sustainers" ("struggling poor") and "belongers" ("middle-class, conservative, conforming shoppers, low to moderate income") tend to be more value oriented and more likely to shop at K-Mart and J. C. Penney.[54]

The average American visits a mall every ten days and spends more than one hour and fifteen minutes there. The most commonly mentioned reason for making these weekly pilgrimages is entertainment.[55] "The mall is like three-dimensional television," says Kowinski.[56] Its rush of images and fast-changing façades, endless commercial messages and dramatic settings, are familiar to a generation that grew up with TV. The only difference is that in the mall, the viewer crosses over onto the set and becomes an actor in the unfolding drama. In both mediums, elaborate cultural productions are staged with the goal of entertaining the "audience" or "customers" and, in the process, selling them some form of commodified experience, either a product, service, or memorable event.

Malls pride themselves on their unique stage sets. In Scottsdale, Arizona, the Borgata—an open-air mall in the desert—is a scaled-down version of San Gimignano, a quaint, picturesque hill town in Tuscany, Italy. The mall includes a central plaza and tower made of Italian bricks. In Connecticut, Old Mystic Village is a reproduction of a New England main street of the early eighteenth century.

The West Edmonton Mall in Canada, the world's biggest shopping mall, is also the largest stage set for cultural productions in the world. Encompassing an area that extends more than 100 football fields, the enclosed structure houses the world's largest indoor amusement park, the world's largest indoor water park, a fleet of submarines, the world's largest indoor golf course, 800 shops, 11 department stores, 110 restaurants, an ice-skating rink, a nondenominational chapel, a 360-room hotel, 13 nightclubs, and 20 movie theaters. Visitors can meander along Parisian boulevards or boogie down New Orleans' Bourbon Street as they make their way from one stage set to another.[57] The internal "grounds" are lush with vegetation, and the ceilings are made from special reflective materials that give the appearance of natural sunshine.[58]

The developers of the West Edmonton megamall envisioned bringing the culture of the world into a giant indoor space, where it could be commodified in the form of bits of entertainment to delight and amuse visitors and stimulate the desire to buy. At the opening ceremony, one of the mall's developers, Nader Ghermezion, exclaimed, "What we have done means you don't have to go to New York or Paris or Disneyland or Hawaii. We have it all for you here in one place, in Edmonton, Alberta, Canada!"[59]

The West Edmonton mall is a wraparound theater where in any direction one goes, one is surrounded by cultural fragments, performances, and every kind of entertainment. One can ride a rickshaw; go onboard a full-length replica of the Santa María; pet farm animals in the petting zoo; be photographed with a live lion, tiger, or jaguar; and take part in an "authentic" Mongolian barbecue. Ghermezion sees his commercial venture as a surrogate for—not just a simulation of—culture. The mall, he says, is "to serve as a community, social, entertainment, and recreation center."[60] Except in this private world, culture is bought and access is determined by the mall owners. The architects' and designers' mission, writes Peter Hemingway, was to provide "a sugarcoated dream world where we can shop, play, and experience danger and delight without once stepping outside; where we can change experiences like flipping TV channels . . . where the plastic credit card is the open sesame to every experience."[61]

The West Edmonton Mall is on the cutting edge of the vast changes taking place in the global economy as its makes the transition from an industrial- to a cultural-centered capitalism. In the early malls, cultural productions and entertainment were backdrops for selling goods. In the new malls, entertainment and lived experiences are fast becoming the primary commercial activity, and buying goods is becoming, for some at least, more of an accompanying activity.

The new malls of the future are called "destination entertainment centers." Giant department stores like Bloomingdale's and Nordstrom are no longer the primary attractions. Instead, IMAX movie theaters, themed nightclubs like the Hard Rock Café and the Rainforest Café, high-tech video amusements, virtual-reality games, and motion-simulator rides are becoming the core commercial business.

Sony's new Metreon in San Francisco, which is estimated to have cost upward of $160 million to construct, is a state-of-the-art "urban entertainment destination." The 350,000-square-foot complex houses twelve movie theaters, a 3-D IMAX theater, eight upscale eateries, a games parlor called the "Airtight Garage," and a Sony Play Station where people can order video games at the "computer bar." Other stores showcase Sony electronics, Microsoft software, and the Discovery Channel's line of items. The complex also hosts two major entertainment attractions, "The Way Things Work" and "Where the Wild Things Are." The latter, patterned after Maurice Sendak's children's classic, is a playground the size of a football field, inhabited by giant fanged yellow-eyed monsters hanging from the ceiling and hiding behind various landscapes. Kids pay a seven-dollar admission fee to scamper through caves and tunnels, build their own towers, and yank on ropes and levers that make the monsters jump and dart around. Metreons—the word comes from *Metropolis* and the Greek suffix *eon,* or meeting place—are being readied for Tokyo and Berlin.[62]

In an Age of Access, the megamalls and the entertainment destination theme centers are primary gatekeepers to a new commercialized culture. As more and more of people's social encounters and lived experiences take place in these enclosed commercial environments, access to these domains becomes an increasingly important social issue.

"Nothing gets in here unless we let it in," warns the manager of the Westmoreland Mall in Greensburg, Pennsylvania.[63] At Tyson Corners in Virginia, notices posted on the entrances read:

> *Areas in Tyson Corner Center used by the public are not public ways, but are for the use of tenants and the public transacting business with them. Permission to use said areas may be revoked at any time.*[64]

The issue of who is to be granted access to malls and under what conditions has become highly charged in both the political arena and the courts. Much of the concern in the United States is centered around First Amendment rights. In the public sphere, every citizen has a constitutional right to congregate, assemble, speak, and petition. But does the Bill of Rights extend to the private megamalls, the new gathering places? Mall owners argue that First Amendment rights end at the front entrance. "I don't mind that people are trying to save the whale," says a manager of a Florida mall, "but I don't want my shoppers stopped to sign petitions."[65]

The United States courts have been wrestling with the issue of political rights versus commercial access for years with ambiguous and often contradictory rulings. In a California case, *Diamond v. Bland,* the court allowed antipollution activists access to a San Bernardino mall, arguing that "in many instances the contemporary shopping center serves as the analog for the town square."[66] However, in a later Supreme Court case in 1972 involving antiwar activists distributing literature, the majority of the justices sided with the mall owner, saying that such exercises of freedom of speech and petition are an "unwarranted infringement" of the proprietary interests of the owner.[67]

The late Supreme Court justice Thurgood Marshall is among a minority of judges who worried that the continuing commercial enclosure of the cultural sphere and the public square inside giant megamalls poses a serious danger to basic constitutional safeguards. He warned that in these new domains, "it becomes harder and harder for citizens to find means to communicate with other citizens."[68]

The megamalls and entertainment destination centers, like common-interest developments and tourist spaces, are part of a new competitive environment where success is measured by who has access to cultural production and commodified forms of lived experience and who is left outside the gates. These kinds of access issues are likely to dominate the political agenda in the twenty-first century as society struggles with the question of who is to be included and who is to be excluded from the cultural economy.

From Being Cultured to Being Entertained

Culture is meant to be a shared experience—a coming together in communion around common values. Cultural production, on the other hand, is the sectioning off of bits and pieces of culture and their reappropriation as personal commercial entertainment. Historian and media critic Neal Gabler argues that the entertainment revolution is, in fact, already the single most powerful economic and social force of our times. "By the late twentieth century the chief business of Americans was no longer business; it was entertainment," says Gabler.[69] "America's growth industries," he continues, are increasingly "those that . . . [are] directly tied to conventional entertainments or those that in one way or another [enable] people to perform their lives."[70]

The statistics support Gabler's claim. By the mid 1990s, entertainment, in all of its forms, was indeed the fastest-growing industry in the United States, with more than $480 billion in consumer expenditures a year. That's more than was spent on all public and private elementary and secondary school education.[71]

According to the U.S. Department of Commerce, spending on entertainment and recreation—as a percentage of all nonmedical consumer spending—grew from 7.7 percent in 1979 to 9.43 percent in 1993.[72] The entertainment and recreational industries employed more than 5 million workers in 1993 and accounted for 12 percent of all new employment. That's more new hires than in the nation's health-care industry that same year.[73] In Southern California, entertainment has replaced aerospace as the leading revenue-producing industry, a clear example of the shift in economic priorities from making things to making experiences.[74] Americans spend more money on entertainment and recreation than they do on automobiles, health care, apparel and shoes, or housing and utilities.[75] "The entertainment industry is now the driving force for new technology, as defense used to be," says Edward R. McCraken, former CEO of Silicon Graphics, Inc.[76]

Many historians date the beginning of the entertainment economy to the graphics revolution of the second half of the nineteenth century. Printers began producing high-quality chromolithographs in the United States, creating a mass market for visual images for the first time. Original paintings, which had long adorned the walls of the rich and were made available to the public in a limited fashion in public art museums, suddenly became available to the masses in the form of cheap, vivid reproductions. Chromos were sold in stores, given away in mail advertisements, or made available as premiums. The arts and aesthetic pleasures, previously the preserve of the well-to-do and part of haute couture, were democratized by a fledging cultural marketplace and made into a form of popular entertainment for everyone. In 1893, a spokesperson for the National Lithographer's Association waxed:

> Within a few decades, public taste has been lifted out of the sluggish disregard for the beautiful . . . and now seeks to adopt the decorative accessories, which beneficent enterprise has so cheapened as to place them within reach of all.[77]

The democratization of images elicited a certain amount of ridicule from the rich, who viewed it as a cheapening of high culture. But for most Americans, the new images seemed a beacon of the better life to come, a visual promissory note to the edenic land that loomed just over the horizon.

Former slave and social critic Frederick Douglass viewed the spread of chromos as a liberating force, a way to break down the old barriers of culture and class and make available, to even the poorest members of society, the enjoyment of art. He wrote:

> Heretofore, colored Americans have thought little of adorning their parlors with pictures. . . . Pictures come not with slavery and oppression

and destitution, but with liberty, fair play, leisure, and refinement. These conditions are now possible to colored American citizens, and I think the walls of their houses will soon begin to bear evidence of their altered relations to the people about them.[78]

If chromolithography laid the initial groundwork for mass cultural production, it was the advent of films that established cultural production as a truly significant force in the capitalist marketplace and elevated commercial entertainment to the center of American social life. With film, high and pop culture became "consumer culture," and cultural capitalism was born.

For millions of immigrants in transit from traditional cultures to a society so young that culture barely had time to create itself, the movies became the substitute acculturation process. The movies introduced waves of immigrants, especially women, to an "idealized" version of what America was supposed to be all about. For first-generation Americans looking for clues to the American way of life and anxious to find ways to integrate their own lives into the new culture, the movies became both teacher and inspiration. By 1909, New York City alone had more than 340 movie houses, and a quarter of a million people paid the price of admission on weekdays and more than half a million on Sundays.[79]

"The movies," write Stuart and Elizabeth Ewen in their book *Channels of Desire,* "became for immigrants a powerful experience of the American culture."[80] Most of the moviegoers—more than 72 percent—came from the laboring class, according to a study conducted in 1911. By contrast, less than 3 percent of moviegoers came from the leisure class, a clear sign that in the early years, the movies appealed to those newer Americans who had not yet been shaped by the American experience.[81]

Going to the movies was as much a matter of escape as a cultural learning experience. In the dimly lit rooms of the cinema, people of all ages could leave behind the ennui of their day-to-day lives and be transformed into another, more glamorous and inviting world. For a moment of time each week, they could transcend the ordinary and live an idealized existence. The movies, like Cook's tours, packaged lived experience as a commodity in the marketplace. For just a nickel, people could be transported to other places and milieus, where they could fantasize, frolic, express their deepest emotions, and live out their hopes and dreams.

Cecil B. DeMille and other filmmakers that followed added sex, money, and romance to the film equation, creating "a channel of desire" for the emerging consumer culture, say the Ewens. The screen became a surrogate of the department store window. On the other side lay a world of beautiful people surrounded by every comfort and luxury; all things to desire and hopefully buy in the new consumer culture. The movies, observes Neal Gabler, "provided a new set of shared experiences for the entire nation, naturalizing every viewer as citizen of a country of the imagination that would eventually supersede and devour the country of the material."[82]

Today, the entertainment economy, the economy of fantasy and play, of intense and pleasurable lived experiences, is an omnipresent force in the lives of a growing number of Americans whose interests are turning from industrial products and services to cultural production. Buying access to enjoyable and meaningful lived experiences, especially among the middle class around the world, has become a way of life. The meteoric rise of the entertainment economy bears witness to a generation in transition from accumulating things to accumulating experiences and from property to access relationships. Americans spend hundreds of billions of dollars a year on movies, video rentals, toys, sporting equipment, live entertainment, spectator sports, gambling, amusement parks, books and magazines, recorded music, and other forms of entertainment and recreation.[83]

Every Business Is Show Business

The economy is being transformed from a giant factory to a grand theater. Even the imagery and metaphors used to organize commerce are changing, reflecting the ascendancy of cultural production in the global economy. Machine images like efficiency, productivity, utility, deliverability, and computability are falling by the wayside, replaced by the theatrical images of cultural production. Business gurus are turning out books with titles like *Management As a Performing Art: New Ideas for a World of Chaotic Change; Jamming: The Art and Discipline of Business Creativity; The Experience Economy: Work Is Theatre and Every Business a Stage;* and *The Entertainment Economy: How Mega-Media Forces Are Transforming Our Lives.* John Kao, in his book *Jamming,* exclaims that "management is a performing art."[84] Kao, like a number of other management consultants, believes that "large companies can capitalize on adopting some variation of the *studio model*" by bringing together independent contractors and creative artists for the task of reproducing the culture in commodity form.[85] "The person at the top," says Kao, "must be like a media mogul who is able to use every tool at his or her disposal to communicate the culture with relevance."[86]

Management consultants B. Joseph Pine and James Gilmore probe even deeper into theatrical metaphors in their book *The Experience Economy*, suggesting that the entire organization of business, in the era of cultural production, be redesigned along the lines of the performing arts. "Applying theatre principles to a business," they observe, "begins with *casting*, the process of selecting actors to play specific roles" in an enterprise. The producers, say Pine and Gilmore, are the men and women who financially back the business and determine the nature of the production they want to stage. The directors, in turn, are responsible for transforming the "treatments" (conceptual material) into operational scripts and staging the performance. Scriptwriters are those responsible for defining "the processes [that] will generate the end performance"—what businesses used to call "total quality management" and "business process reengineering." Technicians design the sets, provide the props, select the costumes, and are responsible for overseeing the physical layout for the production. Finally, the stage crew serves behind the scenes, making sure the various elements of the production unfold smoothly and without hitches.[87]

While the manufacturing phase of capitalism was characterized by output, the cultural phase is characterized by performance. Management consultant Tom Peters claims that "it's barely an exaggeration to say that *everyone* is getting into the entertainment business." Peters counsels his corporate clients that "the bottom line in commercial life is the sum total of conjured-up dramas created by our customers." The new operative words, says Peters, are *myth, fantasy,* and *illusion.*[88]

In the new era, *industrious* gives way to *creative,* and business comes to be less defined in terms of work and more in terms of play. Businesses in every field are beginning to reinvent their organizational environments to make them more compatible with creativity and artistry—the cornerstones of cultural commerce. Many business managers no longer even refer to personnel as workers but rather prefer to use the term *players.*

The work environment is steadily being transformed into a play environment, reflecting the new emphasis on cultural performance and the marketing of lived experiences. Companies have introduced all sorts of "playful" innovations to create a relaxed atmosphere more conducive to artistic creativity. Canon Inc. in Tokyo has installed meditation rooms. Kodak, in Rochester, New York, has a "humor room" stocked with toys, videos, and games. The Body Shop has lined its walls with stuffed sculptures to amuse and entertain its "players."[89]

Much of the intellectual footing for the theatricalization of business has been borrowed from the field of sociology. In the post–World War II era, scholars like Kenneth Burke, Erving Goffman, and Robert Perinbanayagam developed a radical new approach to analyzing and understanding human behavior based on the principles of drama and theater. The "dramaturgical perspective" is founded on the notion that all human interaction is drama and follows principles similar to those used in the theater. Kenneth Burke broke down human interaction into five broad theatrical concepts. First, there is the "act"—what actually occurs between people when they interact. The "scene," says Burke, is the background in which the act unfolds. The agents are the "actors" who interact with each other. Burke defines the "agency" as the way the act is performed. Last is the "purpose," that is, why the act is performed.[90]

Although Burke introduced the new behavioral paradigm, Erving Goffman, in his landmark work *The Presentation of Self in Everyday Life,* was the first to apply the drama metaphor to human behavior in rigorous detail. Goffman describes all intentional social behavior as theatrical in nature and observes that in every performance, the actors shuffle between a back region (backstage), where they rehearse their performance, and a front region (stage), where they deliver the lines.

In recent years, marketing professionals have taken up Goffman's work and applied it to service performances and increasingly to the commodification of human experiences. The methodology underlying Goffman's dramaturgical perspective has become as important a tool in diagnosing and understanding the marketing orientation as Max Weber's analysis of bureaucracy was in describing organizational behavior in manufacturing and white-collar office work.

Stephen J. Grove, professor of marketing at Clemson University College of Business and Public Affairs, and Raymond P. Fisk, professor of marketing at the University of Central Florida, argue that the marketing of services—and experiences—is fundamentally theater and can be properly understood only in that context. They observe that "just as theatrical performers must commit themselves to a plethora of considerations to stage a believable performance, the service 'actors' must subscribe to a variety of concerns to foster a desired impression before their audience."[91] A service provider's dress code, gestures, deportment, manners, style of engagement, knowledge, and communicative abilities all contribute to the dramatic exchange and the success of the performance vis-à-vis the client or audience.

The service performance is particularly important in more intimate encounters between servers and clients—for example, between waiters and their diners. The British medical journal *Lancet* published a controversial article several years ago suggesting that doctors engage in a theatrical performance—whether conscious of the fact or not—every time they interact with their patients. Drs. Hillel Finestone and David Conter of the University of Western Ontario write:

> *If a physician does not possess the necessary skills to assess a patient's emotional needs . . . and to display clear and effective responses to those needs, the job is not done. Consequently, we believe that medical training should include an acting curriculum, focused on the conveying of appropriate, beneficial responses to those emotional needs.*[92]

Both the Kellogg Graduate School of Management at Northwestern University and the Columbia Business School have introduced dramaturgical principles into their advanced management programs. Professional actors and directors coach business executives in the art of theatrical presentation and engage them in intensive role-playing sessions to familiarize them with how to use drama techniques to elicit the desired response from coworkers and clients. Grove and Fisk say that the dramaturgic approach to social behavior is relevant to every phase of business and every kind of industry and field, as it provides both a vocabulary and a conceptual foundation—what they call a "unifying framework"—for analyzing exchanges in the marketplace.[93]

In the 1980s, some critics disparaged the American marketplace as the "Mickey Mouse economy." No more. American exports of entertainment- and other cultural-based products are setting the pace for the global economy. Kim Campbell, the former prime minister of Canada, observes that cultural production has been a vehicle for the Americanization of the globe. "Images of America are so pervasive in this global village," says Campbell, "that it is almost as if instead of the world immigrating to America, America has emigrated to the world, allowing people to aspire to being Americans even in their distant countries."[94]

Cultural production is going to be the main playing field for high-end global commerce in the twenty-first century. In the Age of Access, cultural production ascends to the first tier of economic life, while information and services move down to the second tier, manufacturing to the third tier, and agriculture to the fourth tier. All four tiers will continue the process of metamorphosing from a system based on property relations to one based on access. And all four tiers will do more of their business in embedded network relationships operating between the worlds of geography and cyberspace.

Chapter Nine

Mining
the Cultural
Landscape

In *The Truman Show,* the 1998 movie about a fictional character who grows up inside a totally simulated televised environment, the protagonist is, for a long time, unaware of his captive circumstances. When Truman finally finds out where he is, he desperately tries to escape back into the "real world" outside the enclosed television stage set. The irony is that while Truman is running away from his artificial surroundings, most of the rest of us are journeying in the opposite direction.

We are engulfed by simulated electronic mediums, and more and more of our experiences occur inside artificial environments. This represents an extraordinary change in how human beings live out their lives. Remember that just a hundred years ago, *broadcast* was still an agricultural term and meant the scattering of seeds.

Now for most people in the industrialized nations, media consumption is second only to work. In Japan, the average household watches eight hours and seventeen minutes of television per day.[1] In the United States, the television set is on for more than seven hours a day and viewed, on the average, for four and a half hours a day by adults.[2] By the mid-1990s, there were more than 1 billion television sets in the world.[3]

Electronic communications are simulated media environments designed to recreate the real. Telephones, film, radio, and television all are meant to deceive, to fool the senses. A phone conversation, for example, gives one the appearance of "being there" even though one may be a thousand miles away. The word *phony* became popular in the early years of the twentieth century as a pejorative way of referring to voices that are not "real" and therefore cannot be trusted.[4]

Similarly, films and television play tricks with our conventional notions of time, space, and reality. We come to think of the people on the screen as real, and we interact with them in very intimate and personal ways. The progression of new electronic communications technologies has drawn us into a succession of technologically mediated environments, each of which is better able to produce the sensation of the "real" in simulated forms. This is particularly true in cyberspace.

This powerful new communications tool distills the symbolic essence out of cultural experience and transforms it digitally into make-believe images and forms, which, when communicated, seem even more vivid and real than the original phenomena and therefore become the experience. Cyberspace, then, replaces reality with virtual reality—symbolic, electronically mediated environments that people experience as if they were real—and of course, the very act of living these experiences in cyberspace makes them real. Postmodern philosophers and media consultants like to characterize these simulated experiences in cyberspace as hyperreal experiences.

At MIT's media lab and at other high-tech research and development media centers, scientists are even experimenting with the creation of total environments that can substitute for the whole of the natural world. Ken Karakatsios, a former Apple employee, once remarked that "the only thing wrong with the universe is that it is currently running on someone else's program."[5] Imagine a high-tech ecosystem made up of a "forest of machines," says English professor Mark Slouka of Columbia University, "that can know you and sense your moods: computers that can look at you and recognize you, phones so sensitive they can pick up the 'information carried in stutters, pauses, gulps, tones of voice'—in short, an infinitely personalized universe, entirely subject to human will."[6]

The digital revolution has the potential to make much of lived cultural experience fungible as commodities in cyberspace in the same way money made the exchange of physical goods fungible in the geographic marketplace. Manuel Castells captures the impact that the digital revolution and electronic commerce is having on the culture. He writes, "All messages of all kinds become enclosed in the medium, because the medium has become so comprehensive, so diversified, so malleable, that it absorbs in the same multi-media text the whole of human experience, past, present, and future."[7]

Because cyberspace is such an encompassing communications environment, other forms of traditional communications that take place in the shared culture through direct face-to-face communications—rituals, ceremonies, festivals, theater, the arts, religion, civic discourse—become less relevant and have less and less impact on human relations.

Simulated lived experience in cyberspace is, at its core, theatrical experience, says artist and business consultant Brenda Laurel of the Interval Research Corporation in Palo Alto, California.[8] In cyberspace, however, one goes from watching the screen to going behind the screen and becoming the performance. Cyberspace theorist Randall Walser observes:

> Whereas film is used to show a reality to an audience, cyberspace is used to give a virtual body, and a role, to everyone in the audience. Print and radio tell; stage and film show; cyberspace embodies. . . . Whereas the playwright and the filmmaker both try to communicate the idea of an experience, the spacemaker tries to communicate the experience itself. A spacemaker sets up a world for an audience to act directly within, and not just so the audience can imagine they are experiencing an interesting reality, but so they can experience it directly.[9]

Cyberspace is the new world stage where cultural productions of every imaginable kind will be performed in the future. And like other commercial performances, one will have to buy a ticket, pay a subscription, or take out a membership to gain access. Unlike in traditional theater, however, the performances being acted out are the lived experiences of each of the ticket holders who pay the price of admission. "We are on the brink of having the power of creating any experience we desire," says author and syndicated columnist Howard Rheingold.[10] Mark Slouka agrees. He writes:

> As more of the hours of our days are spent in synthetic environments . . . life itself is turned into a commodity. Someone makes it for us; we buy it from them. We become the consumers of our own lives.[11]

Rheingold warns that "reality is disappearing behind a screen" and predicts that in the new world coming, "reality itself might become a manufactured and metered commodity."[12] He wonders, what will human beings think of one another and themselves when "we begin to live in computer-created worlds for large portions of our waking hours?"[13]

It remains an open question as to exactly how much of our lives we will experience in physical space and how much of it in cyberspace in the new century. Of one thing, however, we can be fairly sure. Much more of our day-to-day experience is likely to take place in artificial electronic environments. In the hyper-real world of virtual reality, where everything is abstract and made symbolic and immaterial, the notion of property and old-fashioned concepts of ownership will be less relevant. In cyberspace, cultural production eclipses industrial production, and access becomes the basis of the competitive struggle.

Marketing the Culture

Not surprising, as cultural production becomes the high-end sector of the economic value chain, marketing assumes an importance that extends well beyond the commercial realm. Marketing is the means by which the whole of the cultural commons is mined for valuable potential cultural meanings that can then be transformed by the arts into commodified experiences, purchasable in the economy.

The shift from a production orientation to a marketing perspective— a phenomenon we've discussed at length—represents one of the more important events in the history of capitalism. By the mid 1990s, U.S. businesses alone were spending more than $1 trillion a year—or one out of every six dollars of GDP—on marketing. Advertising made up $140 billion of the total, while sales promotions made up more than $420 billion.[14] Marketing is the capitalist system's way of translating cultural norms, practices, and activities into commodity forms. Using the arts and communications technologies, marketers ascribe cultural values to products, services, and experiences and imbue our purchases with cultural meaning. By controlling the information and telecommunications technologies by which more and more people communicate with one another, marketers come to play the role that schools, churches, fraternal organizations, and neighborhood and civic institutions used to in interpreting, reproducing, and creating cultural expression and maintaining cultural categories.

Nowhere is this new marketing reality more in evidence than in the selling of designer labels. When someone buys a Zegna shirt, a Bill Blass lamp, or an Eddie Bauer customized car, he or she is purchasing access to a lifestyle, an image of a way of life he or she would like to have and experience. Ralph Lauren's label now appears on paint at Home Depot stores. Giorgio Armani's name is now attached to a handful of upscale eateries in places like Beverly Hills and New York City. The designer licensing business topped $12.6 billion in licensing fees in 1997 and shows no sign of slowing.[15]

Buying the label puts one in the make-believe cultural world of shared values and meanings that the designers create. The fact that it is all just a come-on, a sophisticated marketing device, is of little consequence. Millions of people have shown their willingness to suspend disbelief and buy their way into these stylized environments. The designer clothes, appliances, and whatnots become costumes and backdrops for living out imagined lifestyles and experiences. With everyone else playing the same game in the cultural marketplace, the substitute, by default, becomes the reality.

The marketing function has changed over the years, reflecting the shift in emphasis from selling the product to selling the experience. In the industrial era, when the focus was on selling the good, marketing played an important but ancillary role by using cultural expressions to draw customers to the product. Now the primary task of cultural workers in the marketing industry is to select snippets of meaning from the popular culture and, with the help of the arts—music, film, design, advertising—package products in such a way that they elicit an emotional response in the customer that reproduces a particular cultural category. Selling the product becomes secondary to selling the experience. Remember, Nike doesn't so much sell shoes but rather an image of what it would be like to be in those shoes. A. Fuat Firat, professor of marketing at Arizona State University, and Alladi Venkatesh, professor of marketing at the Graduate School of Management at the University of California at Irvine, observe that in the new era of marketing, "*the image does not represent the product,*" but rather, "*the product represents the image.*"[16]

As cultural production comes to dominate the economy, goods increasingly take on the qualities of props. They become mere platforms or settings around which elaborate cultural meanings are acted out. They lose their material importance and take on symbolic importance. They become less objects and more tools to help facilitate the performance of lived experiences. Unlike property, which is generally regarded as an autonomous entity and an end in itself, props are thought of more as instruments employed in the creation of a performance.

Marketing's new, more expansive role is that of impresario of cultural productions. Marketers create elaborate fantasies and fictions woven out of the bits and pieces of contemporary culture and sell them as lived experiences. Marketing manufactures the hyper-real. Its success is marked by its ability to make the counterfeit or simulation more attractive than, and a substitute for, the real. For example, while some experience-oriented consumers would rather venture out into the real world of nature, millions of other consumers choose to journey through Disney World's Wild Kingdom, where they can enjoy the animals amid artificial surroundings. They prefer the drama of the stage performance. It appears more vivid. In the Wild Kingdom, new surprises are around every corner. In nature, by contrast, one often has to be patient and wait for encounters, sometimes without result by the end of the journey. Cultural production breathes excitement into lived experiences. Emotional response is guaranteed, or your money back.

Marketing's job is to continue to rifle through the culture to find new themes for eliciting human response. Often marketers will plumb the depths of culture and borrow images from the most unlikely sources to sell products. Several years ago, Benetton created a maelstrom of controversy with its stark and deeply disturbing advertising images portraying a dying AIDS victim, oil-covered birds, a priest kissing a nun, and a terrorist bombing incident. In these instances, juxtaposing the drama of human misery, hypocrisy, and cruelty with the Benetton logo gained worldwide publicity for the company's products. Critics railed that the campaign was a cynical attempt to capture headlines and draw public attention to the company. Indeed, Benetton saw the campaign as a way of positioning its brand at the center of the popular culture—in effect, appropriating the culture by way of the arts for the purpose of cultural production.[17]

Countercultural trends have become particularly appealing targets for expropriation by marketers. Environmental issues, feminist concerns, human rights advocacy, and social justice causes all are themes that have found their way into marketing campaigns. By identifying products and services with controversial cultural issues, companies evoke the rebellious antiestablishment spirit in their customers and make the purchases stand for symbolic acts of personal commitment to the causes they invoke. When people buy soaps and perfumes at The Body Shop, they are really buying the experience of being a friend of animals.

In the new economy, say Firat and Venkatesh, "the consumer increasingly becomes a consumer of culture and culture increasingly becomes a marketable commodity."[18] Nowhere is this trend more evident than in the relatively new field of lifestyle and event marketing. A growing number of companies are attaching their brand names, products, and services to cultural activities and events, sometimes even taking over cultural fare and managing it directly under their auspices.

The first such lifestyle marketing event to receive widespread media and public attention was Hands Across America, billed as the "largest single participatory event in history."[19] The event was conceived by nonprofit cultural organizations to draw public attention to global hunger and to help feed the poor. The sponsoring organizations planned a 4,000-mile human chain to stretch from coast to coast across America, with people linking hands in solidarity with the poor.

Early on, Coca-Cola joined the community and national nonprofit organizations and began to turn the event into a commercially sponsored and run cultural experience. Coca-Cola established a Hands Across America radio network made up of more than 2,000 radio stations, which aired public service announcements to recruit people for the human chain. Local Coca-Cola bottlers managed sign-up drives in baseball parks and distributed hundreds of thousands of bumper stickers. Seventeen major theme parks served as registration centers for people signing up to join the chain. Schools and colleges hosted pre-event teach-ins and rallies and lined up buses to transport students to the event.

On May 25, 1986, more than 4 million people linked hands across America, while another 2 million participated in support events in local schools and churches. The event was covered live by the major networks and broadcast around the world. Front-page stories appeared in virtually every leading newspaper. Meanwhile, Coca-Cola's corporate image appeared everywhere. The company even produced miles of red and white Coca-Cola cord to link participants together in sparsely populated areas of the country.

For the company, the event proved priceless. Anthony J. Tortorici, at the time vice president of Coca-Cola's public affairs division, summed up his company's reasons for joining in and co-orchestrating what was essentially a cultural event. He said:

> Hands Across America was right for the time in America, and right for Coca-Cola. American concern for the homelessness and hunger were at an all time high. We had just come off the controversial New Coke introduction and Classic Coke reintroduction. We needed something to rebond the company with America. It was perfect.[20]

Alfred L. Schreiber, a lifestyle marketing consultant who advises corporations on how to leverage their brand names by engaging in lifestyle marketing, argues that Hands Across America was the pivotal event that turned corporations toward greater institutional involvement in social activities. In his book *Lifestyle and Event Marketing,* Schreiber writes that the single-day event "sent a clear signal that a new age of partnership between business and consumers was already under way." From that point on, says Schreiber, businesses were saying they didn't want just our dollars but also "to become involved in our lives . . . to share our values."[21]

Companies spend more than $3 billion a year on sponsorship of community and cultural events around the world. Carlsberg beer sponsors the European Soccer Cup, Citgo Petroleum has sponsored the Boston Marathon, Beefeater gin sponsors the Oxford Cambridge boat races, Philip Morris contributes funds to the Houston Grand Opera, and Omega watch company sponsors the Bermuda Gold Cup and other world-class sailing races. Dewars Scotch has even hosted literary readings in New York City.

The corporate presence is becoming nearly pervasive in the cultural sphere. It seems that no cultural icon is immune any longer to the corporate stamp. College football bowl games, once an expression of community spirit and regional rivalries, have become largely commercial affairs. Fans now attend or tune in to the Nokia Sugar Bowl, the Outback Bowl (sponsored by Outback Steakhouse), the Insight.Com Bowl, the Micron PC Bowl, the Tostidos Fiesta Bowl, the Chick-Fil-A Peach Bowl, and the Jeep Aloha Bowl.

The goal of lifestyle event marketing is to create lifelong relationships with niche communities and interest groups by positioning the company as an active cultural partner and player. Schreiber advises his clients that in selecting a lifestyle or event opportunity, they should attach the company to a cultural activity or institution that is "already playing an active role in the lives of the people you are trying to reach."[22] He offers up a potpourri of potential cultural targets for sponsorship and event marketing, including country music or arts festivals, hospitals, service organizations, performing arts organizations, amateur sports programs, disease foundations, day care, environmental cleanup or renovation, historic preservation, and local school programs.

Most important, says Schreiber, is to have a clear understanding of your goals—the things you hope to obtain through your sponsorship.[23] He says that lifestyle event marketing is particularly appropriate for positioning a company's product, launching a new product line, opening up a new market, and countering negative exposure to your products or company.

Marketing forecasters predict that the next major wave of lifestyle and event marketing initiatives will involve grass-roots community events and activities. The International Events Group Newsletter tells its subscribers that "community based events and causes are the place to be for corporate America" because they are closer to the lives of their potential customers. For example, neighborhood and community-wide festivals have risen by 10 percent every year for the past five years, and companies have made sure to be very visible in both the financing and the overseeing of the events.[24]

The financial and technological resources at the disposal of transnational companies engaged in cultural production are staggering. "Each day of our lives," writes Ronald Collins in the *Columbia Journalism Review*, "twelve billion display ads, two and one half million radio commercials, and over three hundred thousand television commercials are dumped into the collective consciousness."[25] The average American is now bombarded by more than 3,500 advertising messages a day—more than double the number thirty years ago. During that same period of time, ad spending in all media increased by ten times. U.S. television networks now broadcast 6,000 commercials per week, up 50 percent since 1983. In addition, every American receives more than 600 pieces of sales-related material every year. *Business Week* observes that "the buying public has been virtually buried alive in ads." The magazine notes that companies are now "stamping their messages on everything that stands still." Companies are advertising in every conceivable space, from urinals to classroom walls. In the U.S. alone, corporations spend more than $555 per year on every human being living in the country. In Europe and Japan, advertising expenditures are rising even faster than in the U.S.[26]

Advertisers realize that people are first and foremost consumers of symbols rather than of mere products. Advertising, as such, assumes the role of interpreter of cultural meanings. It serves as a bridge, continually mediating the individual's own life story with the larger stories that make up the culture. Consumers gain access to the culture and its various meanings in part through the many advertising messages directed toward them. Advertising informs consumers about the culture and instructs them as to which purchases will evoke the appropriate cultural connotation and lived experience. Advanced capitalism, then, is no longer just about the manufacture of goods or the performance of services or even the exchange of information but rather the creation of elaborate cultural productions.

The New Gatekeepers

Power, in the coming era, belongs to the gatekeepers who control both access to the popular culture and the geographic and cyberspace networks that expropriate, repackage, and commodify the culture in the form of paid-for personal entertainment and experiences. *Gateways* and *gatekeepers* are words heard with increasing frequency in private and public discourse. These are terms that just a few decades ago enjoyed very limited use. *Gateways* conjured up the notion of geographic passage—as in St. Louis, the "Gateway to the West." Gatekeepers were thought of as toll collectors on the interstate highways. Today, the terms are all but ubiquitous. *Gateways* is used increasingly to define the various passages and routes into networks, parallel worlds, and virtual realities of one sort or another. *Gatekeepers* refers to the institutions and individuals who determine the rules and conditions of admittance and control who gains access and who is shut out of a network-based society.

Like property relations, access relations are meant to create distinctions. With property, the distinction is between those who possess and those who are dispossessed. With access, the distinction is between those who are connected and those who are disconnected. Both property relations and access relations, then, are about inclusion and exclusion. In the former case, the separation is between the haves and the have-nots. It is measured in quantitative terms by the value of the property one holds, and in qualitative terms by the power and control one can exercise over the labor of others by dint of one's wealth. In the latter case, the separation is between those who are inside and those whose are on the outside. It is measured in quantitative terms by the number of networks one is a part of, and in qualitative terms by the embeddedness of one's relationships and connections with others. In a society built around private property, whoever owns the physical capital and controls the means of production is in a position to determine who succeeds. In a society built around access relations, whoever owns the channels of communication and controls the passageways into the networks determines who is a player and who sits out.

The term *gatekeepers* became part of the popular genre with the widespread use of the Internet. To gain access to the World Wide Web, users subscribe to Internet service providers like America Online and CompuServe. To access specific information sites on the World Wide Web, users rely on search engines like Excite, Infoseek, and Lycos. The companies are both gateways and gatekeepers to the many worlds that populate cyberspace. Millions of cyberspace travelers have become comfortable with the idea of paying gateway companies for securing access to the labyrinthine passageways of the electronic domain. These gatekeeping companies become more powerful as people around the world log on and carry on more of their business and social lives in cyberspace. Yahoo, for example, attracts more than 31 million different visitors to its site every month.[27]

The world's leading entertainment, software, and telecommunications companies, aware of the commercial potential of being the gatekeepers, have positioned themselves at the entry point to the new world of electronic commerce and are buying up the more successful access providers and search engine companies. They realize that whoever controls the gates to cyberspace exercises vast potential control over people's day-to-day lives in the twenty-first century. Thus in June 1998, Disney swept up Infoseek for $473 million.[28] In January 1999, At Home Network, a high-speed Internet service for cable television subscribers, acquired Excite Inc. for $6 billion.[29]

The giant media companies see a number of advantages in controlling the gateways. To begin with, people using access providers and search engines are a potentially captive audience for advertisements at the entry sites after they log on. Internet advertising, while still in its infancy, already boasted revenues of more than $500 million in 1997 and is expected to reach $6.5 billion by the year 2001.[30] Access providers and search engine companies also get a "piece of the action" when they direct users to companies selling goods and services on the Internet. The potential commercial gains of being positioned at the gateways are enormous.

With so much money at stake, Jeff Mallett of Yahoo warns that the world's media giants are likely to control the gateways and serve as the gatekeepers to all of cyberspace within a few short years, giving them the power to dictate the terms by which users are granted access to the new world of electronic commerce. "You'll turn on the computer and there will be three big networks," predicts Mallett.[31]

"Gatekeeping," say Elihu Katz of the Annenberg School of Communication and the late sociologist Paul F. Lazarsfeld, "means controlling a strategic portion of a channel—whether that channel is for the flow of goods, or news, or people—so as to have the power of decision over whether whatever is flowing through that channel will enter the group or not."[32]

Now that all of society is reorganizing itself in terms of geographic and electronic networks of various kinds, the gatekeeping function becomes critical. It establishes the terms of access into these network worlds. In the era of property relations, ownership was the precondition for exercising one's will in the world. Recall that for a long time, being propertied was the only way to be guaranteed the political franchise and a vote. In a wired world, however, having access to networks is the guarantor of full engagement in society. All networks act as gatekeepers, says Manuel Castells. "Inside the networks," he says, "new possibilities are relentlessly created. Outside the networks, survival is increasingly difficult."[33]

Gatekeeping as a social concept was first explored in an article written by social psychologist Kurt Lewin and published in 1947. Lewin was interested in how decision making occurs at a gate. He traced the process of how food decisions are made in the household with an eye toward understanding who in the family controls the gates—as far as what kinds of foods are purchased and how they are prepared and consumed. Lewin was interested in the social dynamics of the process, including how the gatekeepers were selected, how they exercised influence over the decisions, what their psychological predispositions were, and how their own motivations both drove and biased the gatekeeping decisions. He believed that gatekeeping is a fundamental process and that understanding the nature and dynamics of gatekeeping would open the door to a deeper understanding of how people structure their lives and institutions. Lewin cited the institutional discrimination problems that society faced as an example of the powerful but little understood role that gatekeeping plays in perpetuating the process. He wrote:

> Discrimination against minorities will not be changed as long as forces are not changed which determine the decisions of the gatekeepers. Their decisions depend partly on their ideology—that is, their system of values and beliefs which determine what they consider to be "good" or "bad" . . . Thus if we think of trying to reduce discrimination within a factory, a school system, or any other organized institution, we . . . see that there are executives on boards who decide who is taken into the organization or who is kept out of it, who is promoted, and so on. The techniques of discrimination in these organizations are closely linked with those mechanisms which make the life of the members of an organization flow in definite channels. Thus discrimination is basically linked with problems of management, with the actions of gatekeepers who determine what is done and what is not done.[34]

Pamela J. Shoemaker, professor of communications at the S. I. Newhouse School of Public Communications at Syracuse University, points out that millions of gatekeeping decisions—momentous and trivial—are made every day, deeply affecting everyone's most personal as well as public lives. Gatekeepers serve as the mediators and arbiters of our lives and times. They control what gets in and what's left out of the social process.

"As a result," says Shoemaker, "the way in which we define our lives and the world around us is largely a product of the gatekeeping process."[35]

Most Americans have become familiar with the power of the gate-keeping function through their health maintenance organizations (HMOs). At the heart of the HMO practice is the primary care physician, who is referred to as the member's gatekeeper. He or she is the "exclusive portal of access to medical services." The gatekeeper determines whether or not a member should be referred to other specialists, undergo various therapies, take medical tests, be admitted to the hospital for surgical procedures, or receive drug prescriptions, nursing care, and other medical services. He or she is positioned at the gateway to access to medical care and is the critical link in the whole HMO process.

The gatekeeping function is as important a factor in understanding the dynamics of access as the "invisible hand of the market" was in understanding the rules governing the exchange of goods and property. It's not surprising, then, that the study of gatekeeping is gaining momentum and spreading across academic disciplines as society at large begins to make the transition into the Age of Access.

Journalism students and scholars study the gatekeeping function to better understand how information flows in and out of the newsroom and how editorial decisions are made as to which stories should be covered and which stories should be ignored and put aside.[36] Radio researchers look at how the gatekeeping function operates in the selection of music and in determining what people will hear. Similarly, television media critics fret over the nature of the gatekeeping decision process that determines the television fare millions of viewers will have access to.

Gatekeeping often is a complex multistage process involving several gatekeepers. For example, a literary agent serves as the first gate in the book publishing industry. Without proper representation by a respected agent, would-be authors are generally unable to gain access to editors at publishing houses. Editors and publishers act as gatekeepers at the next stage of the process. They decide which among the many agented manuscripts will make it through the gate and be published. Reviewers often are the final gatekeepers. Studies have shown, for example, that favorable or unfavorable reviews in the *New York Times Book Review* can influence whether bookstores, libraries, and the public will purchase the books. Those same studies also show that books published by companies that advertise heavily in the *New York Times Book Review* are more likely to receive the most review space in the paper. Thus, the *Times* is positioned at a strategic gatekeeping point and can play a significant role in determining the level of access an author enjoys.[37]

A study of art galleries in New York City showed that over the years, some thirty-six galleries have served as gatekeepers for showcasing styles and painters, and they exercise considerable influence over the arts market.[38]

Cultural Intermediaries

In the industrial era, it was the bourgeois class of propertied business owners who came to dominate the political sphere and dictate the social values and norms of society. As capitalism makes the shift to cultural production and the commodification of lived experience, a new elite class is beginning to exercise vast influence in both the political arena and civil society. The real power of the new class of "cultural intermediaries" lies in their intangible assets—their knowledge and creativity, their artistic sensibilities and impresario skills, their professional expertise and marketing acumen. They are the artists and intellectuals, advertising geniuses and communicators, stars and celebrities employed by international companies and domestic enterprises to bring audiences and cultural productions together in a web of lived experience. Although at one time they were semi-independent players in the cultural sphere, they now have journeyed over to the commercial sphere, where they act as instruments of the marketing function. In an era in which access to experience becomes even more coveted than ownership of property, the new cultural intermediaries become the gatekeepers between the individual and the cultural experiences they seek. "The new tastemakers," says Mike Featherstone, "constantly on the lookout for new cultural goods and experiences, are also engaged in the production of popular pedagogies and guides to living and lifestyle."[39] As a social group, they are characterized by an "endless quest for new experiences," which they cull from the popular culture and then fashion into commodified forms of consumption.[40]

In the mid 1990s, a new genre of cultural intermediaries was born. Called "cool hunters," the mostly young men and women prowl the byways of youth culture looking for new cultural trends that can be packaged, commodified, and sold in the commercial marketplace. Companies like Trendology, Brain Reserve, Cool Works, Lambesis, Youth Intelligence, Bureau de Style, Icono Culture, Sputnik, and Agent X send their representatives to the basketball courts of Harlem, the school yards of Chicago, the malls of Atlanta, the skateboard parks of Denver, and the clubs of San Francisco in search of interesting cultural resources that can be prospected and converted into advertising gold and retail sales. Their target audience is the 104 million consumers—four out of every ten Americans—who make up the youth market and spend more than $300 billion a year.[41] Corporate clients like Nike, Coca-Cola, Disney, Chanel, Polo, McDonald's, Sony, IBM, and Calvin Klein pay cool-hunting firms handsome fees to gain a foothold into the youth culture and an inside track into the latest cultural waves. Being able to forecast cultural trends and transform them quickly into commercial fare can mean millions of dollars in additional revenue for companies.

Cool hunter DeeDee Gordon was the first to sniff out the sandal craze. Working the streets of Los Angeles, Gordon kept noticing teenage girls wearing tight white tank tops called "wife beaters," tube socks, and shower sandals. Convinced that shower sandals were going to be the next big hit, Gordon teamed up with a designer, who made a retro sneaker sandal, similar to the Converse One Star, a sneaker popular in the 1970s. The craze took off, earning Converse millions of dollars.[42]

Cool hunter Baysie Wightman, vice president of Mullen Advertising, noticed in her recent travels through the youth subculture that more and more kids are wearing flannel pajamas as separates to school, a trend of interest to one of her corporate clients, flannel outfitters L. L. Bean.[43] The "pajama look" is part of the newest trend in youth culture—the staying-at-home phenomenon that is becoming fashionable among Generation Y (twelve to twenty-one). "Young people are less interested in just going to the next new club and more interested in hanging out with their friends and chatting," says cool hunter Greg Chapman.[44] Hosting dinner parties is now in.

Jane Rinzler Buckingham, president of Youth Intelligence, reports that spirituality is the next big thing among the clubbing generation on both sides of the Atlantic. "Madonna wearing a bindi dot is by itself not that important," says Buckingham. "But that fad indicates people are searching for more spirituality in their lives."[45] Cool hunters like Buckingham pass along this kind of cultural reconnaissance to their corporate clients, who then commodify the trend with the manufacture and sale of "products like Hindu-inspired body jewelry or Chinese charm bracelets."[46] Knowing that the youth culture is yearning for spirituality, companies can incorporate spiritual symbols, images, and themes into their advertising and marketing campaigns "to show the target audience that the company speaks their language."[47]

The new cultural intermediaries have come under heavy attack from other artists, intellectuals, and academics, who remain staunch defenders of a semi-independent cultural sphere. The critics worry about the dangers of expropriating the whole of the culture for commercial gain. Norman Denzin denounces "these cultural intermediaries, who play to the market oriented consumer culture." He warns that the new gatekeepers perpetuate "a hegemonic control over popular culture, defining in every instance proper images of the American dream."[48]

The influence of the new cultural intermediaries stretches well beyond national boundaries in the age of electronic commerce. By shaping much of the cultural content that is filmed, broadcast on TV, and sent over the Internet, they are able to affect the lived experiences of people around the world. Since many of the cultural intermediaries work for U.S.- and Japanese-based global transnational companies who have communications links and distribution channels spanning the globe, there is legitimate concern among critics that local cultures will be either pillaged for commercial content, leaving them in shambles, or, worse still, bypassed and ignored altogether and allowed to atrophy and pass into extinction. "What will happen to our collective consciousness," asks Michel Colonna d'Istria in Le Monde, when a handful of U.S. and Japanese information, entertainment, and telecommunications giants control most of the global media markets?[49]

The statistics more than justify the concerns. American films now claim 70 percent of the film market in Europe—up from 56 percent in 1987—and 83 percent of the film market in Latin America. Hollywood, which grossed more than $30 billion in worldwide film revenues in 1997, now gets more than 50 percent of its revenue from overseas—up from 30 percent in 1980. Much of the television programming seen around the world also originates in the United States. According to a 1998 UNESCO study, 62 percent of the television programming in Latin America comes from Hollywood.[50]

With world trade in cultural goods of all kinds more than tripling in just the past decade, there is growing alarm about the spread of a *homogenized* global culture.[51] The homogenization process, already well under way, is reflected in the wholesale extinction of many of the world's languages and the substitution of English as the standard-bearer of the new cultural commerce. There are currently 6,000 languages still spoken in the world, but fewer than 300 of those are spoken by more than a million people and nearly half will be lost by the end of the twenty-first century. Meanwhile, English, the language of much of the film and television fare, as well as the language most used in cyberspace, is on the rise. More than 20 percent of the world's population now speak English, largely because of the hold U.S. media companies enjoy over world cultural commerce. In a century from now, English is likely to be all pervasive.

"When we lose a language, it is like dropping a bomb on the Louvre," says Ken Hale, professor of linguistics at MIT.[52] That's because language communicates the shared meanings, expressions, values, and understandings of a culture, as we learned in chapter 8. "As languages disappear, culture dies," writes Wade Davis in a recent *National Geographic* issue on global culture. "The world becomes inherently a less interesting place, but also we sacrifice raw knowledge, the intellectual achievements of millennia," with the loss of each language, laments Davis.[53] The French government has been so concerned over the possibility that their own language and culture might succumb to the influence and power exercised by American cultural intermediaries and the companies they work for that they have floated proposals in Brussels at the European Union that would ensure that 51 percent or more of the content shown on European television and in movie theaters is made in Europe.[54]

In the industrial era, the geopolitical struggle centered on the question of colonial and later neocolonial control over local natural resources and labor pools. The issue of ownership and property rights defined the nature of the contest between peoples and countries. In the new era, as we have seen, the geopolitical struggle is increasingly fought over the question of access to local and global culture and the channels of communications that carry cultural content in commercial form. The new cultural intermediaries, working on behalf of the transnational enterprises, play the pivotal role of gatekeepers in a world where access determines the parameters of lived experience for millions of people.

Chapter Ten

A
Postmodern
Stage

A new human archetype is being born. Comfortable living a part of their lives in cyberspace in virtual worlds, familiar with the workings of a network economy, less interested in accumulating things and more interested in having exciting and entertaining experiences, able to interact in parallel worlds simultaneously, quick to change their own personas to match whatever new reality—simulated or real—is put before them, the new men and women of the twenty-first century are a breed apart from their bourgeois parents and grandparents of the industrial era.

Psychologist Robert J. Lifton calls this new generation "protean" human beings. They have grown up living inside of common-interest developments; their health care is administered through HMOs; they lease their automobiles; they buy things online; they expect to get their software for free but are willing to pay for services and upgrades. They live in a world of seven-second sound bites, are used to quick access to and retrieval of information, have short attention spans, and are less reflective and more spontaneous. They think of themselves as players rather than workers and prefer others to think of them as creative rather than industrious. They have grown up in a world of just-in-time employment and are used to being on temporary assignment. In fact, their lives are far more temporary and mobile and less grounded than their parents'. They are more therapeutic than ideological and think more in terms of images than words. While they are less able to compose a written sentence, they are better able to process electronic data. They are less analytical and more emotive. They think of Disney World and Club Med as the "real thing," regard the shopping mall as the public square, and equate consumer sovereignty with democracy. They spend as much time with fictional characters on television, film, and in cyberspace as they do with peers in real time, and even integrate the fictional characters and their experiences into social conversations, making them a part of their own personal stories. Their worlds are less boundaried and more fluid. They grew up with hypertext, Web site links, and feedback loops, and have a perception of reality that is more systemic and participatory than linear and objective. They are able to send e-mail to people's virtual addresses without ever having to know or even care about their geographic addresses. They think of the world as a stage and their own lives as a series of performances. They are continually remaking themselves as they try on new lifestyles with each new passage of life. These protean men and women are less interested in history but are obsessed with style and fashion. They are experimental and court innovation. Customs, conventions, and traditions, on the other hand, are virtually nonexistent in their fast-paced, ever changing environment.

These new men and women are only just beginning to leave ownership behind. Their world is increasingly of the hyper-real event and the momentary experience—a world of networks and gatekeepers and connectivity. For them, access is what counts. Being disconnected is death. They are the first to live in what the late British historian Arnold Toynbee called the Postmodern Age.[1] This new age lies in sharp contrast to the Modern Age, in which private property relations and ownership informed virtually every economic transaction and colored most social interaction. Distinctions in the Postmodern Age are increasingly ones of access rather than ownership.

What makes the Postmodern Age so very different from the Modern Age? The simple but complex answer is to be found in the fact that the Postmodern Age is bound up in a new stage of capitalism based on commodifing time, culture, and lived experience, whereas the former age represents an earlier stage of capitalism grounded in commodifying land and resources, contracting human labor, manufacturing goods, and producing basic services.

Modernity

Modernity—a period that stretches roughly from the European Enlightenment in the eighteenth century to the end of World War II—saw both the triumph of private property as the foundation for the structure of human relations and the rise of rationalism, scientism, materialism, ideology, and linear notions of progress as the grand philosophical superstructure built on top of a private property regime. The Enlightenment ideas about nature, society, and human consciousness reinforced, in their every detail, an incipient capitalist system based on private ownership and market exchange of property and capital.

The Modern Age was characterized by a belief—some might call it a faith—that the world runs by immutable laws that are knowable and that can be exploited to advance the human condition. The moderns replaced faith with ideology, convinced that the human mind is capable of synthesizing the vast store of available knowledge into testable theories that could explain the origin, development, and workings of the natural world. Francis Bacon, sometimes called the father of modern science, developed a methodology for the proper exploration of nature's secrets. He said it was possible for the human mind to detach itself from nature and study it as a neutral observer. Bacon viewed nature as a "common harlot" whose wildness could be "squeezed, molded and shaped" to "enlarge the bounds of human empire to the effecting of all things possible." Armed with the scientific method, Bacon was convinced that we had at long last a methodology that would allow us "the power to conquer and subdue" nature and to "shake her to her foundations."[2]

In turn, Enlightenment philosopher and mathematician René Descartes replaced St. Thomas Aquinas's great chain of being with a mechanical vision of a clockwork universe whose workings are as automatic and predictable as the hands of the great Strasbourg clock. Descartes stripped nature of any remaining substantive qualities and reduced it to what he considered to be its basic mathematical and quantitative components. His computational universe is fixed, regular, and divisible. It is a world in which location and speed provide the overarching frame for organizing reality itself.

The modernists introduced the idea of progress. The Golden Age, they argued, lay not in a distant past but in a negotiable future. Human ingenuity and will, not divine intervention, would lead humanity to a new earthly paradise—a utopian world of material abundance. French aristocrat the Marquis de Condorcet confidently predicted:

> No bounds have been fixed to the improvement of the human faculties . . . the perfectibility of man is absolutely indefinite; . . . the progress of this perfectibility henceforth above the control of every power that would impede it, has no other limit than the duration of the globe upon which nature has placed us.[3]

The worldview of the Enlightenment provided a grand metanarrative—an all-encompassing theory—for explaining the workings of a new social order steeped in propertied relations and propelled by capitalist development. Philosophers and intellectuals of the period were convinced that rational thought and rigorous mathematical calculation could unlock the secrets of the universe and give humankind Godlike powers to control nature and even human nature. As late as the twentieth century, the great British philosopher and mathematician Bertrand Russell wrote that science would eventually produce a mathematics of human behavior as precise as the mathematics of machines.[4]

Underlying all of this newfound confidence was the fervently held notion that there exists, in fact, a knowable objective reality. If science were used to explore its workings, and technology to harness its products, then private property would be the institution to divide up the spoils of conquest.

The new reality modern philosophers came to see was best described by Isaac Newton. The Englightenment scientist and mathematician viewed the world as populated by autonomous material things—both inert and alive—that interact with one another in predictable fashion according to the unshakeable laws of gravity. Newton's universe has been likened to a field full of billiard balls—hard objects with discrete boundaries bombarding one another according to the laws of physics.

The modernist sensibility worked well alongside the idea of private property relations. If the natural world is both knowable and exploitable, then those who, by dint of their ingenuity and hard work, transform nature into artifice and commodities ought to reap the rewards by being able to own the fruits of their labor. This is, of course, exactly what John Locke argued in his labor theory of property. And if, in fact, everything in the world—inert or alive—were autonomous and boundaried and easy to define as discrete objects, then it would be equally easy to assign everything as property.

The philosophers of the Englightenment ran roughshod over the medieval mind. They even changed the very notion of human perception, substituting subjects and objects for the medieval notion of a hierarchically organized universe. Thinking of the world in terms of subjects and objects owes much to the development of perspective in art during the European Renaissance. While perspective was not unknown to medieval artists, it was rarely used. In a world made up of a seamless web of relationships that is hierarchical and stretches from the fiery furnaces of hell to the gates of heaven in a great chain of being, relationships spill over on top of one another—a reality expressed in most medieval paintings.

In the new horizontal world of enclosed landscapes, colonial territories, and capitalist markets, one's gaze is redirected from the heavens to the horizon, and perspective becomes the vantage point for taking in one's surroundings. Perspective, by its very nature, makes the artist the center of the universe and reduces everything within his or her sight to an expropriatable object. Bacon's scientific method, and much of the later Enlightenment ideas about nature, are centered on the notion of a bifurcated world of subjects and objects. In Bacon's world, all activity boils down to a life-and-death struggle between competing subjects each attempting to expropriate and possess objects of value that lie around them. In the end, there is only the subjective will. Everything else becomes a potential object to nourish and inflate the will. A private property regime based on the exclusive possession and control of "things" flourishes in a milieu in which everything is either an active subject or a passive object.

Postmodernity

The Postmodern Age, by contrast, is built on an entirely different set of assumptions about the nature of reality—assumptions that ultimately undermine modern ideas about property and give support to the restructuring of human relations around principles of access.

To begin with, postmodern scholars reject the very idea of a fixed and knowable reality. The first chink in the Enlightenment armor occurred in the twentieth century when German scientist Werner Heisenberg introduced the idea of indeterminacy into the scientific debate. According to Heisenberg's indeterminacy principle, the notion of a detached, impartial observer—the core assumption of Bacon's scientific method—recording nature's secrets in an objective fashion is an impossibility. The sheer act of making observations brings the observer into direct participation with the object of his or her inquiry, therefore biasing the results. Heisenberg demonstrated that everything we do—even our observations—effects outcomes. Far from being detached, every human being is both player and participant, always affecting and being affected, by the world we attempt to manipulate and influence. After Heisenberg, it was difficult to continue to hold to the Baconian idea that the world is made up solely of knowing subjects acting on passive objects. Newton's notion of autonomous agents careening through the universe became equally suspect. If even the act of observation brings the observer into participation with the things he or she observes, then autonomy is more fiction than reality.

New theories about matter and energy did still more damage to the Enlightenment metanarrative. Recall, classical physics defines matter as impenetrable physical substances. Newton's laws are based on the proposition that two particles can't possibly occupy the same place at the same time because each is a discrete physical entity that takes up a certain amount of space. By the early years of the twentieth century, however, the orthodox view of physical phenomena was giving way to an entirely new conception. As the physicists began to probe deeper into the world of atoms, they began to realize that their earlier ideas about solid matter existing in a fixed space were naïve. What we call hard physical objects, said the physicists, are really just patterns of energy. The seeming physicality of things—their fixity and beingness—is merely an approximate notion.

Much to their surprise, physicists found that an atom is anything but still. In fact, it became apparent that the atom is not a thing, in the conventional material sense, but rather a set of forces operating in relationship to one another. Relationships, however, cannot exist independent of time. As the late historian and philosopher Robin G. Collingwood of Oxford University has pointed out, relationships can exist only in "a tract of time long enough for the rhythm of the movement to establish itself."[5] The Nobel Laureate philosopher Henri Bergson once remarked, "A note of music is nothing at an instant."[6] It requires notes preceding and following it in time. If each atom, then, is a set of relationships operating over time, then "at a certain instant of time the atom does not possess these qualities at all."[7]

Thus the old idea of structure, independent of process, is abandoned. The new physics contends that it is impossible to separate what something is from what it does. Nothing is static. Therefore, things no longer exist independent of time but rather through time.

According to the new physics, matter is a form of energy, and energy is pure activity. Gone forever is the quantitative notion of hard substances existing within a "static framework of spatial relations." Scientist and philosopher Alfred North Whitehead delivered a devastating blow to the idea of space as the dominant feature of nature: "The notion of space with its passive, systematic, geometric relationship is entirely inappropriate . . . there is no nature apart from transition, and there is no transition apart from temporal duration."[8]

What then of property? The physicists were beginning to deconstruct the hard physical reality of the modern world. How does one own a force, a pattern of activity, a relationship over time? How does one distinguish between what is mine and thine in a world in which boundaries are a mere social fiction? It's interesting to note that in cases where persons have lost their eyesight in early infancy and regained it later in life, the experience can be traumatic. Because their minds never were fully trained to distinguish individual objects in isolation, they see the world as a blur of colors and shades and a kaleidoscope of ever changing patterns. All is process and movement. Discrete forms with boundaries are not easily distinguishable, all of which suggests that even our commonsense perception of bounded objects existing in isolation is a learned experience and part of our cognitive development.

While most human beings continued to act as if the world was made up of subjects and objects and solid expropriatable things, the physical sciences quietly but inexorably established a new philosophical framework for the rethinking of reality. Today, chaos theory, catastrophe theory, complexity theory, and the theory of dissipative structures all reflect the new scientific emphasis on contingency, indeterminacy, embeddedness, and diversity in the natural world. Where modern science looked for ultimate truths and fundamental particles, the new science looks for unexpected possibilities and emerging patterns. Nature is seen more as a series of continuously creative acts than an unfolding of reality based on unalterable laws. Nature is full of surprises at every juncture and creates its own reality as it goes.

Nowhere have the new ideas in physics, chemistry, and mathematics been more deeply felt than in the humanities. If there is no fixed and knowable reality but only the individual realities we create by the way each of us participates in and experiences the world around us, then the idea of an overarching metanarrative—an all-encompassing view of reality— must not exist. The world, according to the postmodernists, is a human construct. We create it, say the semioticians, by the stories we concoct to explain it and by the way we choose to live in it. This new world is not objective but rather contingent, not made up of truths but rather of options and scenarios. It is a world created by language and held together by metaphors and agreed-upon shared meanings, all of which can and do change with the passage of time. Reality, it seems, is not something bequeathed to us but rather something we create, whole cloth, by communicating it into existence.

The Spanish philosopher José Ortega y Gasset once remarked that there are as many realities as there are points of view. His theory of perspectivism challenged the modern notion of a simple, knowable, objective reality with the idea of multiple realities, each representing the unique life story of every human being that lives on earth. He summed up the new postmodern way of thinking about reality by positing the dictum "I am I and my circumstances."[9] Even science, argue the postmodernists, is an elaborately constructed set of texts or stories whose authority rests ultimately on their ability to sway and convince their readers of their validity.

Heisenberg observed that when it comes to the exploration of science, "what we observe is not nature itself, but nature exposed to our method of questioning. Our scientific work in physics consists in asking questions about nature in the language we possess."[10] Reality, then, is a function of the language we use to explain, describe, and interact with it, or, to paraphrase Hamlet, reality is "words, words, words."

In the postmodern world, stories and performances become as important as, or even more important than, facts and figures. The new era revels in semiotics—the study of signs and signifiers—and is as concerned with the laws of grammar and semantics as the modern era was with the laws of physics. The scientific preoccupation with truth becomes less interesting to scholars than the personal and collective quest to find meaning. Language is the key to exploring meaning because it is the vehicle we use to communicate our thoughts and feelings to one another. Language, then, says psychologist William Bergquist, "is itself the primary reality in our daily life experiences" in a postmodern world.[11]

If people of the modern world searched for purpose, those of the postmodern world seek playfulness. Order of any kind is considered restraining, even stifling. Creative anarchy, on the other hand, is tolerated, even pursued. Spontaneity is the only real order of the day. Everything is less serious in the postmodern environment. Irony, paradox, and skepticism are rampant. There is no great concern with making history but only making up interesting stories to live by. Because there is no overarching historical frame governing either nature or society, interest in history, per se, wanes. History is less a reference for understanding the past and projecting ourselves into the future and more loose story fragments that can be recycled and made part of contemporary social scripts.

The fast pace of a hyper-real, nanosecond culture shortens the individual and collective temporal horizon to the immediate moment. Traditions and legacies become fading interests. What counts is "now," and what's important is being able to feel and experience the moment. Climax and catharsis subsume efficiency and productivity in both personal and social life. It is a world full of spectacles and entertainments and highly sophisticated performances acted out on elaborate stages. In this new era, the "reality principle," which governed human conduct from the Protestant Reformation through the industrial revolution, has been dethroned, or, more appropriately, abandoned. The "pleasure principle" reigns.

Playfulness and pleasure seeking are everywhere. Take, for example, architecture. In contrast to the seriousness of modern architecture, with its emphasis on regularity and functionality, postmodern architects stress irony and amusement. Postmodern buildings are often collages of historic styles drawn together to shock, titillate, and entertain. Classic Greco-Roman columns and cornices might be juxtaposed with neo-Baroque bric-a-brac. The façade of an old nineteenth-century brownstone building might be saved and used for a space-age-looking structure. A Rube Goldberg–type contraption might adorn an atrium, while trompe l'oeil art on a nearby lobby wall creates a three-dimensional representation of a French village. Architectural orthodoxy has given way to iconoclasm and an anything-goes attitude as long as the result is likely to capture attention and be the subject of conversation and debate.

In the social sciences, postmodern scholars say that the modern effort to create a unified vision of human behavior has led only to ideologies of classism, racism, and colonialism. Postmodern sociology stresses pluralism and ambivalence and preaches toleration for the many different stories that make up the human experience. There is no one ideal social regime to which to aspire but rather a multitude of cultural experiments, each equally valid. The idea of inescapable linear progress toward an agreed-upon future utopian ideal is eschewed. The postmodernists celebrate the diversity of local experiences that together make up an ecology of human existence.

The new era is ambiguous and diverse, entertaining and humorous, tolerant and chaotic. It is eclectic and highly irreverent. Ideology, unalterable truths, and ironclad laws are cast aside to make room for performances of all kinds.

The Postmodern Age, then, is punctuated by playfulness, while the Modern Age was characterized by industriousness. In a regime built around work, production is the operational paradigm and property represents the fruits of human labor. In a world orchestrated around play, performance reigns and commercial access to cultural experiences becomes the goal of human activity. Making things and exchanging and accumulating property become ancillary in the Age of Access to scripting scenarios, telling stories, and acting out fantasies.

Gone are the hard edges of an age dedicated to harnessing and transforming physical resources. The postmodern era is softer, lighter, and bound up with feelings and attitudes. It is a world turned upside down. The conscious mind of rational and analytical thought becomes suspect, while the unconscious mind of erotic desires, illusions, and dream-states comes to the fore and becomes, in effect, reality, or, more appropriate, hyper-reality. The underworld of fantasy is glorified and made manifest.

Jean Baudrillard, Frederic Jameson, and other postmodern scholars credit this historic turnaround—this triumph of the unconscious—to the vast changes in communications technologies and commerce that have made the whole world a stage and all experience a simulation. A French postmodernist once remarked that if a child grows up spending most of his or her waking hours in front of a screen, peering deep inside a virtual reality, after a while it is no longer virtual. It is their reality. Baudrillard says that TV, for example, is no longer a surrogate for reality. TV no longer interprets or dramatizes the world. "TV is the world."[12]

A 1999 survey conducted by the Kaiser Family Foundation, entitled "Kids and Media at the New Millennium," reports that American children now spend an average of five hours and thirty minutes a day, seven days a week, interacting with electronic media for recreation. For youngsters eight and older, the total is even higher, with the average child spending six hours and forty-five minutes a day engaged with television, computers, video games, the Internet, and other media (outside the classroom) as a part of their leisure-time activity. Equally important, the survey found that most children interact with electronic media alone. Older children, for example, watch television alone more than 95 percent of the time, while children between the ages of two and seven watch TV alone more than 81 percent of the time.[13]

MTV captures all of the various features of the new postmodern ethos better than any other television fare. Millions of preteens and teenagers all over the world spend hours in front of their screens, watching rock promos. MTV blurs all the many distinctions that have been carefully built up over the course of the modern era. In this sense, it is a revolutionary art form. It is also, don't forget, a marketing mechanism. The goal is to sell music CDs. *Rolling Stone* writer Stephen Levy notes that "MTV's greatest achievement has been to coax rock and roll into the video arena where you can't distinguish between entertainment and the sales pitch."[14]

MTV destroys boundaries of every kind. It levels all the rich gradations of human experience to a single, flat playing surface in which all phenomena exist in the form of pure images, one following the other at lightning speed, with no seeming context or coherence. The whole of human culture is ransacked for images that are then jumbled together to create a blitzkrieg of hot, evocative visual stimuli designed to both disorient and fix the gaze of the viewer. Categories are meant to be reshuffled, borders destroyed. The separateness of things in time and space—what makes them unique—is eliminated. Ann Kaplan, director of the Humanities Institute at the State University of New York at Stony Brook, observes that "MTV refuses any clear recognition of previously sacred aesthetic boundaries: images from German Expressionism, French Surrealism, and Dadaism . . . are mixed together with those pillaged from noir, gangster, and horror films in such a way as to obliterate differences."[15]

MTV is not parody but rather pastiche. There are no judgments to render, no critiques to make. In fact, there is no point of reference from which to even make commentary—just an endless procession of cultural fragments creating what Jean Baudrillard calls "the ecstasy of communication."[16]

MTV is experiences without context. It has the feel of the unconscious—a timeless realm in which fantasies of all kinds bubble up onto the screen, only to fade away in the wake of the next and the next. . . . MTV is dreamlike entertainment, unencumbered by the weightiness of either history or geography. MTV repackages snippets of culture in the form of simulated fantasies that entertain and excite and provide a kind of simulated lived experience for millions of young people. It is the ideal signifier of the postmodern world.

TV and cyberspace have become the places where we spend much of our time and where we create much of our individual and collective life stories. Today's generation is as likely to compare the "real" world and events that take place there to something they saw or experienced on television. The late cultural critic O. B. Hardison mused that "for many people today, an event is not authenticated—is not 'real'—unless it has been seen on television."[17] The question, then, is, which is reality and which is illusion? The answer, say the postmodernists, is the experience that is the most powerful—and for more and more young people that often means the simulation. Says Baudrillard, "Today we live in the imaginary world of the screen, of the interface . . . and networks. All our machines are screens. We too have become screens, and the interactivity of men has become the interactivity of screens. . . . We live everywhere already in an 'aesthetic' hallucination of reality."[18]

Changing Forms of Consciousness

Postmodern scholars and social critics like to talk of the "dot-com generation"—the first generation to grow up in a simulated commercial world. But how different are today's youngsters from the bourgeois children of the late nineteenth and early twentieth centuries? While there are many similarities, the differences are profound and suggest that a new type of human being is being readied for the twenty-first century—individuals whose sense of self is bound up less in how much output they produce and how many things they accumulate and more in how many vivid experiences and relationships they have access to.

The last great change in human consciousness came at the dawn of the modern era with the rise of the bourgeois class. A product of the new cities that were the hubs of an incipient capitalism, the bourgeoisie were the merchants, factory owners, shopkeepers, academicians, and professionals who spearheaded the industrial way of life. In a world that was being transformed from caste to class, they were the upwardly mobile middle, sandwiched between a dying feudal aristocracy on top and an oppressed and volatile proletariat of workers and disenfranchised small farmers and peasants on the bottom. They were the entrepreneurs and accumulators of capital, the champions of nationhood and extended markets, the realists who believed that human reason could unlock the secrets of nature and codify the truths of a knowable objective reality. They were the class that gradually abandoned theology for ideology and heavenly salvation for an earthly utopia. They spread the gospel of materialism and extolled the virtues of private property.

Unlike medieval life, which was conducted openly and in public, the bourgeoisie lived mostly behind closed doors. Their life was an interior one—lived out in small shops and drawing rooms. The bourgeoisie organized their lives the way they organized their property. Every aspect of their being was enclosed, privatized, controlled, boundaried, categorized, protected, hoarded, and hidden away from public scrutiny. Everything in this private world was composed and organized. Nothing was out of place.

The interiorization of physical life was accompanied by the internalization of consciousness. It was in the bourgeois period that human beings began to turn their attention to self. While the concept of self had been developing slowly and inexorably throughout Western history, it became the object of near obsessive attention among the bourgeoisie. Mirrors were to be found everywhere in the homes of the new bourgeois class. Self-inspection and self-reflection became both preoccupation and pastime. Words like *self-confidence, self-love, self-pity, self-esteem, self-worth, character, ego,* and *conscience* became reference points for personal development and social discourse. Self-portraits and biographies became popular cultural forms.

During the late Victorian era, material comfort came to define the life of the bourgeoisie. When one thinks of a bourgeois person, one is likely to conjure up images of overstuffed furniture, heavy drapery, and layers of carpeting on the floor—the feeling of comfort and security, of quiet and decorum, walled off from the hustle and bustle and vagaries of the outside world. Donald M. Lowe, author of *History of Bourgeois Perception,* observes that "the bourgeoisie had a compulsion to fill up the visible space of the home with excessive furniture and intricate decoration. They cluttered every room in the house with objects. The eye seemed to abhor any visible, empty space."[19]

In an age structured around private property relations, the bourgeoisie organized their own lives in ways that glorified that ideal. They surrounded themselves with possessions and created every kind of boundary to separate mine from thine. They even internalized the concept of possession into their very consciousness. To be "self-possessed" was a much sought-after personal goal of every member of the bourgeois class.

In the Medieval Age, when personal attention was focused more on securing a place in the next world, virtue was what every good Christian aspired to. To lead a virtuous life and to be of good virtue assured eternal salvation. In the Modern Age, virtue began drifting to the margins as society became increasingly production oriented. The bourgeoisie began to substitute character for virtue. By the nineteenth century, *character* had become one of the most important descriptive words in the English vocabulary. To be of good character was the highest compliment one could extend to a bourgeois man or woman. Character, more than anything else, conjured up the notion of self-control and self-mastery. The term *character* became associated with citizenship, hard work, industriousness, determination, frugality, integrity, and, above all else, adulthood. It represented both a secularization of the values of the Protestant work ethic and a reaffirmation of the kind of producer values deemed so important to advancing the capitalist agenda and a propertied regime.

By the early 1920s, however, character was beginning to wane in importance and a new concept of self was beginning to emerge, first in the pages of self-improvement manuals and books and later in the popular culture. Commentators of the day urged Americans to develop their personalities. Orison Swett Marden, who just a generation earlier had written on the qualities of good character, published a new book, *The Masterful Personality,* in 1921, in which he urged his readers to learn to exhibit personal charm. Marden reminded his followers that "so much of our success in life depends upon what others think of us." He counseled that manners, proper clothes, good conversation ("to know what to say and how to say it"), energy, life efficiency, and poise all are qualities that everyone can use to "sway great masses."[20]

The words used to describe personality were quite different from those used to describe character. Someone is said to have personality if he or she is attractive, creative, fascinating, forceful, magnetic, engaging, vivacious, demonstrative, and warm. To have personality is to stand out in a crowd, to be noticed, to command attention, to influence others. To "be yourself," to "express your individuality," to "have self-confidence" became the rallying cry of a generation. Those very qualities, in turn, became the psychological raw material for mass marketing techniques and national advertising campaigns designed to turn a nation of savers and producers into a nation of spenders and consumers.

While the bourgeoisie of the nineteenth century accumulated property and wealth, they maintained an ascetic approach to life that was opposed to too much reveling in consumption for its own sake. By the 1920s, America was awash in goods and in need of a new kind of human being who might be more open to a consumer lifestyle—someone less serious and more playful, less in control and more adventurous, someone anxious to "make an impression."

The marketing experts were more than glad to provide the appropriate counsel. Keeping up with fashion—being stylish, modern, and avant-garde—was the way to make a statement, to express one's unique personality in a very visible manner. Modern marketing and the "cult of personality" worked hand in hand to create a new human being for whom self-fulfillment was as important as self-control. While private property remained the central value of society throughout the long journey from character to personality, its importance shifted, reflecting the change in emphasis from production to consumption values.

The Protean Persona

Today, as the global economy shifts emphasis once again—this time from consuming goods and services to consuming culture and lived experience—human nature is changing once again. The new protean men and women of the Age of Access view themselves and their world quite differently from their parents and grandparents. If past generations thought of themselves as people of "good character" or "strong personality"—in conformance with producer and later consumer values—the new generation is beginning to think of themselves more as "creative performers," moving comfortably between scripts and sets as they act out the many dramas that make up the cultural marketplace.

The new protean self owes much to the increasing density of human interaction occasioned by modern transportation and communications and city living. The twentieth century has been the century of urbanization. Villages grew into towns, and towns into giant cities, greatly increasing human interaction for the first time in history. The railroad, steamship, automobile, airplane, telegraph, telephone, and later radio and television further compressed time and space. Where 100 years earlier one's circle of acquaintances might never have exceeded more than several hundred people in a lifetime, in the twentieth century, one might encounter that many people in less than a week. The qualitative change in human interaction requires a more flexible person, one able to continually readjust to changing environments, new circumstances, and varying expectations. In a small community, where everyone knows everyone else, one's core self is generally set at an early age and remains consistent and predictable throughout a lifetime. In the more anonymous and challenging setting of the city, one is forced to be more of a chameleon, to address the multiplicity of opportunities that present themselves.

The philosopher Georg Simmel, reflecting on the new kind of person emerging in the fast-paced urban world of the twentieth century, wrote of the "essential restlessness" of life. The pace of human activity is so pronounced, thought Simmel, that even form itself is giving way. "We gaze," said Simmel, "into an abyss of unformed life beneath our feet."[21] Human activity is so speeded up, and human consciousness is so fluid, remarked Simmel, that life "constantly struggles against its own products, which have become fixed and do not move along with it."[22]

In the nineteenth century, one's sense of self was far more static. It wasn't uncommon to think of one's life as a product whose value increases over time. In the twentieth century, people slowly came to think of themselves more as works in process. "Being" gave way to "becoming" in the new streamlined world.

The changes taking place in the concept of self found their counterpart in the weakening of property as an all-encompassing metaphor for defining both the individual and social relations. Sociologists Michael R. Wood of Hunter College and Louis A. Zurcher, Jr., of the University of Texas, in their book, *The Development of a Postmodern Self,* take note of the transformation "from a self thought of as an object built up through cumulative effort to a present oriented self, realized, discovered, and actualized in a continual process."[23] Instead of thinking of oneself as one might think of a piece of property—i.e., making something out of oneself—the new self is more likely to be regarded as an unfolding story continually being updated and re-edited.

The property metaphor was further undermined by what scholars refer to as the fall of historical consciousness and the rise of therapeutic consciousness. The bourgeoisie of the eighteenth, nineteenth, and early twentieth centuries viewed themselves in historical terms. They saw themselves as participants in the unfolding of a great historical drama whose outcome would be a material utopia. For the capitalists, the end of history meant the final enclosure of the earth's vast commons and the broad distribution of property in the hands of the people. For the Marxists, the end of history meant the dissolution of a propertied regime and its replacement with a society whose material resources and capital were collectively owned. Still, capitalists and socialists alike saw property relations as the driving force of history and each human being as a small player in the unfolding of a larger metanarrative. It was an age propelled by ideology and the sure conviction that each person's productive efforts were leading inextricably to a future cornucopia.

By the middle decades of the twentieth century, historical consciousness was giving way to a new therapeutic consciousness. People thought less in terms of their place in history and more in terms of making their own personal history. In the new posthistorical era, observed sociologist Philip Reiff, "men . . . feel freer to live their lives with a minimum of pretense to anything more grand than sweetening the time."[24] The therapeutic man and woman, said Reiff, are "able to enjoy life without erecting high symbolic hedges around it."[25] Being productive and making something out of oneself—values that went well with a production-oriented historical consciousness—seemed more like sheer drudgery. Life is too short to sacrifice oneself for history and some future state of well-being—especially when self-fulfillment and well-being are available here and now for the taking. While "historical man" sacrifices in the present and lives for the future, "therapeutic man" lives for the present and gives up any pretense of a grand historical mission. The late social philosopher Christopher Lasch described the therapeutic sensibility. He wrote:

> People today hunger not for personal salvation, let alone for the restoration of an earlier golden age, but for the feeling, the momentary illusion, of personal well-being, health, and psychic security. . . . To live for the moment is the prevailing passsion—to live for yourself, not for your predecessors or posterity.[26]

Lasch said that "we are fast losing the sense of historical continuity, the sense of belonging to a succession of generations originating in the past and stretching into the future. It is the waning of the sense of historical time."[27] The fall of historical consciousness and the rise of therapeutic consciousness, according to Lasch, parallels the shift from a world where the accumulation of property is a measure both of one's accomplishments and one's contributions to history to a world where the accumulation of lived experiences is a measure of one's personal psychological journey and quest for transformation. Lasch wrote: "The pursuit of self-interest, formerly identified with the rational pursuit of gain and the accumulation of wealth, has become a search for pleasure and psychic survival."[28] Therapeutic consciousness has laid the groundwork for a new man and woman—a postmodern human being.

Reprogramming the Mind

While there are countless other factors that have contributed to the changes occurring in human consciousness none perhaps is more important than the shift in communication technologies from print to computer. Great changes in human consciousness have always accompanied changes in the forms of communication human beings use to create their social relations. The last great shift in communications technologies, from oral and script culture to print culture, came at the dawn of the modern era and changed forever the nature of human consciousness. The print revolution facilitated a way of thinking that was ideally suited to a society organized around the notion of private property relations and market exchanges.

To begin with, the new print medium redefined the way human beings organize knowledge. The mnemonic redundancy of oral communication and the subjective eccentricities of medieval script were replaced by a more rational, calculating, analytical approach to knowledge. Print replaced human memory with tables of contents, pagination, footnotes, and indexes, freeing the human mind from continually recalling the past so that it might fix on the present and future. The shift in consciousness prepared the way for the new commercial idea of unlimited material gain and human progress.

Print introduced charts, lists, graphs, and other visual aids that were to prove so important in creating ever more accurate descriptions of the world. Print made possible standardized, easily reproducible maps, making navigation and land travel more predictable and accessible. The opening up of oceans and land routes spread commercial markets and trade. Printed schedules, continually updated, mass produced, and widely circulated, facilitated rail traffic and ocean voyages.

Print made possible a "contract" commercial culture by allowing merchants and capitalists to coordinate increasingly complex market activity and keep abreast of far-flung commercial transactions. Modern bookkeeping, schedules, bills of lading, invoicing, checks, and promissory notes were essential management tools in the organization of market capitalism. Print also made possible a uniform pricing system without which modern ideas of property exchange could not have developed.

Print also introduced the idea of assembly, a key component of the industrial way of life. Separating the alphabet into standardized units of type that were uniform, interchangeable, and reusable made print the first modern industrial process. With print, objects are uniformly spaced by positioning type on a chase and locking the chase onto a press. The composite type then can be reproduced over and over, each copy identical and indistinguishable from the original. Assembly, uniform and interchangeable parts, predictable positioning of objects in space, and mass production were the foundation stones of the industrial way of life. Print created the archetype technology for this new way of organizing nature.

Print helped spawn the development of nationalism and gave impetus to the creation of nation-states. Vernacular languages, reduced to print, created a larger focus for collective identity. People began to see themselves as French, English, German, Spanish, and Swedish. Print made possible detailed recordkeeping, so indispensable for the creation of modern government bureaucracies.

Print organizes phenomena in an orderly, rational, and objective way, and in so doing encourages linear, sequential, and causal ways of thinking. The very notion of "composing" one's thoughts conjures up the idea of well-thought-out linear progression of ideas, one following the other in logical sequence, a mode of thought very different from that in oral culture, where redundancy and discontinuity in conversation often are the rules.

By eliminating the redundancy of oral language and making precise measurement and description possible, print laid the foundation for the modern scientific worldview. Phenomena could be rigorously examined, observed, and described, and experiments could be made repeatable with exacting standards and protocols, something that was far more difficult to achieve in a manuscript or oral culture.

Print also made important the idea of authorship. While individual authors were previously recognized, they were few in number. Manuscript writing was often anonymous and the result of the collective contribution of many scribes over long periods of time. The notion of authorship elevated the individual to a unique status, separating him or her from the collective voice of the community.

The idea of authorship also went hand in hand with the concept of owning one's own words. Copyright laws made communication among people a commodity for the first time. The idea that one could own thoughts and words and that others would have to pay to hear them marked a seminal turning point in the history of human relations.

Before print, people shared their thoughts together orally, in face-to-face dialogue and exchange. Even manuscripts were read aloud and were meant to be heard rather than seen. The print revolution helped nurture a more meditative environment. Books were read silently and alone, creating a new sense of personal privacy and, along with it, notions of self-reflection and introspection, eventually leading to the creation of a therapeutic way of thinking about oneself and the world.

Print made possible universal literacy for the first time, preparing successive generations with the communication tools they needed to manage the complexities of the modern market and new ways of working and socializing. In short, print created the appropriate mind-set and worldview for an "industrious" way of living and being in the world.[29]

Today, the computer is organizing communications in a revolutionary way that makes it an ideal tool for managing an economy built around access relationships and the marketing of cultural resources and lived experiences. In the process, it is slowly changing the very nature of human consciousness.

Electronic communication is organized cybernetically, not linearly. The notions of sequentiality and causality are replaced by a total field of continuous, integrated activity. In an electronic world of communications, subjects and objects give way to nodes and networks, and structure and function are subsumed by process. The computer's mode of organization—especially parallel computing—mirrors the workings of cultural systems, in which each of the parts is a node in a dynamic network of relationships that is continually readjusting and renewing itself at every level of its existence.

Electronic communication also organizes knowledge differently from the way print technology does. Hypertext replaces the more limited and narrow kind of print referencing. A self-contained book, with a set number of facts, makes room for an open-ended field of information as footnotes and references are expanded indefinitely, creating new subtexts and metatexts.

Whereas a printed book is linear, bound, and fixed, hypertext is associational and potentially boundaryless. A printed book is exclusive in nature and autonomous in form. Hypertext, however, is inclusive in nature and relational in form. In other words, printed books have a beginning and an end. They are complete. Hypertext has no clear beginning and end, but only a starting point from which users make connections between related materials. It is always metamorphosing and never complete. The printed book is a product, while hypertext is a process. The former lends itself to extended ownership, while the latter is best accessed on a moment-to-moment basis.

Hypertext also undermines one of the central features of print consciousness—the idea of the individual author who owns his or her own ideas and words. Hypertext blurs the traditional notion of authorship. Because the medium is based on inclusivity and connectivity rather than exclusivity and autonomy, there is often no clear boundary separating one's contribution from another's. People are continually snipping, recombining, editing, and tweaking material that has been accessed from countless other sources and mediums, then combining the material with their own before sending it on its way to other nodes in the various networks they are linked to. When material of all kinds becomes part of an ongoing open-ended process involving multiple parties distributed over time and space rather than a finished product resulting from a single person's creative effort, exclusive ownership sometimes becomes difficult to assign.

Hypertext leads to what French literary theorist Roland Barthes calls "the death of the author" and with it the concepts of exclusivity and autonomy that were so important in framing both the modern mind and a propertied world.[30] Michael Heim of the graduate faculty in communications and new media at the Arts Center College of Design in Pasadena, California, observes that digital communication "turns the private solitude of reflective reading and writing into a public network where the personal symbolic framework needed for original authorship is threatened by linkage with the total textuality of human expressions."[31] In the network, one is immersed in texts within texts and in continuous collaboration with others, making boundaries between self-expression and collective expression difficult, if not impossible. "As the authoritativeness of text diminishes," says Heim, "so too does the recognition of the private self of the creative author."[32] In the new world of computers, hypertext, nodes, links, and networks, the nineteenth-century idea of the self as an island—an autonomous being, solid and boundaried like the printed books and physical goods bought and sold in the industrial marketplace—succumbs to a new relational self. Philosopher Jean-François Lyotard makes the point that in the electronic networks of cyberspace, "[a] *self* does not amount to much . . . no self is an island; each exists in a fabric of relations. . . . Young or old, man or woman, rich or poor, a person is always located at 'nodal points' of specific communication circuits."[33] Having access to multiple circuits—i.e., being connected—in the new network economy is as important as being autonomous and propertied was in an earlier market economy.

The computer helps nurture the creation of a new kind of relational consciousness, just as print helped foster the notion of an autonomous being. A generation growing up using hypertext and engaged in multiple networks is likely to be increasingly predisposed toward a commercial world steeped in connectivity and access relationships. The new computer consciousness and the new way of conducting commerce are coming together. In time, they will weave a near seamless web.

The New Thespians

The long-term transformation in the concept of self from an autonomous being that exists in space to a relational and ever changing personal story that unfolds over time is only just beginning as we turn the corner into the twenty-first century. The older notion of an autonomous self fit a frontier world where people were separated by great distances and lived in relative isolation from one another. Being self-sufficient, self-possessed, and propertied, in earlier times, was a survival strategy. In this older world, mine and thine are clearly marked. The autonomous, boundaried, bourgeois self is the most appropriate form of consciousness to negotiate a world of vast physical expanses and untapped natural resources.

The current generation, however, is more caught up in time than in space. It finds itself embedded in a far more complex, interdependent, temporal world made up of ever changing webs of human relationships and activity. Everywhere we turn, some form of potential human connection comes careening toward us. The reality, says Kenneth Gergen, professor of psychology at Swarthmore College, is that "we engage in greater numbers of relationships, in a greater variety of forms, and with greater intensities than ever before."[34] We are enveloped in relationships, some virtual, others real. Our cellular phones, voice mail, faxes, and e-mail keep us in instant communication with people everywhere in the world. Our networks—both economic and social—embed us in still more varied relationships. Advertising messages, direct-mail campaigns, radio, television, and cyberspace provide even more interaction. There is virtually no alone time left; every spare moment becomes an opportunity to make another connection. We live in a world in which getting and holding one another's attention becomes paramount, and relationships of all kinds become central to our existence. Descartes's dictum "I think therefore I am" has been replaced by a new dictum: "I am connected therefore I exist."

The old idea of personal autonomy gives way to the new idea of multiple relationships, further eroding the notion of discrete boundaries separating mine and thine. Gergen notes that

> with the multiplication of relationships also comes a transformation in the social capacities of the individual. . . . The relatively coherent and unified sense of self inherent in a traditional culture gives way to manifold and competing potentials. A multiphrenic condition emerges in which one swims in ever-shifting, concatenating, and contentious currents of being.[35]

The near riot of social interaction pulls and tugs on every individual consciousness, forcing a loss of the centered self. Caught up in the waves of competing and often contradictory social discourses that flood over us, we all desperately divide up our limited attention, giving bits and pieces of our consciousness over to each passing demand on our time. In the process, we risk slowly losing ourselves in the labyrinthine network of short-lived and ever changing connections in which we find ourselves embedded. Gergen writes:

> This fragmentation of self-conceptions corresponds to a multiplicity of incoherent and disconnected relationships. These relationships pull us in myriad directions, inviting us to play such a variety of roles that the very concept of an "authentic self" with knowable characteristics recedes from view. The fully saturated self becomes no self at all.[36]

This state, says Gergen and others, is "postmodern consciousness."[37]

In this postmodern world made up of networks and commodified relationships where boundaries are blurred and activity is increasingly connected, the old self-contained, autonomous consciousness is slowly becoming an anachronism. In its stead is a new person who is more like a node operating in a myriad of relationships. "The final stage in this transition to the postmodern is reached," says Gergen, "when the self vanishes fully into a stage of relatedness." In this new world, argues Gergen, "one ceases to believe in a self independent of the relationships in which he or she is embedded . . . thus placing relationships in the central position occupied by the individual self for the last several hundred years of Western history."[38]

A curious phenomenon has gained a toehold among an increasing number of young people in the more affluent neighborhoods and suburbs of industrial countries. Teenagers are more often ending their sentences in a slightly elevated tone and in a more tentative manner, suggesting that everything they are saying is more in the form of a question rather than a statement. Psychologists and sociologists have been intrigued by this widespread practice—known as upspeak—and wonder if it might not be symptomatic of the shift taking place from an autonomous to a relational self. The open-ended and conditional nature of this new way of talking suggests that one's very thoughts need to be continuously linked to feed-back from others in order to make sense and be validated. The declarative sentence, so characteristic of an autonomous nature, appears to be giving way to the inquisitive sentence of the more relational self.

Gergen acknowledges that "the related self is not yet a pervasive condition," but asserts that human consciousness is heading in that direction as we journey farther into the world of cyberspace. Jean Baudrillard shares Gergen's analysis. Deeply pessimistic of the consequences of this new journey, Baudrillard observes that "our private sphere has ceased to be the stage where the drama of the subject at odds with his objects . . . is played out." We no longer exist as subjects at all, says Baudrillard, but rather "as terminals of multiple networks."[39]

The new relational personality is as fluid and transitory as the networks people engage in. MIT professor Sherry Turkle, who has conducted an extensive study of the young men and women who spend much of their time in virtual worlds in cyberspace, says that at least some among the first generation of the postmodern era are beginning to exhibit what psychologists call "multiple personas." In cyberspace, says Turkle, "hundreds of thousands, perhaps already millions of users create online personae who live in a diverse group of virtual communities where the routine formation of multiple identities undermines any notion of a real and unitary self."[40]

Turkle recounts her experience with young people in the virtual worlds of cyberspace. Multiple-user domains (or MUDs) are virtual worlds created by computer participants. In these worlds, players create online versions of whatever characters they choose to be and then act out their new identities through their relationships with the other MUD players. The anonymity of MUDs allows participants to experiment with multiple identities. After a while, say some of the most engaged players, they feel as if the characters they're playing so much of the time in cyberspace are really themselves—or at least some of the many personas they feel themselves to be. One of the players told Turkle, "You are who you pretend to be." Another youngster, who spent the most time in cyberspace, said, "Part of me, a very important part of me, only exists inside Pern-MUD."[41] Turkle reports that some young people move in and out of several virtual worlds each day, taking on the particular persona that inhabits each respective sphere.

For many computer users, says Turkle, windows have become "a powerful metaphor for thinking about the self as a multiple, distributed system."[42] In the new worlds of cyberspace, one plays multiple roles, often on parallel tracks. Each window opens up into a new virtual reality in which one plays out yet another one of his or her personas. Life becomes increasingly decentered, while at the same time more connected in webs of relationships.

Robert J. Lifton is far more sanguine about this new protean archetype than Baudrillard and other critics of postmodernity. Lifton believes that having multiple personas is a coping mechanism, a way for the psyche to accommodate the escalating demands being placed on it in the emerging hyper-real, postmodern society. Lifton contends that having multiple personas, far from representing the disappearance of self, is really a more plastic and mature stage of consciousness—one in which a person is able to live with ambiguities and complex and often competing priorities. He makes the point that today, anyone who can afford the price can "have access to any image or idea originating anywhere in the contemporary world or from any cultural moment of the entire human past."[43] Lifton says that this "eerie omniaccess" is without precedent in human history. Being able to live and experience as many potential realities as possible, sometimes even at the same time, requires a protean consciousness.

The new postmodern man and woman is constantly casting about for new lived experiences, just as their bourgeois parents and grandparents were continually in search of making new acquisitions. The new cultural industries, in turn, are creating an almost infinite number of scripts for acting out one's life experiences, just as the manufacturing industries provided a vast number of consumer products to buy.

While buying things is a linear affair, a sequential activity in which one transaction follows another, a lived experience is polymorphous and cybernetic in nature. When one is surrounded by commercially mediated cultural experiences—some of it in virtual worlds, others in real time and space—the mind has to be everywhere at once, continually negotiating access, evaluating experiential outcomes, opening up new channels of communications, rearranging relationships, and networking new worlds of potential engagement. "Proteanism," says Lifton, "is a balancing act between responsive shapeshifting, on the one hand, and efforts to consolidate and cohere on the other."[44]

But if Lifton is correct, does the new protean consciousness necessarily have to lead to a commodified future in which all of life becomes a series of paid-for performances, entertainments, and fantasies? Some might argue that emphases on connectivity, embeddedness, and relatedness free up the human consciousness to migrate to an entirely different realm— one punctuated by a newfound sense of oneness and participation with others. After all, the older autonomous consciousness of the industrial era, mired in mine and thine distinctions, spatial expropriation on a grand scale, and a craving for the accumulation of property and possessions, has given us a divided world: the rich against the poor, humanity against the other creatures, and a planet greatly diminished and depleted.

As long as human beings continue to perceive the earth almost exclusively as an object for expropriation and to view one another as combatants in a life-or-death struggle to make everything mine rather than thine, a perpetual state of warfare is inevitable. This, unfortunately, is much of the legacy of the modern era of property and markets.

Is it possible that the more relational consciousness of the postmodern era might break the mine-thine divide, ending the long struggle of each against the other to secure as much of the earth as possible in the form of private property? Certainly there is evidence that at least some people of today's younger generation are less competitive than previous generations weaned on market relations and a property ethic. Systems thinking, teamwork, and consensus building all are part of the network ethos. Moreover, parallel processing—multitasking—which is becoming more common among youngsters, might help engender a deeper sense of the interconnectiveness of all phenomena and give rise to a more participatory way of thinking and acting in the world.

Experimentation with multiple personas might also lead to a better understanding of and tolerance for differences among people and a willingness to be more open in our dealings with others. It is perhaps no accident that people in the theater have long been thought of, justifiably, as being more open and tolerant in their views and sensibilities. Being able to adopt another persona—putting oneself in someone else's shoes and imagining what it might be like to be that other person—is a powerful conceptual tool for breaking the mine-thine divide. While a protean consciousness could result in a fragmented sense of being, as some psychologists have warned, it is possible also that the experimentation with multiple personas might engender a new sense of empathy for others and, in the process, help lay the foundation for cultural renewal.

The critics are skeptical. Some, like Frederic Jameson, are likely to regard the new more plastic psyche a bit more cynically. In an economy consumed with selling cultural commodities and lived experiences, Jameson and others might argue that the fragmentation of each psyche into multiple personas only increases the number of potential cultural markets. After all, if each person's lifetime potential for lived experience is the market for cultural production, then the more personas each person manifests, the more markets there are to exploit.

All the World Is a Stage

What is so transparent in surveying the many aspects of the Age of Access is the theatrical nature of it all. The network mode of organization, relationship marketing, common-interest developments (CIDs), entertainment destination centers, themed cities, tourism, cultural production, and virtual worlds all resonate with theatricality. In the Industrial Age, which was structured around the transformation of resources into products, human beings readily accepted Charles Darwin's notion of nature as a battleground and life as a competitive struggle to accumulate scarce resources. Holding on to reconstituted bits of nature, in the form of exclusive private property, represented the high-water mark of the evolutionary sojourn. In an age structured around cultural production and the consumption of lived experience, nature is viewed as a giant theater of potential performances. The more versatile one is, the more access one has to crafting his or her own scripts.

The metamorphosis of human beings from productive workers and informed consumers to creative performers represents a great change in human social relations. That's not to suggest that theatricality went unnoticed as a defining metaphor for life in earlier periods of history. Human beings always have used the theatrical arts to mimic nature and create symbolic worlds. When primitive men and women painted their faces, tattooed their skin, mutilated their body parts, adorned themselves with feathers and skins of other animals, staged elaborate rituals, choreographed dances designed to re-create the hunt or the birth of nature, buried the dead with pomp and circumstance, they were theatricalizing their lives. "The birth of a child, education, hunting, marriage, war, the administration of justice, religious ceremonies and funeral rites—every important event in life is made by the primitive man . . . the occasion for a purely theatrical spectacle," writes Russian playwright Nicolas Evreinoff.[45] A primitive person's entire life, says Evreinoff, was a "succession of such 'shows.'"[46]

Human beings are continually engaged in the process of transformation—altering their states of being, becoming something or someone else. In cultural gatherings, social settings, and business environments, human beings suspend disbelief and take on a role. The very word *person* comes from the Latin *persona,* which means to wear a mask.

While the theatrical metaphor is but one of many lenses from which to view human behavior, what makes the postmodern sense of theatricality so different is that at least for the more affluent members of society, performance has become far more self-conscious and commercial in nature. Growing numbers of people, especially young people, see themselves as performance artists and their lives as unfinished works of art. The cultural industries both create and exploit the new consciousness. Neal Gabler reminds us:

> *An ever-growing segment of the American economy is now devoted to designing, building and then dressing the sets in which we live, work, shop and play; to creating our costumes; to making our hair shine and our faces glow; to slenderizing our bodies, to supplying our props.*[47]

"Image managers," like Ralph Lauren and Martha Stewart, prepare the costumes and sets that people use as backdrops for the performances they act out. One can be outfitted in Lauren's Western cowboy motif, or be made to look like a successful New York broker or a California surfer. Each costume is designed to make the appropriate visual statement to go along with whatever persona is being projected. Martha Stewart is perhaps the most successful of the new genre of personal set designers. She advises her customers how to put their props together in just the right way to maximize the theatrical effect. As in traditional stage performances, nothing is left to chance but rather carefully scripted out. Stewart counsels her clients that when shoveling snow from their sidewalks they should always take care to "leave one inch of snow so it looks nice and white." "Aesthetics," says Stewart, "are very important in snow removal."[48]

The theatricalization of much of lived experience and its near total absorption into the commercial sphere is a powerful social phenomenon—so powerful, in fact, that historian Daniel J. Boorstin suggests, "We risk being the first people in history to have been able to make their illusions so vivid, so pervasive, so 'realistic' that they can live in them."[49] Boorstin wrote these words before the advent of cyberspace. The new virtual worlds in which people work and play are, by their very nature, simulated environments, electronic stages for the acting out of millions of individual performances.

It's no wonder, then, that the dramaturgical perspective that we examined in chapter 8, which has been used so effectively to reconceptualize marketing techniques, is also becoming an equally popular methodology for understanding and modeling human behavior itself. If life is the acting out of a series of personal and collective social dramas, then the more complex the economic and social networks in which one is embedded, the more diverse roles each person is called on to play.

In the dramaturgical way of looking at human behavior, the self is no longer a private possession of an individual, as John Locke would have us believe, but rather, says Erving Goffman, "a sense given to [a person] by the very people he wishes to share it with." The self, then, is not an entity, say University of Minnesota professor of behavioral science Dennis Brissett and Oklahoma State University professor of sociology Charles Edgley, but rather "a kind of fictional, constructed, consensually validated quality" that results from the interaction and communication between people.[50] If so, then one's very being in the world depends on having access to others, of being part of networks of relationships, each of which validates a part of one's selfhood. This view is quite different from Hegel's notion that each person's unique self is both imprinted in and manifest by the possessions he or she acquires over a lifetime. Property, in the postmodern era, as we have seen, is no longer "the sole measure of a man."

Clearly, dramaturgists do not see their methodology as a mere metaphor for explaining the sociology of human behavior. Rather, they believe that life itself is, in fact, deeply dramaturgical. Robert Perinbanayagam makes the point that "it is not that reality is theatrical or dramatic; rather what is considered reality by society, or a part thereof, is theatrically realized and constructed."[51] The reason why, writes Perinbanayagam, is that dramatism

> *takes off from the premise that humans cannot help but communicate with symbols, on the one hand, and cannot help but be aware that the others around us are interpreting the world around them. . . . The world consists of communication-worthy social facts or social objects that dramatistically develop and present a theme. . . . The theater, then, is not something apart from society. . . . Rather it is a crystallization and typification of what goes on in society all the time—or more sharply, what a social relationship in fact is.*[52]

Even our possessions, argues Perinbanayagam, become part of the larger dramas we act out. We surround ourselves with material objects and continually rearrange them in various ways, "converting them into symbols so as to elicit particular responses from others," says Perinbanayagam. They become what Goffman calls part of "the presentation of a self."[53]

At a time when the commercial sphere is transforming itself from the selling of goods and services to providing access to commodified relationships, cultural productions, and lived experiences, the dramaturgical perspective provides just the right methodology for making sense of this new way of conducting business. It places communications at the heart of human activity, redefines the self in relational terms, makes experience itself a theatrical affair, and transforms property into symbols that help people act out their many dramatic roles as they flit in and out of networks of lived experiences, each representing a different aspect of their life story. The dramaturgical perspective is, in the final analysis, a vivid description of the state of mind that accompanies the newest stage of global capitalism. Our perceptions of human behavior are being transformed—this time to fit the requisites of cultural production and the commodification of lived experience.

As for the young people who have grown up in front of the screen and inside virtual worlds, their protean nature and theatrical consciousness serve them well for the many challenging roles they will have to perform on the electronic stage. We can be sure that the marketing experts, advertisers, and cultural intermediaries will be ready and waiting at the gateways, offering up access to all sorts of meaningful new cultural commodities and lived experiences for the price of admission. They will prospect local cultures for fresh fragments of cultural experience that can be mined and commodified. They will make their way back into history in search of story lines for creating exciting and entertaining new experiences. They will glorify the notion that each person's own story is the most important reality, and create simulated worlds that every individual can buy his or her way into. There are millions of personal dramas that need to be scripted and acted out. Each represents a lifelong market with vast commercial potential. In these new worlds, the only vestige of personal property likely to remain are the props that provide context for the performances that take place. For the thespian men and women of the new era, purchasing continuous access to the scripts, stages, other actors, and audiences provided by the commercial sphere will be critical to the nourishing of their multiple personas. Being able to perform and be transformed, in turn, will become the sine qua non of their existence.

Chapter Eleven

The Connected
and the
Disconnected

The question of access is likely to be as passionately debated in the coming century as questions of property rights were during the whole of the modern era. That's because access is a potentially more encompassing phenomenon. While property dealt with the narrow material question of what's mine and thine, access deals with the broader cultural question of who controls lived experience itself.

The shift from geographic markets to cyberspace, made possible by the digital communications revolution, opens up new ways to organize human relationships. The coming together of computers, telecommunications, cable television, consumer electronics, broadcasting, publishing, and entertainment in an integrated communications web allows commercial enterprises to exercise unprecedented control over the ways human beings communicate with one another.

More than twenty years ago, Daniel Bell made the observation that in the coming era, "control over communication services [will be] a source of power, and access to communication [will be] a condition of freedom."[1] The French philosopher Jean-François Lyotard tightened Bell's observation by suggesting that "increasingly, the central question is becoming who will have access" in this new postmodern world.[2]

The New Corporate Moguls

A handful of global media companies are locked in an epic struggle to control the communications channels and cultural resources that together will make up much of the commercial sphere in the twenty-first century. Whereas in the twentieth century, companies like Standard Oil, DuPont, Ford, U.S. Steel, and Sears were at the center of a marketplace dedicated to the production and sale of propertied goods, in the twenty-first century it's companies like Disney, Time Warner, Bertelsmann, Viacom, Sony, News Corporation, TCI, General Electric, PolyGram, and Seagram who will dominate the global media market and determine the conditions by which the public gains access to cultural resources and commodified experiences. These ten companies alone enjoyed annual sales ranging from $10 billion to $25 billion in 1997. A second tier of forty or so regional media giants from Western Europe, the United States, Asia, and Latin America controls much of the remaining communications channels and content, with annual sales of between $1 billion and $5 billion.[3]

U.S.-based media companies are the world leaders and have set the ground rules for the global contest to control communications and commodified cultural resources. The editors of *Vanity Fair* recently reflected on the historic importance of the post–Cold War shift from industrial to cultural production in the United States. They wrote:

> The power center of America . . . has moved from its role as military-industrial giant to a new supremacy as the world's entertainment-information superpower.[4]

The Disney empire is a prime example of the new commercial forces that are consolidating their control over large swathes of the media and cultural markets. Disney merged with Capital Cities/ABC in 1995. The $19 billion deal created a global entertainment production and distribution company with combined revenue of $16.5 billion.[5] Disney also has interests in Hyperion and Chilton book publishing; 4 magazine publishing groups, including *Women's Wear Daily;* 681 Disney retail stores; and interest in television and cable networks, including Lifetime, A&E, The History Channel, and ESPN. Disney also owns a National Hockey League team, a major league baseball franchise, 11 newspapers, and 4 music companies.[6]

Other companies have entered into similar megadeals designed to control much of the communications and cultural landscape. Paramount and Viacom's merger brought together Paramount's library of 50,000 films, Simon & Schuster's 300,000 book titles, Blockbuster Entertainment's 500 music stores, Nickelodeon and MTV, as well as several theme parks and television and radio stations all under one roof, giving this single company vast power in the cultural production industry.[7] Adding to its clout, Viacom merged again in the fall of 1999, this time with CBS. The new merger makes Viacom the industry leader in the media and entertainment fields. The $36 billion deal creates a global enterprise worth $80 billion, with revenues of more than $20 billion per year.

The transformation to cultural capitalism was helped along in 1996 with the passage of the Telecommunications Act, a landmark piece of legislation that opened the media field to new competitors, including the large regional telephone companies and cable companies. Now, telephone companies, Hollywood studios, television companies, cable companies, and software companies are creating strategic alliances and entering into megamergers to control as much of the communications market as they can. The goal for each is to become the single provider for homes and businesses for the full range of communications and cultural services. For example, immediately after the passage of the Telecommunications Act, U.S. West, one of the largest telephone companies, acquired Continental Cablevision, the nation's third-largest cable system. Sprint, the long-distance telephone company, scurried to catch up with the competition by forming a joint venture with the cable companies TCI, Comcast, and Cox.[8]

Meanwhile, local telephone and cable companies are beginning to understand the strategic advantage of controlling the last mile of wire that goes to customers' homes and businesses. Controlling wired access to the customer puts the regional telephone companies in a particularly favorable position to market a variety of services from data delivery to entertainment. A few years ago, Pacific Telesis, Bell Atlantic, and Nynex entered into a joint venture with what was then Michael Ovitz's Creative Artists Agency to create video entertainment for distribution over their VDT lines. The local phone companies realize that success depends on controlling both the pipeline and the content. The former gives them access to the customer, while the latter is where the profits are made. Says Paris Burstyn, an analyst with GeoPartners Research, Inc., in Cambridge, Massachusetts, "Delivery is a commodity. Content is a value-added service, and profits are higher on a value-added."[9]

In the global arena, the media giants are either acquiring one another outright or entering into joint ventures to share market opportunities. The ten largest global media companies have, on the average, joint ventures of one kind or another with six or more of the other companies. They also enjoy various strategic partnerships with smaller media firms in regional markets. Seagram, for example, which owns Universal, also owns 15 percent of Time Warner. TCI, on the other hand, is also a major shareholder in Time Warner.[10] In a network economy based on short-term alliances, "nobody can really afford to get mad with their competitors," says TCI chairman John Malone, "because they are partners in one area and competitors in another."[11]

Until 1997, it was difficult for global companies to enter into joint ventures and mergers because of the many restrictions imposed on the telecommunications industry in each country. In some countries, telecommunications were government-owned utilities. In others, the companies were privately owned but publicly regulated monopolies. In 1997, however, officials from sixty countries signed an accord, through the auspices of the World Trade Organization, to end state monopolies and open up the $600 billion global telecommunications market to free competition and foreign investment in domestic markets.[12] Renato Ruggiero, then director general of the WTO, heralded the accord, saying it is "good news for the international economy, it is good news for businesses and it is good news for ordinary people around the world who use telephones or who want to use them."[13] President Clinton echoed the enthusiasm, saying the pact would "spread the benefits of a technology revolution to citizens around the world."[14] While some critics questioned whether the deregulation of state telephone monopolies and their entrance into an unfettered world market would appreciably benefit the world's less advantaged populations, especially in the developing nations, everyone agreed that the pact would hasten mergers.

Under the terms of the Global Telecommunications Agreement, a foreign carrier can, for example, own 100 percent of an American telephone company if its native country provides reciprocal access to its domestic markets. (Some countries, like Japan and Canada, have set somewhat more restrictive conditions).[15] During the early stages of deregulation, much of the effort is aimed at securing access to the lucrative global business markets—some 5,000 corporate customers—who spend more than $90 billion per year on sophisticated telecommunications services to maintain their commercial networks and operations.[16] Typical of the powerful new joint ventures being assembled in the aftermath of the WTO accord is the partnership announced in July 1998 between AT&T and British Telecom, two of the largest phone companies in the world. They have formed a jointly owned company that will provide $10 billion worth a year of telephone, Internet, and data services to multinational companies in more than 100 countries.[17]

Even before the WTO accord was signed, MCI's president Gerald H. Taylor was predicting, "There's probably going to be only four to six global gangs to emerge over the next five years as all of this sorts out."[18] The *Financial Times* agrees with Taylor's forecast, saying that at the end of the day there will likely be only "a handful of giants straddling the world market."[19] The stakes are huge. The telecommunications market now ranks third in the world behind health care and banking and is growing at twice the rate of the global economy.[20] With revenues expected to exceed $1 trillion by 2010, the battle for market share is going to be hard fought and intense.[21]

The telecommunications companies are targeting much of their efforts on securing the gateways to the Internet and cyberspace, hoping to control the electronic worlds in which hundreds of millions of people will be spending much of their personal and business time in the coming century. Like the telecommunications industry, cyberspace was deregulated in 1995 when the government-sponsored NSFnet turned over operating functions to commercial vendors. Today, access to cyberspace is secured through commercial network providers. Tomorrow it will be the captive of "global gangs" of telecommunications giants, broadcasters, and computer companies. The goal, once again, is to control digital voice, data and video transmissions, and products in every region and market of the world. Most of the major television broadcasters, including CNN, NBC, ABC, and Fox, have launched online services. Meanwhile Microsoft has integrated its Web browser into its Windows operating system and begun to acquire content companies.

Much of the early enthusiasm for the Internet's potential to create a more participatory public sphere has been dampened in the rush to commercialize the medium. Commercial advertising is rampant on the Net. With consumers simply unwilling to pay higher access fees, the portal companies have little choice but to connect with commercial advertisers to underwrite their operations. Customers already are being exposed to a blitz of commercial messages when they log on as part of the price they have to pay for securing access to cyberspace.

Being able to control both the communications infrastructure and access to the portals and gateways that hundreds of millions of people will use to communicate with one another, as well as much of the cultural content that flows over the wires and spectrum, gives global media companies unparalleled power. Media historian and critic Ben Bagdikian observes:

> Nothing in earlier history matches this corporate group's power to penetrate the social landscape. Using both old and new technology, by owning each other's shares, engaging in joint ventures as partners, and other forms of cooperation, this handful of giants has created what is, in effect, a new communications cartel. . . . At issue is not just a financial statistic, like production numbers or ordinary industrial products like refrigerators or clothing. At issue is the possession of power to surround almost every man, woman, and child . . . with controlled images and words, to socialize each new generation of Americans, to alter the political agenda of the country. And with that power comes the ability to exert influence that in many ways is greater than that of schools, religion, parents, and even government itself.[22]

The End of the Nation-State

The deregulation and commercialization of the world's telecommunications and broadcasting systems is stripping nation-states of their ability to oversee and control communications within their borders. Global media companies are establishing a worldwide network of communications that bypasses political boundaries altogether and, in the process, changing the fundamental character of political life on earth.

At the dawn of the global media age more than twenty years ago, an American government official remarked that "trade doesn't follow the flag anymore; it follows the communications systems."[23] Private communications networks are forging new communities of interest that have fewer and fewer ties to geography. Many professionals now spend more time in cyberspace than in geographic space, and identify more with their virtual addresses than their geographic ones. Today, the larger multinational companies rely on sophisticated communications technologies to maintain their networks of worldwide operations. Their global reach is impressive. Less than 500 transnational companies now account for ⅓ of all manufacturing exports, ¾ of commodity trade, and ⅘ of the total trade in technology and management services.[24] The partnership between global media companies and the world's largest manufacturing and service-based companies is a powerful one. Their combined ability to control the flow of communications, goods, and services represents a formidable challenge to the traditional political powers exercised by states.

Market libertarians argue that the deregulation of telecommunications, broadcasting, and other media services is the most efficient way to reduce barriers to entry into markets and to spawn innovations. Encouraging competition, they believe, will ensure commercial opportunity and result in greater access to the many new networks that are being forged. Esther Dyson, George Gilder, George Keyworth, and Alvin Toffler, four of the leading proselytizers of the cyberspace revolution, argue that "technological progress is turning the telecommunications marketplace from one characterized by 'economies of scale' and 'natural monopolies' into a prototypical competitive market. The challenge for government," they say, "is to encourage this shift—to create the circumstances under which new competitors and new technologies will challenge the natural monopolies of the past."[25]

Lending institutions, like the World Bank, have made deregulation of telecommunications a quid pro quo for extending loans to developing countries in the belief that the marketization of media is the most effective way to spur development. Others argue that such policies only encourage a new form of colonialism, further impoverishing the most dis-advantaged countries.[26] Jill Hills, professor of international political econ-omy at City University in London, says that when a Third World country hands over its telecommunications networks to a foreign operator, it often results in "the loss of ongoing network revenues and capital outflow in the repatriation of profits."[27] The bottom line, say the critics, is that "where private companies own both the domestic infrastructure and interna-tional links, developing countries are returned to their prewar situation of colonial appendages."[28]

The international telecommunications accord of 1997 went a long way toward weakening national governments by taking away from them one of the most basic regulatory powers in their political arsenal: the right to determine the terms and conditions on how communications are structured and accessed within their borders. Now, a new proposal being floated in U.S. policy circles threatens to complete the deregulation process altogether. If it succeeds, governments around the world will have lost the last remaining vestige of power they have over communications within their borders.

The electromagnetic spectrum is the entire range of radio frequencies in the earth's atmosphere, which is used to transmit radio, television, and other broadcast media. In each country, the spectrum is treated as a "com-mons" and controlled and administered by government on behalf of its citizenry. The United States was one of the first governments to take own-ership of the spectrum in 1927 with the establishment of the Federal Communications Commission (FCC). Since then, the FCC has allocated parts of the spectrum to radio, television, cellular telephone communica-tions, paging and messaging, satellite services, point-to-point microwave and taxi dispatching, and other media, and licensed it to broadcasters for fixed durations, subject to renewal. To keep their licenses, local broadcast-ers have to comply with government regulations designed to safeguard the "public interest." Now a coalition of some of the nation's most powerful public policy think tanks have suggested that the FCC relinquish its long-standing control over all spectrum frequencies and institute a one-time massive sell-off of the entire band to private broadcasters, who would then own and trade the frequencies in the open marketplace in the form of private "electronic real estate."

The suggestion that spectrum frequencies be enclosed in the form of private property was first made by attorney Leo Herzel in the 1950s in an article in the *University of Chicago Law Review*.[29] In the 1990s, the idea was resurrected by the Progress and Freedom Foundation, a Washington think tank with close ties to the former Republican speaker of the U.S. House of Representatives Newt Gingrich. The foundation makes the point that the global information industry is expected to be a $3 trillion market by the early twenty-first century. Yet, they argue, the government's statutes and regulatory regime now in place was established in the 1930s and is so antiquated and outmoded that it is acting as an impediment to innovation. The think tank cites what it calls procrastination and endless delays in assigning frequencies and granting licenses, all of which, it contends, undermines the entrepreneurial spirit.

The solution, say the architects of the foundation's spectrum report— entitled *The Telecom Revolution: An American Opportunity*—is to convert the entire electromagnetic spectrum to private property to be freely used, sold, leased, or otherwise developed.[30] The FCC itself would be eliminated altogether and replaced by a small government agency inside the executive branch, to be called the Office of Communication, whose responsibilities would be limited to auctioning off the spectrum and certain administrative chores. Under the plan, broadcasters holding existing licenses would be granted title to the spectrums they currently use and would henceforth be free to use, transfer, and develop them as they see fit. Shortly thereafter, applicants whose licenses are pending before the FCC would be granted title, and nonallocated parts of the spectrum would be sold to private bidders. "The key," says the report, "is to sell title in property, not in mere licenses." The authors of the report make it clear that the spectrum is to be treated exactly like any other property, and owners would have exclusive rights to control its use, exclude others from using it, and determine the conditions upon which it can be sold to another party.[31] The foundation concludes with a plea to restore "ownership of the entire electromagnetic spectrum to America's entrepreneurial, innovative private sector, where it can contribute to the prosperity potential of the information revolution."[32]

The U.S. Congress has already held hearings on the sell-off proposal, and observers close to the communications industry believe that it is only a matter of time before the spectrum is transferred into private electronic real estate. Once that happens, other nations will be encouraged to follow suit, eventually transferring the entire spectrum around the world to privately traded spectrum real estate. In the Age of Access, spectrum real estate is likely to be the single most important asset in the world. Only a handful of global media players will be able to afford to buy large parts of the electromagnetic spectrum. Owning the global frequencies will allow these companies to control access to the channels of communication over which millions of people conduct their day-to-day lives.

The transformation of the spectrum from public commons—held in trust by government on behalf of its citizenry—to private electronic real estate—controlled by global media giants—fundamentally changes the relationship between the people and global commercial enterprises. Without public ownership over the spectrum, the citizenry becomes beholden to a handful of media companies for access to the means of communicating with one another in a highly sophisticated network-based civilization.

What, then, are we to make of the fate of the nation-state in this new era? Up to now, governments have been rooted in geography. They are institutions designed to control and administer land. But with so much of the commercial and social life of humanity migrating to the nonmaterial world of cyberspace, will political institutions wedded in geography become increasingly less important and less viable?

In a world in which more and more first-tier economic and social activity takes place in cyberspace in the form of commodified cultural experiences, governments find themselves with a greatly diminished role to play. That role is further eroded as governments give up their authority to control the frequencies and communications channels that are the pipelines to cyberspace. In cyberspace, the only megaproperties really worth owning are the radio frequencies, the fiber optic cable, the communications satellites, the hardware and software technologies that make up the channels of communication, and the content that flows through the pipelines. With these forms of property firmly in the hands of a few global commercial networks, other forms of property become less important. While personal property and even commercial property continue to exist, they become ancillary to the more important requisite of securing access to the communications channels and content that link people together in networks of shared meaning.

The decline of the nation-state is becoming most apparent in issues of trade. Global companies have successfully lobbied governments for major concessions that have further weakened traditional rights of sovereignty. International treaties and conventions like NAFTA and GATT have stripped governments of their right to impose domestic restrictions on such things as unfair labor practices or egregious environmental violations, if they interfere with the free exercise of global trade. New institutions like the World Trade Organization, whose officials are unaccountable to any specific government, can impose sanctions on countries who violate trade agreements and norms.

Nowhere, however, is the diminished nature of nation-states becoming more at issue than in the question of tax collection. With a growing amount of personal and commercial business being conducted in cyberspace, it becomes more difficult to assess and collect taxes. In a network economy, in which so much commercial activity is "broken up into small packets of information which do not mean anything until reassembled," says Diane Coyle, economic editor of the *Independent* in London, "it will be impossible for tax authorities to monitor all transactions."[33] Coyle adds that "it would be impossible to say where those transactions had taken place even if they could be monitored and therefore knotty to decide which government is entitled to any tax on them."[34] Then too, when so many products and services are the result of small, value-added contributions made by many players scattered over time and space but working together in shared networks and joint ventures, how does any particular government make the determination about exactly how much value added is assignable to taxation within its geographic borders? Finally, in a market economy made up of the production of things, taxing the labor that went into the process and the value added at each step of the manufacturing and sale of the products is a relatively easy undertaking. In a network economy made up of the commodification of connections, relationships, and lived experiences, how does the government determine gradations and value added for the purposes of taxation?

As long as human activity was grounded in geography, governments made sense. But now that economic and social life is becoming increasingly spaceless, do governments still matter? And when communities are no longer grounded in geography but rather defined by temporary, shared interests among people who interact with one another in virtual worlds, how does one retain any notion of collective solidarity and loyalty to place and country, long regarded as requisites for maintaining any sense of national cohesion? Jean-Marie Guéhenno, in his book *The End of the Nation-State,* makes the point that "in the age of networks, the relationship of the citizens to the body politic is in competition with the infinity of connections they establish outside it. So politics, far from being the organizing principle of life in society, appears as a secondary activity, if not an artificial construct poorly suited to the resolution of the practical problems of the modern world."[35]

Living Outside the Electronic Gates

While nation-states are beginning to buckle under the pressure of a new global economic and social order made up of vast networks of shared interests that bypass national boundaries, eclipse geography, and exist in cyberspace, we need to understand that most people on earth are not connected to these new worlds. They exist outside the electronic gates in another world of poverty and despair, in which sheer physical survival dictates the terms of daily life. For them, life is one of toil and drudgery made up of modest efforts to eke out an existence. In an era in which the affluent fifth of the population is leaving property behind in search of cultural experiences and personal transformation, the remaining four-fifths have meager belongings and still wish to be propertied.

Despite all of the euphoria surrounding the communications revolution and the bold projections about a future wired world, the realities are that 65 percent of the human population today have never made a single telephone call and 40 percent have no access to electricity.[36] There are more telephone lines in Manhattan than in all of sub-Saharan Africa.[37]

Access to electricity, telephone lines, radio and television broadcasting, and the Internet has understandably become the litmus test for connectivity in a wired world. The twenty-four OECD countries—the wealthiest nations in the world—make up less than 15 percent of the world's population but account for 71 percent of all telephone lines.[38] Together, Europe and North America own ⅔ of the world's radios and TVs, even though they make up only 20 percent of the global population.[39] In the Pacific Rim, Hong Kong is the most wired city, with 59 phones per 100 people, putting it slightly ahead of Singapore, which boasts 49 phones per 100 people. Taiwan and South Korea each has 35 phones per 100 people, while Thailand has only 3 lines per 100 people. Indonesia has only 6 phones per 1,000 people, and China has 9 phones per 1,000 people.[40] The most wired place in the world is the island of Bermuda. With its offshore insurance companies, investment brokerage houses, and accounting firms, it has become the prototype market in the new commercial world of electronic communications.[41] Meanwhile, Africa represents the other extreme—a continent virtually disconnected from the global network economy. Africa has only 37 televisions and 172 radios per 1,000 people, a stark contrast to North America, where there are 798 television sets and 2,017 radios per every 1,000 people.[42]

Meanwhile, the highly industrial countries accounted for more than 88 percent of Internet users in 1998, even though they make up less than 15 percent of the human population on earth. North America alone, with less than 5 percent of the global population, boasted more than half of the Internet users. South Asia, with 20 percent of the world's human population, accounted for less than 1 percent of the Internet users.[43]

The communications gap between the developed nations and the developing nations is so great that many observers believe that the world is fast dividing into the informationally rich and the informationally poor. Columnist David Kline, writing in the high-tech magazine *Hot Wired*, worries that "the future may become a wonderland of opportunity only for the minority among us who are affluent, mobile, and highly educated. And it may at the same time become a digital dark age for the majority of citizens—the poor, the non–college educated, and the so-called unnecessary."[44]

With governments around the world deregulating and selling off their telecommunications and broadcasting infrastructures, the commercial sphere becomes the ultimate arbiter of who is connected in a wired global economy. Those who can afford access to cyberspace and the shared networks and virtual worlds that make up the new ethereal plane of human existence will be connected, and everyone else will remain outside the electronic gates.

The disparity in income and wealth between the top fifth of the world's population—who already are beginning to live in simulated worlds—and everyone else is increasing so rapidly that any talk of guaranteeing universal access is likely to be greeted with deep suspicion and cynicism by most observers. According to a study conducted by the United Nations Development Program, the world's 358 billionaires now have combined assets that exceed the total annual income of nearly half the people who live on earth.[45] While Bill Gates is now richer than half the American people put together, more than a third of the world's 3 billion workers find themselves without jobs or underemployed, according to a 1998 report of the International Labor Organization.[46] The result is that while the wealthiest human beings on earth are increasingly preoccupied with entertainment and living creative and expressive lives, nearly 1 billion other human beings are living in poverty and several billion more are barely making ends meet.[47] And the projections for the immediate future are even more grim. More than 100 countries, with a combined population of 1.6 billion people—more than a quarter of the world's population—continue to experience economic decline. Eighty-nine countries are worse off now in terms of income than ten years ago, and thirty-five have experienced a greater fall in per capita income than occurred at the height of the Great Depression in the 1930s.[48] In Africa the average household consumes 20 percent less today than it did twenty-five years ago.[49]

Worldwide, more than 600 million people are homeless or living in unsafe and unhealthy housing, and the World Bank estimates that by the year 2010, more than 1.4 billion people will live without safe water and sanitation.[50] Meanwhile, the top 20 percent of high-income earners in the world now account for 86 percent of all the private consumption, while the poorest 20 percent consume only 1.3 percent of the global economic output.[51] The reality is that Americans spend more on cosmetics—$8 billion annually—and Europeans on ice cream—$11 billion (in U.S. dollars)—than it would cost to provide basic education, clean water, and sanitation for the 2 billion people in the world who currently go without schooling or even toilets.[52]

The growing disparity in income between rich and poor is affecting the developed nations as well as the developing countries. In Britain, for example, income inequality has risen faster in the past twenty years than in any other industralized nation.[53] In the U.S. the Census Bureau reports that income disparity between rich and poor is higher now than at any time since the end of World War II in 1945.[54] Today, the top 20 percent of Americans receive half the income in the country, while 50 percent of American families have less than $1,000 in financial assets.[55] Middle- and working-class families have been particularly hard hit. The median household income in 1996 was 4 percent below where it was in 1989.[56]

At the same time that the more affluent part of the population is migrating behind electronic gates, many of the nation's poorest and least educated citizens are being put behind prison gates. More than 1.5 million Americans are currently behind bars, making the U.S. the most incarcerated population in the world. In California, the state legislature, which used to spend a mere 2 percent of its budget on prisons in 1980, spent 9 percent in 1995 and is projected to spend nearly 18 percent of its funds on prisons by the year 2002. California now spends more public funds on prisons than on higher education.[57]

All the talk about access to global networks, cultural production, cyberspace, and simulated lived experiences falls largely on deaf ears for the millions of Americans who have yet to experience even the rudimentary benefits of ownership and a propertied way of life. Bill Gates's vision of a wired world is meaningless to the more than 7 million American families who are without even basic telephone service.[58] Millions of others—the working poor and lower-middle-income families—lack the financial resources, educational skills, and time to become active players in the new electronically mediated network worlds. They risk being left even farther behind as the more affluent connect with one another, erect commercial and social networks of shared interest, and leave everyone else isolated, alone, and forced to fend for him- or herself in an increasingly inhospitable and impoverished world.

The disenfranchised and dispossessed also are becoming the disconnected in the Age of Access. *Time* magazine glimpsed their plight in a special issue dedicated to cyberspace. The editors noted that access to electronically mediated worlds will be essential to one's "ability to function in a democratic society."[59]

The Right and Left of Access

Access issues are not new in the communications arena. Questions surrounding access were raised when the telephone was first introduced, and later when radio and television appeared. Debates on how best to guarantee universal access to phone lines and broadcasting technologies have reared up periodically throughout the whole of the twentieth century. Federal laws in the U.S. were passed early on to ensure rural households cheap and affordable access to telephone service. When the FCC began to regulate radio, provisions were written into the legislation to make sure license holders served local community needs. The public interest, however, quickly capitulated to commercial interests. The Communications Act of 1934 handed over vast control of the airwaves to communications companies like RCA, General Electric, and Westinghouse, who wasted little time converting the new medium to an advertising forum for commercial sponsors. Lee de Forest, the inventor of the vacuum tube that made radio broadcasting a reality, was so upset by the way the new medium was being used that he openly condemned the industry in a letter to the National Association of Broadcasters in 1946. He complained that "you have made of [radio] a laughing stock to intelligence . . . you have cut time into tiny segments called spots (more rightly stains) wherewith the occasional fine program is periodically smeared with impudent insistence to buy and try."[60]

The advent of television in the 1940s led to similar public calls to advance popular education and the community interest. Television stations were expected by law to provide public service announcements, local public affairs shows, and children's programming. They also were required to provide equal time to people and groups in the community to air differing views on topics covered by the station management. In addition, the Fairness Doctrine required every station to present programs on controversial topics and make sure to provide a balanced set of opposing views. By the 1980s, however, most of the Fairness Doctrine had been whittled away in the wake of the deregulating fervor spawned by the Reagan administration. As was the case earlier with radio, commercial interests were able to thwart any effort to make television an instrument to serve public education and community interests. While public television has attempted to fill that role, even it has had to compromise along the way. Although in theory public television is free of advertising, in practice it relies heavily on the private sector to underwrite and sponsor its programming and has become increasingly subject to market pressures to beef up its entertainment content, often at the expense of its educational content.

Again, with the birth of cable television, the issue of public access was raised once more—this time in the halls of Congress and state legislatures and by professional and community organizations. Many championed the new medium as a powerful tool to serve communities. The National Science Foundation's report on the future of cable television was bullish over the possibilities. The foundation wrote:

Public access channels can be made available to individual citizens and community groups. . . . Churches, Boy Scouts, minority groups, high school classes, crusaders for causes—can create and show their own pro-

grams. With public access, cable can become a medium for local action instead of a distributor of prepackaged mass-consumption programs to a passive audience.[61]

The NSF envisioned cable TV performing a broad educational mission, including offering "instruction for homebound and institutionalized persons, preschool education, high school and post-secondary degree courses in the home, career education and in-service training, and community information programming . . ."[62] Although some vestiges of community programming still can be found on cable, most of the fare is commercial in nature and driven by advertising.

Today, the issue of access has become far more significant. The digital revolution is bringing all of the major forms of technologically mediated communications—voice, data, video—together in an integrated web. More and more personal and commercial communications take place in electronic networks, making them indispensable to survival in a wired world. The issue is no longer simply one of access to the mediums themselves but rather access—through the mediums—to the culture. Our very abilities to connect with our fellow human beings, to engage in commerce, to create communities of shared interests, and to establish meaning in our lives are increasingly mediated by these powerful new forms of electronic communications. While cyberspace may not be a place in the traditional sense, it is a social arena in which millions of people are beginning to engage one another in human discourse. Much of the life of human civilization is going to occur in electronic worlds in the future. The question of access, then, becomes one of the most important considerations of the coming age.

Chapter Twelve

Toward
an Ecology
of Culture
and Capitalism

Until now, issues of access in cyberspace have been narrowly con-
strued. Concerns have been raised over the affordability of hardware
and software, the availability of service, computer literacy, First Amendment rights, privacy, and the control over data flows. While important,
these issues are symptomatic of more fundamental concerns that need to
be raised—concerns that go to the very heart of the kind of civilization we
are creating for ourselves in the twenty-first century.

What does it mean to live in a wired world where market transactions are replaced by complex commercial networks? Where holding
property is less important than having access? Where more and more of
our economic and social life is lived in cyberspace? Where culture itself
becomes the ultimate commodity? Where paid-for human relationships

become the norm, and lived experience becomes something to purchase? Where an autonomous self gives way to multiple personas and a thespian consciousness? Where society is viewed in theatrical terms, and each person's own life is perceived to be made up of countless scripts and texts acted out on both geographic and virtual stages?

The Age of Access brings with it not only new tools for organizing human existence but also new definitions of what it means to be a human being. The central question, as we approach the new era, is, what exactly do we mean by "access"—not the limited notion of access to technology and data but rather the broader teleological notion of access? The propertied age offers an instructive analogy. While narrow legal and economic questions of mine and thine were always central to the discussion of structuring human relationships, the deeper philosophical issue of the purpose of property, of its role in defining the essential nature of a human being and the workings of society, provided an overarching framework for explaining the metaphysics of human existence. The various philosophies that attended the era of propertied relations and market exchanges served to define the meaning of an age. Similarly, the new communications technologies and the networks we create out of them are not ends for which we seek access but only the gateways and portals to new ways of reenvisioning the human journey in the coming age. Defining the sociological nature and political import of access relations remains the unfinished business at hand.

A New Rights Theory

Not surprising, the shift from ownership to access is being accompanied by new theories about property relations. A growing number of intellectuals, legal scholars, and economists are looking anew at the nature and philosophy of property relations in an effort to readjust their assumptions to the new realities of a network economy and wired world. Although the libertarian theme, with its emphasis on a conventional, private property regime, continues to be touted in public policy circles in the U.S. and U.K.—less so in Europe and Asia—some scholars are beginning to suggest, at least in academic circles, that our traditional notions of property are outmoded. Fragments of a new theory of access relations are beginning to appear in the literature, if not yet in public discourse. Even though a full-blown theory of access relations has yet to be articulated, the discussion is far enough along to suggest the possibility of a wholesale rethinking of social relationships in the coming decades as the global economy makes the transition from markets to networks, from geography to cyberspace, and from industrial to cultural capitalism.

The most advanced thinking on the matter of ownership versus access is found in the collective works of University of Toronto professor Crawford MacPherson. While MacPherson didn't anticipate all of the many specific changes that are now transforming the global economy, he understood that postindustrial technologies were beginning to change the nature of the game. His insights were all the more prescient given the fact that they were made in the mid 1970s, in the very earliest days of a technology revolution whose weight and impact are just now being felt around the world.

MacPherson began his analysis by noting that our current concept of property is, for the most part, an invention of the seventeenth and eighteenth centuries. The first characteristic of modern property, says MacPherson, is the right to exclude others. So convinced have we become of this cardinal principle of property that we have lost sight, says MacPherson, of the fact that previously in history, property was defined also as the right *not* to be excluded from the use or benefit of something. To that end, society sets aside a second category of property—public property—which includes such things as parks, city streets, common lands, and waterways. Each person enjoys the legal right not to be excluded from the use or enjoyment of these forms of public property. Both forms of property, private and public, make up the full spectrum of individual property rights enjoyed by every human being in society: The first guarantees each person the right to exclude others from the use or benefit of something, and the second guarantees each person the right not to be excluded from the use or benefit of something.

In the Modern Age, notes MacPherson, common property "drops virtually out of sight."[1] While governments retained the notion of public goods, and most people had a vague understanding of the idea of public property, the thought that every individual enjoyed a dual property regime—the right of inclusion as well as exclusion—was all but lost. The rise of the modern marketplace and industrial capitalism catapulted exclusive property to the forefront of economic and social relations.

MacPherson contends that an individual right to exclude others from the use or benefit of something is no longer adequate to define the conditions and terms for structuring human economic relationships. He argues that in a complex, highly interdependent world, the most important form of property is "as an individual right not to be excluded from the use or benefit of the accumulated productive resources of the whole society."[2] MacPherson favors bringing back the older definition of property that existed before the days of industrial capitalism. Property needs to be broadened, says MacPherson, to include the "right not to be excluded from access."[3]

The right not to be excluded from access has gained currency in recent decades in the wake of the civil rights, women's rights, and environmental movements. African-Americans fought for their rights to sit down at lunch counters in the South in the 1960s. The owners argued that their establishments were private property and therefore they had a right to exclude anyone they so chose from entering the premises. The Civil Rights Act and subsequent statues established the principle, in law, that an African-American's right not to be excluded from access is more important than an individual owner's right to exclude. When feminists in the 1970s and 1980s brought lawsuits against exclusive men's clubs, arguing that by being denied the right to access they were being excluded from important social interactions that were critical to their ability to engage competitively in business, they too eventually prevailed in the courts. Similarly, the right to clean air and water and a healthy environment, says MacPherson, "is coming to be regarded as a property from which nobody should be excluded."[4]

Property, MacPherson reminds us, has always been a vehicle for structuring human relationships in a world of physical scarcity. Property relations provided a legal means for securing the right to material revenue. Now, at least for the top fifth of the world's population, for whom material scarcity has been conquered, "property must become rather a right to an *immaterial* revenue, a revenue of enjoyment of the quality of life."[5] He adds that "such a revenue can only be reckoned as a right to participation in a satisfying set of social relations."[6] Ironically, notes MacPherson, this idea is closer to traditional notions of property than those that were prevalent as late as the seventeenth century. Political writers of the time spoke of man's property as "including not only his rights in material things and revenues, but also in his life, his person, his faculties, his liberty, his conjugal affection, his honor, etc.; and material property might be ranked lower than some of the others, as it was specifically by Hobbes."[7]

MacPherson points out that in a society of abundance, property—as the right to exclude others—diminishes in importance. If there is material plenty and more than enough to go around and to satisfy everyone's material needs and desires, then organizing material relationships around excluding others makes little or no practical sense. Rather, in a society that has conquered material scarcity, immaterial values take precedence and the quest for self-fulfillment and personal transformation becomes the goal. In such a society, the right not to be excluded from a "full life" becomes the most important property value that each person holds. Property in the new era, concludes MacPherson, "needs to become a right to participate in a system of power relations which will enable the individual to live a fully human life."[8]

In the new schema, then, access to the entire system of social relations that make a life of quality possible becomes the litmus test for structuring human activity. Of course, it has to be acknowledged that 80 percent of the world's population is still struggling to gain a foothold in material ownership. Still, in a world in which abundance is now at least conceivable, the idea that each person has a right not to be excluded from the totality of human resources and activities that make psychological fulfillment possible is a powerful new social vision. That vision, however, has to be tempered with the observation that daunting challenges still remain in the way of reaching this new plateau of human development. Rising human population, diminishing natural resources, loss of biodiversity, and spreading man-made pollution threaten the biosphere that sustains all of life. Unless these problems can be resolved, any discussion of a new social vision based on material abundance and personal transformation will remain more fantasy than reality for most human beings.

The right not to be excluded—the right of access—becomes more and more important in a world increasingly made up of electronically mediated commercial and social networks. As more of the day-to-day communications among people, as well as much of lived experience, take place in the virtual worlds of cyberspace, questions of access will become paramount and the right not to be excluded will become critical.

Even our most basic ideas about personal freedom and our relationship to governance irrevocably change in this new era. When exclusive property relations were the reigning paradigm for organizing human activity, freedom was associated with autonomy, and autonomy with ownership. To be free was to be autonomous—that is, not dependent on or beholden to others. Autonomy, in turn, depended on being propertied. The more one could claim as mine rather than thine, the more autonomous and independent one could be. The government's role was conceived of as a limited one—to help secure one's private property and, by doing so, preserve each person's individual freedom.

In a network economy of suppliers and users, however, in which embedded relationships become the axial principle for structuring activity, freedom comes to mean something very different. Inclusion and access, rather than autonomy and ownership, become the more important tests of one's personal freedom. Freedom is a measure of one's opportunities to enter into relationships, forge alliances, and engage in networks of shared interest. Being connected makes one free. Autonomy, once regarded as tautological with personal freedom, becomes its opposite. To be autonomous in a network world is to be isolated and disconnected. The right not to be excluded, the right of access, on the other hand, becomes the baseline for measuring personal freedom. Government's role in the new scheme of things is to secure every individual's right of access to the many networks—both in geographic space and cyberspace—through which human beings communicate, interact, conduct business, and constitute culture. Whether governments will, in fact, have the clout to ensue the right of access in an increasingly wired global economy is still, however, very much in doubt.

Two Kinds of Access

The question of access runs even deeper. In all of the discussions surrounding the digital revolution, the new network-based global economy, and cyberspace, there's often an implicit assumption that the only access worth having is the one leading through the corporate portals and gateways to the commercial sphere. We tend to forget that much of what we now access with our purchases were, just a short while ago, freely available cultural goods. We are, in effect, beginning to purchase our own lived experiences, along with the cultural frills and accoutrements that go with them. Our common life is inexorably being sucked into commercial life, with profound long-term consequences for the future of human civilization.

Still, incredibly, we have yet to ask some of the more fundamental questions that attend the transformation to a postmodern society. For example, are commercial relationships an adequate substitute for cultural relationships? Are phrases like "customer intimacy" and "simulated realities" oxymorons? What kinds of collective repercussions flow from pulling the cultural sphere into the commercial sphere? If human life is less ideological and more dramaturgical, less bound up with meganarratives and grand cosmologies and more an expression of billions of individual human dramas, each scripted and acted out in commercial networks and cyberspace, then what are we to make of the human condition and the human spirit? Are there any thoughts to be had on the purpose of human life, or are we left, in the final analysis, with only the airing of endless commercial announcements punctuated by the occasional whisper, "it's showtime"?

If there is an Achilles heel to the new age, it probably lies in the misguided belief that commercially directed relationships and electronically mediated networks can substitute for traditional relationships and communities. The premise itself is deeply flawed. The two ways of organizing human activity flow from very different sets of assumptions and values, making them irreconcilable rather than analogous. Traditional relationships are born of such things as kinship, ethnicity, geography, and shared spiritual visions. They are glued together by notions of reciprocal obligations and visions of common destinies. They are sustained by communities whose mission it is to reproduce and continually secure the shared meanings that make up the common culture. Both the relationships and the communities are regarded as ends.

Commodified relationships, on the other hand, are instrumental in nature. The only glue that holds them together is the agreed-upon transaction price. The relationships are contractual rather than reciprocal in nature. They are sustained by networks of shared interests for as long as the parties involved continue to honor their contractual obligations.

The distinction between social contracts and commercial ones is important. The former has a longer temporal horizon and is bound by custom, on one end, and deliverance, on the other. Social contracts are steeped in the notion of indebtedness to ancestors, unborn generations, the earth and its creatures, and a benevolent God. Membership in traditional communities brings with it restraints on personal action. Obligations to others take precedence over personal whims, and security flows from being embedded in a larger social organism.

Commercial contracts, on the other hand, are generally of short duration. They are bound by neither history nor legacy but rather performance and results. The obligations between the parties are explicit, generally quantifiable, and spelled out in legal terms in the contractual agreement.

Only parts of oneself enter into pecuniary relationships. The rest of one's being is left unencumbered by any additional obligations and free of restraints. Security flows from exercising multiple options and being able to enter into and exit relationships quickly and with the minimum of inconvenience. Commercial networks, through which commodified relationships are expressed, are expected to serve the interests of the client and customer, as opposed to traditional communities, in which members are expected first to serve the interests of the group as a whole.

Commodified relationships are designed to maintain a distance between the parties. It is understood at the outset that the relationship is based on nothing deeper than the exchange of money. Whatever shared experience occurs between the parties in the course of their relationship is meant to be superficial, expedient, and short-lived. The whole process requires a suspension of disbelief, making it the archetypal simulated experience. When a server, for example, shares pleasantries with a client, entertains him or her, shows concern for his or her well-being, offers to help him or her with problems and be supportive of his or her aims and goals, both parties know that the relationship that has been struck is disingenuous. At least some of the emotional flow between the parties is pretense. It is not freely surrendered as a gift but commercially solicited and paid for in advance.

The crucial question, then, in the Age of Access, is, what exactly is the nature of the access we seek? With the marketplace and now cyberspace colonizing more and more of the shared culture in the form of cultural production and cultural commodities, less time and space are available for the expression of traditional relationships and the nurturance of conventional communities. While there is much to be gained—both economically and intellectually—from organizing human activity in networks and engaging one another in the virtual worlds of cyberspace, there is also much to be lost if in the process most remaining human activity migrates to the commercial realm. If that happens, access will be narrowly defined as merely inclusion in the commercial sphere. Were that to occur, it is likely that the much sought-after goal of self-fulfillment, which has come to be so championed in the postmodern era, might be irreconcilably compromised. To understand why, we need to examine the very different functions communities and economies perform and the historic relationship each sphere has to the other.

To begin with, as we discussed briefly in chapter 1, social communities—that is, culture—precede commerce. Throughout history, human beings have always established social communities first. They develop rules of social exchange, embed their members in complex reciprocal relationships, and build social trust. Only when these relationships, and the trust that is built from them, are firm can communities enter into commercial trade and set up markets for exchange. That's because markets, by their very nature, deplete trust. The old adage *caveat emptor* is as true today as it was at the time of the Roman markets more than 2,000 years ago. The point is that markets are secondary rather than primary institutions. They are derivative in nature and exist only as long as there is enough social trust in place to assure the terms of trade. Western European and American businesses learned this lesson the hard way in the aftermath of the fall of the Soviet Empire. Companies rushed into Central and Eastern Europe to set up shop, anxious to establish trade in the former Communist territory. Many of the businesses failed because there was not enough social trust—sometimes called "social capital"—to guarantee trade. The Communists had eliminated much of the third sector, the many cultural institutions that create social trust and allow markets to function. The results were that business agreements were difficult and even impossible to arrange, and commercial contracts, when they were entered into, were often unenforceable.

Every country focuses much of its public policy on the first sector—the market—and on the second sector—the government—and often takes the third sector—the culture—for granted, not realizing the critical role it plays in establishing social trust and making markets and trade possible. The cultural institutions of a society—its churches, secular institutions, civic associations, fraternal organizations, sports clubs, art groups, and nongovernmental organizations—are the wellspring of social trust.

Because they exist, they make markets possible. In communities and countries that have a strong, well-developed third sector, capitalist markets thrive. Where the third sector is weak, capitalist markets are generally less successful. If the third sector in the United States, for example, were to disappear overnight, it's unlikely that the capitalist marketplace—or, for that matter, even government—would survive a fortnight. Although some neoliberals and neoconservatives and most libertarians continue to believe that healthy economies create vibrant communities, in fact the reverse is more often the case. A strong community is a prerequisite for a healthy economy because it alone produces social trust.

The United States boasts more than 1.14 million nonprofit third-sector organizations with annual revenues of $621 billion. Nearly 7 percent of the American workforce is now employed in the third sector. In addition, 93 million Americans volunteered an average of 4.2 hours of their time each week to the third sector in 1995. The time volunteered is estimated to be worth the equivalent of $201 billion.[9]

While the third sector is well developed in the United States, it is a formidable force in other countries around the world as well. In a twenty-two-nation survey conducted in 1998 by the Center for Civil Society Studies at Johns Hopkins University, the third sector was found to be a $1.1 trillion industry that employed more than 19 million full-time equivalent paid workers. Nonprofit expenditures in these twenty-two countries averages 4.6 percent of the gross domestic product and accounts for 10 percent of all service employment. If the third sector in these twenty-two nations were a separate national economy, it would be the eighth largest country on earth.[10]

Third-sector organizations are serving millions of human beings in neighborhoods and communities around the world. They are the institutions most responsible for preserving and enhancing all of the various dimensions of local cultures. The reach and scope of their activities often eclipse that of both the government and commercial sectors. Third-sector organizations carry on many of the most basic functions necessary for the maintenance of democratic societies. They are the lightning rods for challenging institutional abuses of power and for articulating social grievances. They provide a helping hand to newly arrived immigrants and to the nation's poor. Nonprofit organizations preserve the history and cultural traditions of a people by operating museums and libraries. They are the institutions in which people first learn how to practice civic values and exercise democratic skills. Third-sector religious and therapeutic organizations provide refuges where people can explore the spiritual dimensions of their lives, independent of the pull of the market and government. Equally important, the third sector is where people relax and play, seek companionship, make friendships, and experience the joys of life and nature. In short, the third sector is where people create and practice the shared values by which they choose to live. It is the playing field where the culture, in all of its richness, is maintained.

Interestingly, international lending institutions like the World Bank are just beginning to understand the relationship between culture and commerce. For decades, these institutions have funded expensive economic-development projects in emerging countries in the belief that by creating strong economies they could help foster social development. After years of only mixed success and many failed attempts, they have begun to shift their priorities to funding social-development projects first, understanding that strong communities—a robust culture—are a prerequisite to economic development, not a beneficiary of it.

If the capitalist system continues to absorb large parts of the cultural realm into its sphere in the form of commodified cultural products, productions, and experiences, the risk is very real that the culture will atrophy to the point where it can no longer produce enough social capital and thus support an economy. The delicate balance between culture and commerce will have been shattered because social capital, which is produced exclusively by the culture but which serves as the lubricant for commercial operations, will have dried up.

The culture is also the breeding ground for a second value without which human civilization cannot function. Robert Jay Lifton makes the point that "we assert our commonality through our capacity for empathy, for thinking and feeling our way into the minds of others."[11] Empathy is the feeling from which social trust is built. Empathy requires that "one include the other's humanity in one's own imagination."[12] It is among the deepest of all human feelings and the one that creates the bonds of intimacy and civility. To empathize, one needs to reach beyond the confines of the self, to take up emotional residence in the being of another, and to feel another's feelings as if they were one's own. When we empathize with another we are experiencing our shared hopes and sufferings. It is the feeling by which we come to learn about and care for one another.

Empathy is nurtured in real time and in close proximity to

others. The farther removed one is from the lived experience of another human being, the less likely he or she will be able to empathize. One can, for example, watch the gruesome horror of a human massacre in Kosovo or witness a family starving to death in Somalia on television and be moved, but often not sufficiently to have a truly empathetic experience. Being there, however, changes the nature of the reaction. Suddenly the situation and the people become very real, and one empathizes with their plight.

With more and more lived experience—especially among the young—migrating to the simulated worlds of cyberspace, where it is increasingly purchased as a cultural commodity, what happens to the feeling of empathy? How likely is it that members of a generation growing up in front of the screen or inside its virtual worlds—whose communications with one another are mediated by layers of technology and symbols—will be able to empathize sufficiently with others or with their fellow creatures? How does one express empathy in a world of simulation?

Equally important, when much of lived experience is taken out of the culture altogether and pushed into the commercial sphere, it becomes a commodity and therefore impervious to the very notion of empathy. A client-server relationship is always instrumental but rarely empathetic. When we purchase our own lived experiences, we come to expect the proper rate of return on the investment. The other person or persons in commodified relationships are there to "serve" and "perform" in return for the appropriate compensation—hardly the proper soil from which to nurture the feeling of empathy.

A number of psychologists and sociologists are beginning to worry that the generation that is growing up in simulated worlds and becoming comfortable with the idea of buying access to cultural commodities and lived experiences might not have sufficient emotional experience to empathize. Their concerns are compounded by what they observe as the increasing fragmentation of personal consciousness—multiple personas—among members of the dot-com generation, which we discussed at length in chapter 10. Even Lifton, who welcomes the new protean consciousness and views it as a necessary coping mechanism for dealing with the complexities and ever changing realities of a postmodern world, warns of a potentially crippling effect on human behavior. A generation that is unable to feel for one another is incapable of creating the social trust that is so essential to maintain culture.

The price of commodifying and marketing cultural experience is potentially a heavy one. If the culture withers, what is to become of social trust and empathy, its two most important products? And if securing access to a network economy and cyberspace means losing access to social capital in the process, then what has humanity really gained at the end of the day? For that matter, without social trust and empathy, how do we even maintain commerce and trade in the coming era?

The commercial sphere is offering something it cannot, in the final analysis, deliver: access to a life of deep communion and personal transformation. While the economy can provide many valuable things, including material well-being, creature comforts, certain forms of knowledge, and entertainment and amusements, all vital to the experiencing of a full life, it comes up short on being able to produce the most important things—social trust and empathy—the values and feelings from which our culture is shaped and our humanity forged. To the extent that the commercial arena tries to sell access to bits and pieces of human culture and lived experience in the form of bricolage and pastiche, it risks poisoning the well from which we draw these important human values and feelings.

Resurrecting Culture

If this newest stage of capitalism succeeds, its very success could sow the seeds for its destruction. Were the forces of commerce able to deconstruct, reprocess, package, and sell what remains of the cultural sphere, turning virtually all of human activity into commodified lived experiences, its triumph would be short-lived for all the reasons stated above. Markets and networks cannot stand alone. They are, to reemphasize the point, derivative institutions whose very existence depends on the preexistence of strong social communities steeped in social trust and tempered by a measure of empathy.

The economy is a derivative institution in still another sense. Cultural production is always borrowed from the cultural sphere. It never originates in the commercial sphere. In this sense, cultural production relies on the raw resources of the cultural sphere in the same way industrial production relies on the raw resources of nature. Both forms of production are extractive. The culture, like nature, can be mined to exhaustion. If culture is overexploited and wasted, the market risks losing the proverbial hen that lays the golden eggs. Cultural diversity, then, is like biodiversity. If all the rich cultural diversity of human experiences around the world is exploited for short-term gain in the commercial sphere and not allowed to recycle and replenish, the economy loses the broad pool of human experiences that are the stuff of cultural production.

The new genre of world music is a case in point. Today, more than 80 percent of the $40 billion recording industry is controlled by six transnational companies: Sony (Japan), PolyGram (Netherlands), Warner (United States), BMG (Germany), Thorn-EMI (United Kingdom), and MCA (Japan).[13] Always on the lookout for new sounds, the recording companies have begun to search out indigenous forms of music that can be made more contemporary with electronic amplification and synthesizers. Often, native music is combined with other, more contemporary music to create what the industry calls "fusion" or "hybridized music." World music has grown steadily in the global marketplace over the past ten years. The large megastores like Borders Books and Music in the United States stock 300 to 400 titles at any given time. The Gypsy Kings, Puerto Rico's Ricky Martin, Pakistan's Nusrat Fetah Ali Khan, Ravi Shankar, the Cape Verdean songstress Cesaria Evora, and scores of others are routinely turning out popular CDs with their eclectic blend of native and contemporary music. In 1997 and 1998, the soundtracks to Riverdance and Lord of the Dance made Celtic music an international favorite. Cuban salsa, zouk from the French Antilles, rembetika from Greece, raï from Algeria, and qawwali from India are among the many varieties of world music that have become popular.

In its native guise, much of this music represents a form of cultural capital—a medium for communicating the shared values and historical legacy of a people. Indigenous music often expresses the plight and circumstances of a group or speaks to their spiritual yearnings and political aspirations. In its cultural form, music is a strong conveyer of social meaning. It mobilizes deeply held feelings. When appropriated, packaged, commodified, and sold in the form of world music, the central message of the music often is watered down or lost altogether. For example, critics point out that salsa, a musical genre that emerged from the impoverished urban neighborhoods of Cuba and Puerto Rico and originally conveyed the harsh realities of life in the barrios and the pride of Latino solidarity, was made more bland and sentimentalized so it would be more entertaining and palatable to First World audiences. The raï music of Algeria suffered a similar fate. Raï originated in the cabarets of Oran, Algeria's second largest city, and grew out of the economic and political unrest that engulfed the country. Like salsa, the raï sound was transformed into a commodity by the recording industry, and in the process, its deeper political message was defused. The result, writes economist David Throsby in the 1998 *World Culture Report* of UNESCO, is that "while raï music has been transformed in the international context, its capacity to act as a vehicle for expressing the concerns of an anti-establishment constituency in Algeria ('the young, the working class, the unemployed, the illiterate, the dispossessed, the fed up') is threatened."[14]

Proponents of world music argue—with some justification—that providing a global audience for indigenous music helps foster greater understanding and tolerance among people and promotes the idea of living in a multicultural world. The cross-fertilization of musical genres also helps create new musical forms that speak to today's postmodern generation, which is increasingly connected to a single global community. Others, however, argue that the real impact of world music is to seriously weaken local cultures by transforming a primary channel for communicating shared meanings into a kind of packaged mass entertainment that, while it retains the form, eliminates both the substance and context that make the music a powerful expression of human sentiment.

For example, gamelan music of Bali and Java has become popular on world markets and can be found in most major music stores. Gamelan music is played on tuned percussion instruments including gongs, metallophones, drums, flutes, and zithers. American composers combined gamelan instruments with Western ones, including clarinets and electric guitars, to create a hybridized form of world music that has attracted a significant following. The new hybridized music has been enthusiastically embraced even in Indonesia, where it is often integrated into pop songs. Supporters argue that the fusion of gamelan music with more contemporary sounds has given the traditional music a new lease on life, making it more relevant to the sensibilities of today's youth. Traditionalists, however, point out that gamelan musical instruments are embedded with spiritual and magical qualities and are an integral part of rituals that express the shared values and legacy of the Balinese and Java people. What happens, ask critics, when these sacred instruments are taken out of context and their sounds fused with rock and roll and made into a form of mass entertainment, devoid of cultural context? And what happens when even Balinese and Javan youngsters gravitate to this hybridized form of world music, like other young people around the world, and treat it as pure entertainment without any sense of the historical meaning or cultural value previously attached to it?

These questions become particularly relevant in light of the fact that traditional music is designed to reproduce the local culture and the shared values of the community and, therefore, is preserved and passed on, while commercial music is pure entertainment and subject to fad and fancy. The commercial sphere is in a constant search for novelty, which means that when indigenous music is packaged in the form of world music, its life span is likely to be limited to the short attention span of consumers. If, in the process, the native form of that music is lost and the cultural context that gave rise to it is devalued, the local culture is seriously compromised.

Since the commercial sphere relies on the cultural sphere for its very existence, it too will be weakened if indigenous music is absorbed and eventually depleted by the forces of commerce. The economy will have devoured its resource base—the feelings, values, shared experiences, and meanings that human beings nurture in cultural soil and that provide the raw resources for commmodification and exchange in the commercial sphere.

World music is symptomatic of the larger changes taking place as the global economy makes the shift in first-tier commerce from goods and services to cultural production. Mexican anthropologist Néstor Garcia Canclini strikes at the heart of the problem when he observes that "an increasing sector of cultural production is taking on an industrial shape, circulating in transnational communications networks, being received by the consuming masses, who are learning to be the audiences of deterritorialized messages." Canclini points out that "the younger generation, in particular, live their cultural practices in accordance with homogenized information and styles that are received by different societies independent of their political, religious or national context."[15]

The 1998 World Culture Report of UNESCO categorizes the increasing tension between culture and commerce in stark terms. The UN agency argues:

The cultural values which identify and link local, regional or national communities seem in danger of being overwhelmed by the relentless forces of the global marketplace. In these circumstances, questions are raised as to how societies can manage the impacts of globalization such that local or national cultures, and the creativity that sustains them, are not damaged but rather are preserved or enhanced.[16]

The growing animosity between global commerce and local culture has been particularly acute of late around questions of food and cuisine. Transnational franchises like McDonald's, Burger King, Pizza Hut, and Dunkin' Donuts are quickly expanding their retail outlets in Europe, Asia, and Latin America. In Europe, only 16 percent of food distribution is franchised, compared to more than 50 percent in the United States. Realizing that they are reaching saturation in the North American market, U.S. franchisors are looking eagerly to other parts of the world for new opportunities to place their outlets. In Italy, for example, there are approximately 180,000 small, independently owned coffee bars, many of which are in precarious financial straits and vulnerable to a major challenge by Starbucks and other U.S. coffee franchises.[17] American tourists were surprised in the summer of 1999 to see Dunkin' Donuts just a few yards away from the famed Trevi fountain in Rome. Dunkin' Donuts, like other transnational franchises, is mounting a major push into the European market, with plans to open up 110 more stores in Italy and Germany in the next few years.[18]

In Europe especially, where cuisine and culture are tightly linked, the introduction of global fast-food franchises and more recently American-grown genetically modified foods is meeting with stiff resistance. A McDonald's outlet in southwestern France was recently ransacked, and Monsanto's genetically engineered food crops were torn up and destroyed in the English countryside in 1999. French political analyst Alain Duhamel says that "behind all this lies a rejection of cultural and culinary dispossession."[19]

Food and cuisine is currently the most visible arena where the growing war between culture and commerce is being fought. European and other nationals from around the world fear what they call the "Hollywoodization" of food and cuisine, the attempt to impose a homogenized global standard on the types of food crops grown in the fields, the kinds of foods processed for the supermarkets, and the nature of the cuisine prepared in the restaurants. "Culinary sovereignty is imperative," warns Patrice Vidieu, the secretary general of the Peasant Confederation of

France. Vidieu says that an increasing number of Europeans "reject the idea that the power of the marketplace becomes the dominant force in all societies, and . . . multinationals like McDonald's and Monsanto come to impose the foods we eat and the seeds we plant."[20]

Bringing culture and commerce back into a balanced ecology, then, is likely to be one of the most important political tasks of the coming age. Assuring a proper balance requires that equal attention be placed on revitalizing local cultures as on securing access to cultural commodities in the marketplace.

New commercial networks need to be balanced with new cultural networks, new virtual experiences with new real-life experiences, new commercial amusements with new cultural rituals. The emphasis ought to be on dividing human time and attention more equitably between the cultural and commercial spheres in order to find a middle ground between two complementary but often conflicting ways of organizing human activity and relationships.

Finding the middle ground becomes that much more important given the fact that the more connected people become in a range of multifaceted global networks, the less time they have available for the kinds of intimate social relations that can take place only in real time and by way of face-to-face engagement. In a new century dominated by electronically mediated environments, the challenge in every country will be to create new opportunities for direct participation with our fellow human beings in geographic-based communities. Failure to do so could risk a wholesale degeneration of the ability of human beings to connect with one another at the deepest levels of personal experience, and ultimately the loss of our humanity.

The culture needs to be resurrected not simply because it produces the raw resources for cultural production or because it generates social trust and empathy, without which markets could not function. Rather, culture must be rejuvenated for its own sake and on its own terms because it alone is the source for human values. While a restored culture will undoubtedly benefit the market, it can't be allowed simply to be the market's raw resource. To do so would be to devalue the shared human meanings that come out of culture and that create our humanity, and to view them merely as a means to a lesser end, the commodification of lived experience in the form of personal entertainment and therapy.

In a wired world of pure process and sheer temporality, geography counts more than ever. Human connection requires more than electronic transmissions and receptions and computer interfacing. The deepest human connections always occur in geographic space. Cultural experiences can be reproduced by the broadcast media and in cyberspace and directed to other locations, but the farther they journey from their places of origin, the less potent they become as expressions of deeply felt shared meanings. When traditional folk dance is performed in an Irish village, for example, it conveys deeply felt expressions of shared meaning among the participants. But when performed on stage or on television 5,000 miles away to a general audience, it becomes little more than entertainment. Stripped of geographic context, the cultural expression becomes a shadow of the total experience. Although it can be enjoyed and even appreciated by others, it can't evoke the deep feeling of place, which is, after all, what the dance is all about.

All real cultures exist in geography because that's where intimacy takes place, and without intimacy it is not possible to create bonds of social trust and engender true feelings of empathy. Resurrecting and revitalizing culture, then, means paying at least as much attention to geography as to cyberspace and to participation in real communities as to computer interfacing inside electronic chat rooms.

A New Mission for Education

American schools are beginning to wrestle with the question of how to ready students for a network-based global economy and the virtual realities of cyberspace without, however, sacrificing their participation in the broader culture. Every classroom in the United States—and in other countries—is being wired to the Internet and stocked with computers and software in a push to prepare young people with the skills they will need to navigate their way through the electronic domains that make up the new world of e-commerce. Still, educators and a growing number of parents are worried that if students' educational experiences take place more and more in front of the screen or inside virtual worlds, they may not develop the appropriate social skills required to be fully functioning and whole human beings in society.

A quiet grass-roots revolution in education has been making its way across the United States in recent years whose goal is to prepare young people for their responsibilities to the civil society and the larger culture. It goes by many names, including character education, democratic education reform, citizen education, and service learning. Often referred to as civil education, its premise is that students of all ages learn best if their education is experiential and takes place directly in the neighborhoods and communities in which they live. For example, if students are learning the principles of zoology or ecology, they might benefit from a hands-on program at a wildlife rehabilitation center, arboretum, animal shelter, or wildlife refuge. Civil education brings together students, teachers, parents, and community-based organizations in collective partnerships both to create curricula and to execute the learning experience. The idea is to create a relationship between classroom and community and make all learning relevant to a student's whole life. Civil education is a sophisticated mix of traditional apprenticeship, clinical teaching, problem solving, and conceptual systems thinking. It is a revolution in pedagogy that is already gaining a strong foothold in thousands of school districts and hundreds of universities across the United States. If successful, it portends the most significant educational reform movement since the progressive era just before World War I, when the corporate model of efficiency and abstract education was introduced into American schools.

Civil educators argue that access to the knowledge available in cyberspace and virtual worlds, while essential and necessary, must be accompanied by access to the collective knowledge and wisdom embedded in geographic-based communities. Learning, they insist, involves more than just being able to click on to the appropriate information source on the World Wide Web. It also requires direct and intimate participation with others in real time and space. Civil education is increasingly being viewed as a complement to and antidote for the kind of simulated knowledge gathered in cyberspace. Access to both kinds of educational experience, civil educators contend, is necessary if American schools are to produce a generation of young people who are knowledgeable, centered, and equipped for their social obligations to the larger community as well as for the commercial opportunities that lie in cyberspace.

Civil education begins with the premise that the first mission of education is to prepare students for how to access their common culture and become active participants in it. They stress that if approached with rigor and if students, parents, and community organizations all play a role in facilitating the learning experience, academic performance soars because students find their studies more relevant, enjoyable, and ultimately more meaningful to their lives.

Producing marketable skills, long the central mission in many American schools, is like putting the cart before the horse, argue civil educators. Learning skills simply to be able to sell one's labor in the marketplace is, they say, much too narrow a concept of education for the twenty-first century. It produces an adult who thinks of himself or herself more as a salable property than as a whole human being and a responsible member of the society. Civil educators argue for a deepening of the core identity of students to include a sense of their relationship to the culture. Education, they say, should nurture social trust and empathy and promote intimacy with others—as well as with one's fellow creatures—and make students aware of the critical role the culture plays in maintaining the life of civilization. Marketable skills, they contend, are derivative of basic social skills, just as markets are derivative of cultures. While important, they must not come first or at the expense of civil education but rather be viewed as a necessary accompaniment.

Politicizing the Third Sector

Civil education is an essential tool in reestablishing a balanced ecology between culture and commerce. Still, more fundamental changes must be undertaken to restore culture to its former high ground in human relations. Today, the cultural sector exists in a kind of neocolonial limbo between the market and government sectors, despite the fact that it is the wellspring of the other two spheres. It has been stripped of much of its separate identity and made dependent on the other two sectors for its survival. Cultural institutions have lost much of their former independence and become beholden to political and commercial institutions for their very sustenance. Their dependency takes many forms, including the extension of government contracts and grants in return for the performance of service and corporate philanthropy, often extended with the expectation of receiving some kind of marketing or promotional benefit in return.

Contemporary social thought generally divides along a polar spectrum, with the economy on one end and government on the other. The culture, or third sector, if considered at all, is usually an afterthought. With rare exceptions it is relegated to the sidelines, where it plays, at best, a marginal role in the heady decisions that affect the life of the community. That's about to change. To begin with, government, at every level, is paring down its historic role. Many of its functions have been deregulated and turned over to the marketplace. Other functions have been cut—although some would argue they've been reconfigured and streamlined. Either way, governments are playing less of a role in managing the day-to-day affairs of local communities. At the same time, businesses are becoming less local and more global in their activities and operations. Many are migrating from geography to cyberspace and, in the process, loosening or even severing their traditional ties to geography. Like government, they are becoming less involved in local affairs. The steady disengagement of government and commerce from communities around the world is leaving an ever widening institutional vacuum. That vacuum is being filled in some cases by a rejuvenated third sector and, in other instances, by an emboldened fourth sector made up of the informal economy, the black market, and criminal culture. In the coming years, the real race in every geographic region of the world will be between the institutions of the third sector and those of the fourth sector for control over local geography in the wake of its partial abandonment by government and business. For the third sector to prevail, it will have to politicize itself by bringing its various institutions, activities, and interests together in a shared sense of common mission. For that to happen there will have to be recognition of the importance of geography in establishing a common ground.

If the workings of global networks, cyberspace commerce, and cultural production represent one side of the new politics of power in the coming century, then the reestablishment of deep social exchange, the recreation of social trust and social capital, and the restoration of strong geographic communities represent the other side. The contrarian rallying cry, in an era increasingly given over to short-lived facile connections, virtual realities, and commodified experiences, is that geography counts! Culture matters!

The struggle between the forces of global commerce and the interests of local cultures brings with it a new politics. In the industrial era, political sensibilities ran from right to left and were concerned largely with questions of property. The battle to define the parameters of mine and thine consumed the political passions of countless generations. The modern polity has been characterized more by class warfare than by anything else, with the upper class, middle class, working class, and poor continually fighting one another over how best to harness physical capital, produce goods and services, and distribute property. The nagging question of who should control the means of production and determine how the fruits of human labor should be allocated has shaped the political agenda for more than 300 years.

In the Age of Access, right-left politics is steadily subsumed by a new social dynamic that pits intrinsic value against utility value in the political arena. Cultural identity, in the deepest sense, is all about intrinsic value. The shared culture is never a means but always an end. Cultural resources, rituals, and activities are valued in and of themselves. They are not things that can be reduced to quantifiable standards and bought and sold in the commercial market. One cannot attach a dollar sign to a shared cultural experience without doing harm to the reciprocal relationships that give rise to it. When culture loses its communal moorings and becomes reduced to commercial entertainment, intrinsic value dries up. In the marketplace, utility rules.

At a deeper level, then, the struggle between culture and commerce is a struggle between intrinsic and utility values. While both values have played roles in social discourse over the past several hundred years, it's only in more recent times that intrinsic values have become secondary to utility values in human affairs. The tilt toward a utilitarian frame of reference is testimony to the increasing dominance of the commercial sphere and the slow decline of the cultural realm.

Only by making local culture a coherent, self-aware political force will we be able to reestablish its critical role in the scheme of human society. Tens of thousands of strong geographic-based human communities, knit together internally by embedded social relationships and connected with one another externally by a shared sense of the importance of sustaining cultural diversity, represent a powerful social vision as well as an antidote to the politics of global commercial networks operating in cyberspace.

Preserving biodiversity and cultural diversity are the two great social movements of the twenty-first century. The two forces are closely linked. All cultures share common roots in nature because all cultures arise out of an intimate connection to the earth. Music, song, dance, storytelling, the arts, rituals, and festivals are deeply tied to the rhythms and realities of the natural world. Plants, animals, landscapes, the circadian reference, and the changing seasons all have served as inspiration and metaphor for the shaping of cultural forms and expressions. Cultures are born out of an abiding respect for and devotion to the wellsprings of life that make up the natural world. Our many contemporary cultural expressions all trace their lineages back to our first cultural connections to the earth itself. Cultural practices and institutions are, for the most part, life-affirming. They speak to our indebted relationship to nature and wed us to the larger life forces of which we are a part. The reaffirmation of life is at the heart of what intrinsic value is all about. Culture, then, exists in sharp contrast to the commercial sphere, in which all phenomena are reduced to utility, and expropriation and expediency become the accepted behavior norms.

The biodiversity and cultural diversity movements are beginning to work side by side on a wide range of issues including opposition to the introduction of genetically engineered food crops, challenges to provisions of regional and world trade agreements that threaten both the environment and cultural identity, support for indigenous cultures, and efforts to create sustainable farming practices in order to preserve local ecosystems. The coming together of these two powerful movements is a recognition that our ancient social roots are anchored in the natural world. The extent to which these two defining movements are able to find common cause will help shape much of the political activism in the new century.

Interestingly, politicized local cultures are both a countervailing force to a global network-based economy and a necessary precondition for its continued existence. Weaken or eliminate cultural diversity, and capitalist markets will eventually tumble because, as described, social trust and social capital will dry up and no longer be available as a foundation for building and maintaining commerce and trade. If that were to happen, what's left of the capitalist system would find its way to the fourth sector, as is occurring now in Russia, where it would exist largely as an informal or black market economy in an outlaw culture. The prerequisite, then, for securing access to a global cyberspace economy is resecuring access to and rebuilding diversified local cultures.

A word of caution, however, is in order. Restoring culture can just as easily lead to a new and virulent form of fundamentalism as to a revival of cultural diversity. All around the world today, political and religious fundamentalist movements are on the rise. Ultranationalist political parties, separatist groups, ethnic-cleansing movements, and religious revivals represent an extreme counterreaction to the forces of globalization and postmodernization. Fundamentalist movements attempt to close off communication with a world they think is sick and sinful. They seek to purge local culture of contaminating influences from the outside world. At the core of all of these fundamentalist movements is a siege mentality characterized by a frenzied effort to defend the "true faith"—be it ideological, theological, or ethnic—against traitors, infidels, and other poisonous influences.

Fundamentalist movements are always deeply tied to geography. Indeed, defense of territory is the common thread that runs through virtually every fundamentalist credo. Defending ancestral ground, the Holy Land, or the motherland unites people in a life-and-death struggle against "satanic" forces. Behind every one of these movements is the idea of restoring order in a chaotic world by reestablishing borders. They represent the ultimate reaction to a boundaryless world made up of global networks and the flow of communication. They seek constancy in a world of continuous change, and attempt to keep the world at bay by resacralizing territory. In an increasingly temporal world, they remain fiercely loyal to place. They are exclusionary in nature and view any form of access as a corrupting influence.

The sensibilities of fundamentalist movements put them at odds with most civil society organizations (CSOs) who also favor restoration of local culture but are sensitive to and respectful of the rights of other cultures to exist in a culturally diverse world. The adage "Think globally, act locally," while a bit of a cliché after so many years of overuse, still reflects the thinking of third-sector organizations all over the world. Like the fundamentalists, CSOs have deep roots in geography and are wedded to local culture, but they also believe that all of the diverse cultures together make up a shared ecology of human existence. Maintaining a unique cultural identity, while championing a culturally diverse world, becomes the defining characteristic of the burgeoning CSO movement.

Mahatma Gandhi expressed the sentiment of many of today's CSOs when he said, "I do not want my house to be walled in on all sides and my windows stuffed. I want the cultures of all lands to be blown about my house as freely as possible. But I refuse to be blown off my feet by any."[21] Assuring open access to other cultures while preserving the unique features and qualities of one's own culture is what separates the CSO movement from the various fundamentalist movements. Whichever force succeeds in mobilizing and politicizing local culture around the world will determine much of the politics and geopolitics of the coming age.

The Dialectics of a Play Ethos

The struggle between the forces of global commerce and the upholders of the third sector ultimately centers on the issue of who will control access to the many cultural categories that make up the play ethos in the new century. As we have seen, in the Industrial Age, the battle between contending parties over control of the work ethos defined the politics of the era. The work ethos goes hand in hand with property relations. Work is about harnessing nature, extracting resources, and manufacturing goods. Property is the final form the natural world takes when broken up, reworked, and made into commodities. Property becomes a way to remake and allocate nature into mine and thine. Control over the work ethos largely determined how property would be allocated in the Industrial Age and was a decisive factor in the establishment of class distinctions.

Now that we are moving from industrial to cultural capitalism, the work ethos is slowly giving way to the play ethos. Play is what people do when they create culture. It is the letting free of the human imagination to create shared meanings. Play is a fundamental category of human behavior without which civilization could not exist.

Elsewhere, we have explored the change from work to play metaphors in business and commerce. The new era of capitalism brings play to the foreground of global commerce. The commodification of cultural experiences is, above all else, an effort to colonize play in all of its various dimensions and transform it into a purely salable form. Access, in turn, becomes a way to determine who is allowed to participate—to play—and who is not.

The Dutch historian Johan Huizinga was among the first to recognize the importance of play in the making of society. He suggested that Homo ludens (man the player) be afforded equal status to Homo sapiens (man the reasoner) and Homo faber (man the maker) in defining the essence of what it means to be a human being. While other creatures play, human beings excel in the ludenic arts.[22]

Huizinga argues that all cultures arise in play. "It is through this play-ing," says Huizinga, "that society expresses its interpretation of life and the world."[23] All of the critical activities of human society—language, myth, ritual, folklore, philosophy, dance, music, theater, law, even the rules of warfare—are born of play. Social life, says Huizinga, is "an immense game."[24]

Many conventional scholars—especially in the economic field—might blanch at the idea of play's pivotal role, believing as they do that work is a more fundamental category of human activity. Anthropologists, however, remind us that from the very beginning of human existence until the Industrial Age, human beings spent far more time playing than working. In the Medieval Age, for example, nearly half the days of the Christian calendrical year were holidays, feast days, or days of rest. When the French Republic issued a decree replacing the Christian calendar with a secular one containing far fewer holidays, the peasant class revolted, forcing the government to rescind its order. Only in the Industrial Age did work come to dominate human affairs and play recede to the background.

The assumptions and rules governing play are quite distinct from those traditionally governing work. First, play is enjoyable; it's fun. While some kinds of work also are enjoyable, most work—75 percent or more of the tasks in industrial society—are simple and repetitive in nature and for that reason tedious and laborious. Second, play is a voluntary activity. People can't be coerced or forced to play. It has to be entered into freely by choice. Work also can be a matter of choice for the fortunate few—the top 20 percent of the global workforce whose education allows them a great deal of career mobility—but for most people, work is a matter of survival. They have no choice but to accept whatever is available. Work conditions, in turn, often are oppressive and degrading.

Real play also is deeply participatory in nature and generally takes place face-to-face, in close environments. Play is spontaneous. While there are rules—some implicit, others explicit—and the play is often serious, directed, and goal-oriented, it is generally far less rigid than traditional work schedules on the factory floor or in offices. Play also tends to be more intimate than work, more bodily in nature, allowing the full range of human sensibilities to blossom. It is most often experienced as a shared enjoyment rather than as a solitary pleasure. Unlike work, it is not instru-mental to an end but an end in and of itself. It is its own reward. And pure unrehearsed play—as opposed to organized games and sports—is not easily quantifiable like work. It resists the Cartesian stamp. Attention is not focused on production but on having fun.

Openness and acceptance are inherent to playful environments. Although there are consequences that flow from one's actions, all of the players feel free to express themselves, to be vulnerable, because forgiveness permeates play. "I was just pretending" is a standard retort that every child in history has understood when engaged in play.

Finally, the temporal and spatial dimensions of play set it apart from work-related activities. Play requires the suspension of ordinary time. The play world exists in a timeless realm, as anyone who's ever been caught up in play and lost all sense of the passage of ordinary time knows.

Play also takes place in special settings that are marked off from ordinary life. Within these consecrated places, the players are bound by different rules and governed by different behavior. Playgrounds are safe havens where participants can congregate without fear of reprisal. Yet these places are always temporary in nature. When the play is suspended, the playground loses its intrinsic value. The playground is not territory one holds or possesses but rather a pretend setting that people share temporarily. Play, then, takes place in a temporal and spatial dimension but is often experienced as timeless and spaceless. It has both a worldly and an otherworldly dimension. It is grounded and light and elusive at the same time. The players give of themselves freely "for the love of the game." The goal is joy and a reaffirmation of the life instinct. Thus, play is in stark contrast to work, whose object is to expropriate, deaden, process, and produce. Production is always about using things up.

In the Modern Age, humanity reversed the importance of play and work. Work became the primary arbiter of human activity, and play became a marginal activity one engaged in between work and sleep. This shift mirrored the changing relationship between the cultural and market spheres. As the market gained dominance over social exchange and market capital came to eclipse social capital, work continued to gain status while play became trivialized into leisure-time activity.

Now, however, work is beginning to recede once again in importance. The automation of production processes and the increasing substitution of intelligent technology—both software and wetware—for human labor is slowly liberating human beings from toil in the marketplace. It is not difficult to foresee a future in which goods and services of all kinds are produced in sufficient quantity to provide for the needs of every human being on earth, using only a fraction of the total available human labor in the process. We've already demonstrated that possibility in modern agriculture. The fact is, in the U.S., while less than 2½ percent of the labor force is currently engaged in farming, the technological capacity exists to feed millions of people around the world. Unfortunately, because we have not yet found our way to distributing the fruits of commercial success more equitably, millions of people do not have sufficient income and purchasing power to buy the foods that can be produced. As a result, the U.S. and other countries end up paying farmers *not* to grow crops.

Similar technological advances are now at work in the manufacturing, service, and knowledge industries, increasing the productive capacity in virtually every commercial field while reducing the need for human labor in the process. It is likely that with new advances in technology and dramatic increases in productivity, the work week, which at the beginning of the Industrial Age approached seventy hours or more and has been steadily reduced over the past century to forty hours—and now thirty-five hours in France and Italy—will continue its historic decline to thirty, twenty-five, and even twenty hours in the coming century, making human labor far less important as a defining feature of people's day-to-day lives.

At the same time, the steady expansion of production and the reduction in the costs and prices of goods produced are already leading to near satiation among the top 20 percent of the human population who enjoy relatively liberal incomes and who can afford to buy whatever they need or desire. For these people, holding on to the fruits of work in the form of accumulated property is fast reaching the point of diminishing psychic returns. Both the diminution in the number of hours worked and the declining interest in possessing material goods as sufficient and exclusive goals are bringing play back into the human equation once again as a fundamental force.

Play is becoming as important in the cultural economy as work was in the industrial economy. The kind of play produced there, however, is only a shadow of the kind of play produced in the cultural sphere. Because it is purchased, it is not a social experience but rather a contractual one. The participating nature of pure play is replaced by a pecuniary relationship. Enjoyment in the marketplace becomes more of a passive, personal experience than an active, collective experience. The expropriation of play by the forces of the market threaten the wholesale devaluation of the cultural meaning of play and with it a loss of the cultural sphere that is born of and nurtured by play activity.

Pure play represents the highest expression of human freedom—and freedom is not something that can be purchased. In his *On the Aesthetic Education of Man,* written in 1795, Friedrich Schiller observed that "man plays only when he is in the fullest sense of the word a human being, and he is fully a human being only when he plays."[25] That's because pure play in the cultural realm is the supreme expression of human bonding. We play with one another out of love of human communication. It is the deepest act of participation between people and is made possible by a collective trust—the feeling that each player can let down his defenses and abandon himself, for the moment, to the care of others so he can experience the joy that comes from a communion. One can't truly play alone for the same reason one can't truly experience joy in isolation. Both are shared experiences. Even when one is walking alone in a forest, contemplative joy comes from the feeling of deep, unabashed connection to the life force that surrounds.

Freedom and play, then, share a common ground. It is through the experience of pure play in the cultural sphere that one learns to participate openly with one's fellow human beings. We become truly human by reveling in one another. Human beings can never be really free until we are able to fully enter into pure play. It was the French philosopher Jean-Paul Sartre who said, "As man apprehends himself as free and wishes to use his freedom . . . then his activity is to play."[26]

Recall that for most of the Modern Age, we have associated freedom with autonomy, and autonomy with the ability to sell our own labor in the marketplace. The fruits of that labor—property—have been viewed as the tokens of our freedom. The right to exclude others from what we have and hold was regarded as the best way to protect our autonomy and our personal freedom. True freedom, however, is born of sharing, not possessing. One can't really be free if one is unable to share, empathize with, and embrace others.

Mature play, as opposed to passive entertainment, always occurs in the cultural arena. When people voluntarily engage one another through the medium of their fraternal, civic, church, arts, sports, social justice, environmental, and other organizations, they are involved in deep mature play. Their social exchanges create islands of social trust and a largesse of social capital to draw upon. Mature play brings people together into shared community. It is both the most intimate and the most sophisticated form of human communication that exists. Mature play is also the antidote to the unbridled exercise of institutional power, be it political or commercial in nature.

The very notion of the power of play is likely to elicit a snicker of contempt among some analysts of power relations. But it should be emphasized that even the capitalist system views play as the next frontier for commerce. Themed cities, common-interest developments, entertainment destination centers, shopping malls, global tourism, fashion, cuisine, professional sports and games, film, television, virtual worlds, and simulated experiences of every kind represent the new stage of capitalist development. While there is nothing inherently wrong with paying for play in the form of entertainment in the commercial arena, when paid play becomes a near total substitution for mature play in the cultural sphere, civilization risks deconstruction on a grand scale.

It's not enough, then, simply to debate the issue of access to the commercial sphere. While the question of providing educational opportunities so that everyone is computer literate and capable of negotiating his or her way through cyberspace is important, it is not sufficient to address the larger issues of access that accompany the new age. Nor is the issue of access only about assuring an adequate income and standard of living so everyone can afford the admission price to the new electronically mediated worlds of the twenty-first century. If that were the only matter at hand, civilization still would be at risk.

Equally important to assuring access to the new global network economy is assuring continued access to healthy and diverse local cultures. The forces of commerce, if not tempered, could devour the cultural sphere by redirecting it into commodified fragments of commercial entertainments, lived experiences, paid amusements, and purchased relationships. Losing access to the rich cultural diversity of thousands of years of lived experience would be as devastating to our future ability to survive and flourish as losing our remaining biological diversity. Bringing culture and commerce back into a balanced ecology is a pressing concern in the coming era—and one that succeeding generations will have to address with the same passion and conviction as the current generation has shown in its efforts to find the proper balance between nature's economy and the human economy.

The Age of Access will force each of us to ask fundamental questions about how we want to restructure our most basic relationships to one another. Access is, after all, about determining kinds as well as levels of participation. It's not a question just of who gains access but rather what types of experiences and worlds of engagement are worth seeking and having access to. The answer to that question will determine the nature of the society we will create for ourselves in the twenty-first century.

Chapter One

1. Jean-Christophe Agnew, *Worlds Apart: The Market and the Theater in Anglo-American Thought, 1550–1750* (Cambridge: Cambridge University Press, 1986), pp. 41–42, 52–53, 56.

Chapter Two

1. Nathaniel Hawthorne, *The House of the Seven Gables* (Cambridge, MA: Riverside Press, 1932), p. 313.

2. Steven E. Miller, *Civilizing Cyberspace: Policy, Power, and the Information Superhighway* (New York: Addison Wesley, 1996), pp. 44–45.

3. Ibid., p. 46.

4. James Gleick, in *New York Times Magazine*, quoted in Miller, *Civilizing Cyberspace*, p. 47.

5. Kevin Kelly, *New Rules for the New Economy: 10 Radical Strategies for a Connected World* (New York: Viking, 1998), p. 73; "The Global Internet," *Internet Economy Indicators*, 1999, http://www.internetindicators.com/index.html.

6. Beth Belton, "Internet Generated $301 billion in Last Year," *USA Today*, June 11, 1999, p. 1; "Indicators Report," *Internet Economy Indicators*, 1999.

7. Miller, *Civilizing Cyberspace*, pp. 38–39.

8. Ibid., p. 39.

9. Steven Bell, Stan Dolberg, Shah Cheema, and Jeremy Sharrard, "Resizing Online Business Trade," *The Forrester Report*, November 1998, pp. 1–2.

10. Kevin Kelly, *Out of Control: The Rise of the Neo-Biological Civilization* (Reading, MA: Addison-Wesley, 1994), p. 201.

11. Adam Smith, *An Inquiry into the Nature and Causes of the Wealth of Nations,* vol. 1, ed. Edwin Cannon (London: Methuen, 1961), p. 475.

12. Manuel Castells, *The Information Age: Economy, Society, and Culture* (Cambridge, MA: Blackwell Publishers, 1996), vol. 1, *The Rise of the Network Society,* p. 191.

13. Larry Downes and Chunka Mui, *Unleashing the Killer App: Digital Strategies for Market Dominance* (Boston: Harvard Business School Press, 1998), pp. 5, 21, 23.

14. Ibid., pp. 21–22.

15. Ibid., pp. 21, 23.

16. Rashi Glazer, "Marketing in an Information-Intensive Environment: Strategic Implications of Knowledge as an Asset," *Journal of Marketing* 55 (October 1991): 7.

17. Ibid.

18. Ibid.; William Greider, *One World, Ready or Not: The Manic Logic of Global Capitalism* (New York: Simon & Schuster, 1997), p. 47; Don Tapscott, *The Digital Economy: Promise and Peril in the Age of Networked Intelligence* (New York: McGraw-Hill, 1996), pp. 81, 152.

19. George B. Rathman, "Biotechnology Case Study," in Mitchel B. Wallerstein, Mary Ellen Mogee, and Roberta A. Schoen, eds., *Global Dimensions of Intellectual Property Rights in Science and Technology* (Washington, DC: National Academy Press, 1993), p. 325; T. Michael Nevens, Gregory L. Summe, and Bro Uttal, "Commercializing Technology: What the Best Companies Do," *Harvard Business Review,* May–June 1990, p. 155.

20. Michael Borrus, "Global Intellectual Property Rights Issues in Perspective: A Concluding Panel Discussion," in Wallerstein et al., eds., *Global Dimensions of Intellectual Property Rights,* pp. 373–74.

21. Tapscott, *The Digital Economy,* p. 60.

22. Ibid.

23. Steven L. Goldman, Roger N. Nagel, and Kenneth Preiss, *Agile Competitors and Virtual Organizations: Strategies for Enriching the Customer* (New York: Van Nostrand Reinhold, 1995), p. 19.

24. Preston G. Smith and Donald G. Reinertsen, *Developing Products in Half the Time* (New York: Van Nostrand Reinhold, 1995), p. 12.

25. John Markoff, "A Quicker Pace Means No Peace in the Valley," *New York Times,* June 3, 1996, p. D8.

26. Tapscott, *The Digital Economy,* p. 63.

27. Ibid., p. 60.

28. Alvin and Heidi Toffler, *Creating a New Civilization: The Politics of the Third Wave* (Washington, DC: The Progress & Freedom Foundation, 1994), pp. 29–30.

29. Walter W. Powell, "Neither Market Nor Hierarchy: Network Forms of Organization," *Research in Organizational Behavior* 12 (1990): 296–326; Cristiano Antonelli, *The Economics of Information Networks* (New York: Elsevier Science Publishing Co., Inc., 1992), pp. 55–56, 60.

30. Benjamin B. Hampton, *History of the American Film Industry: From Its Beginnings to 1931* (New York: Dover, 1970).

31. Michael Storper, "The Transition to Flexible Specialization in the U.S. Film Industry: External Economies, the Division of Labor and the Crossing of Industrial Divides," *Cambridge Journal of Economics* 13 (1989): 278.

32. Ibid., pp. 278–79.

33. Michael Storper, and Susan Christopherson, "The Effects of Flexible Special-

ization on Industrial Politics and the Labor Market: The Motion Picture Industry," *Industrial and Labor Relations Review,* April 1989, p. 334; Storper, "The Transition to Flexible Specialization," p. 279.

34. Joel Kotlin and David Friedman, "Why Every Business Will Be Like Show Business," *Inc.,* March 1995, p. 66.

35. Storper, "The Transition to Flexible Specialization," p. 286.

36. Asu Aksoy and Kevin Robins, "Hollywood for the 21st Century: Global Competition for Critical Mass in Image Markets," *Cambridge Journal of Economics* 16 (1992): 9.

37. Ibid.

38. Kotlin and Friedman, "Why Every Business Will Be Like Show Business," p. 66.

39. Geoffrey Owen and Louise Kehoe, "A Hotbed of High-Tech," *Financial Times,* June 28, 1992.

40. John Kao, *Jamming: The Art and Discipline of Business Creativity* (New York: Harper Collins, 1996) p. 124.

41. Tom Peters, *Liberation Management: Necessary Disorganization for the Nanosecond Nineties* (New York: Alfred A. Knopf, 1992), p. 12.

42. Powell, "Neither Market Nor Hierarchy," p. 308.

Chapter Three

1. Alan Greenspan, chairman of the Federal Reserve Board, at the 80th Anniversary Awards Dinner of the Conference Board, New York, October 16, 1996, http://www.bog.frb.fed.us/boarddocs/speeches/1996/19961016.htm.

2. Diane Coyle, *The Weightless World: Strategies for Managing the Digital Economy* (Cambridge, MA: MIT Press, 1997), p. viii.

3. Thomas A. Stewart, *Intellectual Capital: New Wealth of Organizations* (New York: Doubleday/Currency, 1997), p. 12.

4. George Gilder, *Microcosm: The Quantum Revolution in Economics and Technology* (New York: Simon & Schuster, 1989), p. 354.

5. Fallon McElligott, "The New Workplace: Walls Are Falling as the 'Office of the Future' Finally Takes Shape," *Business Week,* April 29, 1996, p. 112.

6. Ibid., p. 113.

7. Ibid.

8. Paul Taylor, "As the Information Revolution Gathers Pace, the 'Virtual Office' Will Become the Norm in Many Industries," *Financial Times,* September 23, 1998.

9. Ibid.

10. Stewart, *Intellectual Capital,* p. 26.

11. Stephen P. Bradley, Jerry A. Hausman, and Richard L. Nolan, eds., *Globalization, Technology and Competition: The Fusion of Computers and Telecommunications in the 1990s* (Cambridge, MA: Harvard Business School Press, 1993), p. 129.

12. Matt Richtel, "Sony Plans to Distribute Music On-Line This Summer," *New York Times,* May 12, 1999; Alice Rawsthorn, "Global Internet Music Sales to Reach $4 Billion in Five Years," *Financial Times,* May 12, 1999, p. C2.

13. Heather Green and Seanna Browder, "Cyberspace Winners: How They Did It," *Business Week,* http://www.businessweek.com/1998/25/b3583023.htm.

14. Ibid.

15. Laura Zimm, Gail DeGeorge, and Rochelle Shoretz, "Retailing Will Never Be the Same," *Business Week,* July 26, 1993, p. 56; Gretchen Morgenson, "The Fall of the Mall," *Forbes,* May 24, 1993, p. 107.

16. Nanette Byrnes and Paul C. Judge, "Internet Anxiety," *Business Week,* July 28, 1999, pp. 78–83.

17. Fernand Braudel, *The Structures of Everyday Life: The Limits of the Possible* (New York: Harper & Row, 1981), pp. 442–43.

18. Joel Kurtzman, *The Death of Money: How the Electronic Economy Has Destabilized the World's Markets and Created Financial Chaos* (New York: Simon & Schuster, 1993), p. 17.

19. Ibid., pp. 15–16.

20. Ibid., p. 16.

21. Ibid., pp. 60–61.

22. James Gleick, "Dead as a Dollar," *New York Times Magazine,* June 16, 1996, p. 26.

23. William J. Mitchell, *City of Bits: Space, Place and the Infobahn* (Cambridge, MA: MIT Press, 1995), p. 81; Robert P. Borone, "The Bank and Its Customer: Tomorrow's Virtual Reality Bank," *Vital Speeches of the Day,* no. 59, February 15, 1993, p. 284.

24. Gleick, "Dead as a Dollar," p. 26.

25. William Leach, *Land of Desire: Merchants, Power, and the Rise of a New American Culture* (New York: Vintage Books, 1993), pp. 124, 127.

26. George Fitch, "Charge It," *Credit World* 5 (April 1915): 30.

27. "A Big Store's Advertising," *Merchants Record and Show Window* 47 (November 1920): 5, 48; *Merchants Record and Show Window* 79 (November 1936): 3.

28. Rolf Nugent, *Consumer Credit and Economic Stability* (New York: Russell Sage Foundation, 1939), p. 96.

29. Winifred Wandersee, *Women's Work and Family Values, 1920–1940* (Cambridge, MA: Harvard University Press, 1981), pp. 16–17.

30. Geoffrey Moore, "Changes in the Quality of Credit," *Journal of Finance* (May 1956): 288–300.

31. Roland Vaile, *Research Memorandum on Social Aspects of Consumption in the Depression* (New York: Social Science Research Council, 1937), pp. 19, 28.

32. James Grant, *Money of the Mind: Borrowing and Lending in America—From the Civil War to Michael Milken* (New York: Farrar, Straus and Giroux, 1992), pp. 300, 306–7.

33. James Medoff and Andrew Harless, *The Indebted Society* (Boston: Little, Brown & Co., 1996), p. 11.

34. Stephen Brobeck, "The Consumer Impacts of Expanding Credit Card Debt," *Consumer Federation of America,* February 1997, p. 1.

35. Sylvia Nasar, "The Economists Simply Shrug as Savings Rate Declines," *New York Times,* December 21, 1998, p. A14.

36. Alfred L. Malabre, *Beyond Our Means: How Reckless Borrowing Now Threatens to Overwhelm Us* (New York: Vintage Books, 1987), pp. 4, 21, 27; Robert Kuttner, "Booming on Borrowed Cash," *Washington Post,* January 1, 1999, p. A25; Stephen S. Roach, "Spending Ourselves Into Oblivion," *New York Times,* December 11, 1998, p. A31.

37. Brobeck, "The Consumer Impacts of Expanding Credit Card Debt," p. 2.

38. Saul Hansell, "Personal Bankruptcies Surging as Economy Hums," *New York Times,* August 25, 1996, pp. 1, 38.

39. Matt Murray, "Percentage of Credit-Card Accounts That Are Past Due Rose a Bit in Quarter," *Wall Street Journal,* June 17, 1998, p. A9.

40. Lester C. Thurow, "The Boom That Wasn't," *New York Times,* January 18, 1999, p. A19.

41. Ibid.

42. Kathy Bergen, "Bankruptcy Becoming Prosperity's Partner: Largely a Declaration of the Middle Class," *Chicago Tribune,* July 5, 1998.

43. Jacob M. Schlesinger, "As Bankruptcies Surge, Creditors Lobby Hard to Get Tougher Laws: But Whether Many People Shirk Bills They Can Pay Remains Open to Debate, Changing the Lenders Image," *Wall Street Journal,* June 17, 1998.; Bergen, "Bankruptcy Becoming Prosperity's Partner," pp. A1, A9.

44. Stanley M. Davis and Christopher Meyer, *Blur: The Speed of Change in the Connected Economy* (Oxford: Capstone Publishing Ltd., 1998), p. 182.

45. Ibid., p. 183.

46. Ibid.

47. Ibid., p. 191.

48. Thomas A. Stewart, "The Coins in the Knowledge Bank: Accounting for Intangible Intellectual Assets of a Firm," *Fortune* 133, no. 3, February 19, 1996, p. 101.

49. Equipment Leasing Association, "Professor Lessor," http://elaonline.com/proflesr.htm; Equipment Leasing Association, "Facts About the Equipment Leasing and Finance Industry," http://www.elaonline.com/indfacts.htm.

50. "Significance & Growth of Leasing: Advantages & Disadvantages of Leasing," *Leasing in Industry—Studies in Business Policy, no. 127, A Research Report from the Conference Board.*

51. Elnora M. Uzzelle, "American Equipment Companies Should Consider the International Arena," *Business America,* June 28, 1993, pp. 11–12; Equipment Leasing Association, "Professor Lessor."

52. Kundapur V. Kamath, Sanjiv A. Kerkar, and Tumu Viswanath, *The Principles & Practices of Leasing* (Croydon, Surrey, England: Lease Asia, 1990), p. 3.

53. Ibid., p. 4.

54. Ibid., pp. 8–9.

55. Michael Berke, *Selling Equipment Leasing* (New York: AMACOM, 1994), p. 5.

56. Ibid., pp. 9–10.

57. Equipment Leasing Association, "Facts About the Equipment Leasing and Finance Industry."

58. Peggy Wallace, "Leasing Allows Swapping Up Before Value Drops," *Infoworld,* May 9, 1994, p. 71.

59. David S. Glick, "The Leasing Generation: Leasing Enters the Nineties with a Record of Strong Growth Based on the Benefits It Offers to a Wide Range of Businesses," special advertising supplement in *Forbes,* February 19, 1990, p. A10.

60. David J. Porter, "World Leasing Motors On: Europe Still in the Pits," in *World Leasing Yearbook 1995,* ed. Adrian Hornbrook (Sussex, UK: Grange Press, 1995), p. 3.

61. Ibid.

62. Sallye Salter, "Today's Topic: Commercial Real Estate," *Atlanta Journal and Constitution,* April 16, 1998, p. 2F.

63. David Dabby and Rick Smith, "Retail Properties Hot Commodities in Broward County," *Sun-Sentinel,* August 12, 1996, p. 12.

64. Donna Harris, "Real Estate Trusts Give Dealers a New Path; Potamkin Joins," *Automotive News,* no. 5739, November 10, 1997, p. 1.

65. Jeremy Kahn, "Disownership Is Everything: Dumping Corporate Real Estate—for Profit," *Fortune* 137, no. 6 (March 1998): 44.

66. Richard Whiteley and Dianne Hessan, *Customer Centered Growth: Five Proven Strategies for Building Competitive Advantage* (New York: Addison-Wesley, 1996), p. 37.

67. Outsourcing Institute, "Three Major Areas Companies Outsource," http:// www.outsourcing.com/howandwhy/areas.main.htm.

68. Everest Software Corporation, "Industry IS Spending: An Informational Study on IS Spending in Various Industries," http://www.outsourcing-mgmt.com/ industry/who-2.html#start.

69. Jo Ann Davy, "Outsourcing Human Resources Headaches," *Managing Office Technology* 43, no. 7 (September 1998): 6; "Outsourcing Can Boost Profitability," *USA Today* 127, no. 2639 (August 1998): 3.

70. Everest Software Corporation, "Industry IS Spending."

71. Whiteley and Hessan, *Customer Centered Growth*, p. 37.

72. Joe Vales, "BPO Solutions: New Landmark Survey Demonstrates BPO Growth," *InfoServer: The Journal for Strategic Outsourcing Information*, May 1998, http:// www.infoserver.com/may1998/htm/bpo4.html.

73. Michael J. Mandel, Peter Coy, Pete Engardio, and Karen Pennar, "The 21st Century Economy: Volatility Is Here to Stay, But Technology and Globalization Will Spur Robust Growth," *Business Week*, August 24–31, 1998, p. 110.

74. Saul Hansell, "Is This the Factory of the Future?" *New York Times*, July 26, 1998, section 3, p. 1.

75. James Brian Quinn, *Intelligent Enterprise: A Knowledge and Service Based Paradigm for Industry* (New York: The Free Press, 1992), pp. 39, 43, 45–46, 60–64; Larry Downes and Chunka Mui, *Unleashing the Killer App: Digital Strategies for Market Dominance* (Boston: Harvard Business School Press, 1998), p. 201.

76. Jo-Ann Mort, "Sweated Shopping," *Guardian*, September 8, 1997, p. 11; Bob Egelko, "Suit Accuses Nike of Violating California's False-Advertising Law," *Associated Press*, April 21, 1998; Dion V. Haynes, "Nike Hit with Suit on Labor Practices," *Chicago Tribune*, April 12, 1998, Business section, p. 1; Tammara Porter, "Teens Find Alleged Nike Labor Practices Unfair, But Wait to Act," *Minneapolis Star Tribune*, July 7, 1997, p. 6B; David Meggyesy, "Superrich Superstars in Sports, Moral Jellyfish in Life," *Los Angeles Times*, October 17, 1997, p. B9.

77. Paul Klebnikov, "Focus, Focus," *Forbes*, September 11, 1995, pp. 42–43; Julia King, "Outsourcer: No Money Down," *Computerworld* 32, no. 27 (July 1998): 2–3.

78. King, "Outsourcer," p. 2.

79. Quoted in William H. Davidow and Michael S. Malone, *The Virtual Corporation: Structuring and Revitalizing the Corporation for the 21st Century* (New York: HarperCollins, 1992), p. 6.

80. Davidow and Malone, *The Virtual Corporation*, p. 7.

81. Stewart, *Intellectual Capital*, p. 33; John Plender, "Unbearable Lightness of Being: Never Has So Much Stock Value Been Supported by So Few Tangible Assets," *Financial Times*, December 8, 1998.

82. Fred Moody, "Mr. Software," *New York Times Magazine*, August 25, 1991, p. 56.

83. Margaret M. Blair, *Ownership and Control: Rethinking Corporate Governance for the Twenty-First Century* (Washington, DC: Brookings Institution, 1995), p. 234.

84. Stewart, *Intellectual Capital*, p. 63.

85. Plender, "Unbearable Lightness of Being"; Jeffrey M. Laderman, "Are Stocks Overpriced—Or the Yardstick Flawed?" *Business Week*, July 15, 1996, p. 82.

86. Davis and Meyer, *Blur*, p. 102.

87. George Gilder, "The Fiber Baron," *Wall Street Journal*, October 3, 1997, p. A22.

88. Stewart, *Intellectual Capital*, p. 36.

89. Thomas A. Stewart, "Intellectual Capital," *Fortune*, October 3, 1994, p. 68.

90. Mandel et al., "The 21st Century Economy," p. 63.

91. William H. Davidow, "Why Profits Don't Matter: Until We Measure Intangible Assets Like Goodwill & Management Savvy, Bottom Lines Won't Mean Much," *Forbes* 157, no. 7 (April 1996): S24; Michael Malone, "New Metrics for a New Age," *Forbes* 159, no. 7 (April 1997): S40.

92. Malone, "New Metrics for a New Age," p. S40; Baruch Lev, "The Old Rules No Longer Apply: Accounting Needs New Standards for Capitalizing Intangibles," *Forbes* 159, no. 7 (April 1997): S34.

Chapter Four

1. Thomas S. Dicke, *Franchising in America: The Development of a Business Method, 1840–1980* (Chapel Hill, NC: University of North Carolina Press, 1992), p. 3.

2. David Segal, "Franchisees Unite to Fight for Their Lives: Judgments Against Parent Companies Tip Balance of Power," *Washington Post,* April 17, 1997, pp. A1, A20.

3. Info Franchise News Inc., "What Is Franchising?" http://www.vaxxine.com/franchise/what.html; "Hot Franchising Trends," *The Info Franchise Newsletter* 22, no. 1 (January 1998), http://www.vaxxine.com/franchise/newsletter/jan98.html; John Stanworth and Brian Smith, *The Barclays Guide to Franchising for the Small Business* (Oxford: Blackwell, 1991), p. 26.

4. Conversation with Katrina Schymic, executive director of the Franchise Business Network and the Franchise World Resource Center, International Franchise Association, May 20, 1998; William B. Cherkasky, "Introduction to Franchising and the International Franchise Association," in *The Franchising Handbook,* ed. Andrew J. Sherman (New York: American Management Association, 1993), p. 4.

5. Segal, "Franchisees Unite to Fight for Their Lives"; Cherkasky, "Introduction to Franchising," p. 6.

6. Cherkasky, "Introduction to Franchising," pp. 4, 6; Segal, "Franchisees Unite to Fight for Their Lives," p. A1.

7. Leonard N. Swartz, "Franchising World: Exploring Global Franchise Trends," *International Franchise Association News,* April 1997, http://www.franchise.org/news/fw/marapr97b.asp.

8. E. O. Wright, "Class Boundaries in Advanced Capitalist Societies," *New Left Review,* no. 98 (July–August 1976): 37–38.

9. Jan Kirkham and Timothy McGowan, "Strengthening and Supporting the Franchising System," in *The Franchising Handbook,* p. 11.

10. Ibid.

11. Ibid., p. 12.

12. Ibid.; Dicke, *Franchising in America,* p. 3; Alan Felstead, *The Corporate Paradox: Power and Control in the Business Franchise* (New York: Routledge, 1993), p. 111.

13. John F. Love, *McDonald's: Behind the Arches* (London: Bantam Press, 1987), pp. 156–57.

14. Felstead, *The Corporate Paradox,* p. 112.

15. Ibid., pp. 112–13.

16. Theodore Levitt, "Production-Line Approach to Service," *Harvard Business Review* 5, no. 5 (September–October 1972): 41–52; Love, *McDonald's,* chapter 14; Felstead, *The Corporate Paradox,* p. 118.

17. Felstead, *The Corporate Paradox,* pp. 119–20.

18. Ibid., pp. 101–3.

19. Ibid., p. 114.

20. Ibid., p. 203.

21. *General Electric Co. v. De Forest Radio Co. et al.,* no. 3654, Circuit Court of Appeals, Third Circuit, 28 F.2d 641, 1928 U.S. App. LEXIS 2406, September 18, 1928.

22. Rural Advancement Foundation International, "The Gene Giants: Masters of the Universe?" *RAFI Communique,* March/April 1999, p. 6.

23. Rural Advancement Foundation International, "Seed Industry Consolidation: Who Owns Whom?" *RAFI Communique,* July/August 1998, p. 2.

24. Ibid.

25. Ibid.

26. Ibid.

27. Bernard Le Buanec, secretary-general of the International Seed Trade Federation, speaking on January 16, 1998, cited in Rural Advancement Foundation International, "The Gene Giants: Masters of the Universe?" p. 4.

28. Michael Pollan, "Playing God in the Garden," *New York Times Magazine,* October 25, 1998, pp. 44–51, 62–63, 82, 92.

29. Curt Anderson, "Sterile Seeds Patent Sparks Debate," *Associated Press,* May 23, 1998; "Biotechnology: Sowing Seeds of Discontent," *St. Louis Post-Dispatch,* November 13, 1998, p. C16.

30. Leora Broydo, "A Seedy Business: A New 'Terminator' Technology Will Make Crops Sterile & Force Farmers to Buy Seeds More Often—So Why Did the USDA Invent It?" *Mother Jones Interactive,* April 7, 1998, http://bsd.mojones.com/news_wire/broydo.html.

31. "Biotechnology: Sowing Seeds of Discontent," p. C16.

32. Ibid.

33. *Moore v The Regents of the University of California et al.,* Supreme Court of the State of California, p. 23.

34. John Schwartz, "For Sale in Iceland: A Nation's Genetic Code," *Washington Post,* January 12, 1999, p. A1.

35. Seth Shulman, *Owning the Future* (Boston: Houghton Mifflin, 1999), p. 190.

Chapter Five

1. Art Spinella, "Leasing's Share of Market Slows a Bit in 1998," *Leasing News,* September 1998, http://www.leasesource.com/newsroom/body_news.htm; CNW Marketing Research, "Annual Study: Leasing Showing Its Age; Taken for Granted; Still Potent Siren Song for Many Car Shoppers," *LTR/8+* 11, no. 4 (1998): 2, 5.

2. David Woodruff and Edward C. Baig, "Leasing Fever: Why the Car Business Will Never Be the Same," *Business Week,* February 7, 1995, pp. 92–93.

3. Ibid., p. 96.

4. Ibid., p. 94.

5. Spinella, "Leasing's Share of Market Slows a Bit in 1998."

6. Ibid.

7. Tina Cassidy, "Getting a Lease on Your Dreams," *Boston Globe,* July 31, 1995, p. 73.

8. CNW Marketing Research, "Annual Study: Leasing Showing Its Age," p. 1.

9. Jerry Knight, "Lost But Not Leased? A Used-Car Glut Looms; Analysts Say Consumers, Economy Could Be Hit," *Washington Post,* June 5, 1994, p. H1.

10. Woodruff and Baig, "Leasing Fever," p. 94.

11. Brandon Mitchener, "Frankfurt Auto Show: In This Car Pool, Drivers Can Try Any Car Any Time," *Herald Tribune,* September 14, 1995.

12. Car Free Cities Network, "CityCarClub: Carfree But Carefree," company brochure, 1998.

13. Quoted in Car Free Cities Network, "CityCarClub."

14. Daniel Bell, *The Coming of Post-Industrial Society* (New York: Basic Books, 1973), p. 115.

15. Paul Lafargue, *The Evolution of Property: From Savagery to Civilization* (New York: Scribners, 1901), p. 2.

16. Sir William Blackstone, *Commentaries on the Laws of England,* vol. 1 (Philadelphia: Robert H. Small, 1825), p. 1.

17. Charles H. McIlwain, *The Growth of Political Thoughts in the West, from the Greeks to the End of the Middle Ages* (New York: Macmillan, 1932), p. 181.

18. Richard Schlatter, *Private Property: The History of an Idea* (New York: Russell & Russell, 1973), pp. 63–64.

19. John Locke, *Two Treatises of Government,* vol. 2, ed. Peter Laslett (New York: Mentor Books, 1965), paragraph 27; John Locke, "Of Property," in *Of Civil Government,* book 2, chapter 5.

20. Adam Smith, *Lectures on Jurisprudence* (Oxford: Oxford University Press, 1978), p. 209.

21. Ibid.; Andrew Reeve, *Property* (London: Macmillan Education Ltd., 1986), pp. 58–61, 66.

22. Harry Braverman, *Labor and Monopoly Capital* (New York: Monthly Review Press, 1971), pp. 273–74.

23. Robert Smuts, *Women and Work in America* (New York: Schocken Books, 1971), pp. 11–13.

24. George Stigler, *Trends in Output and Employment* (New York: National Bureau of Economic Research, 1947), pp. 14, 24.

25. Braverman, *Labor and Monopoly Capital,* p. 276.

26. Ibid., p. 248.

27. James Brian Quinn, *Intelligent Enterprise: A Knowledge and Service Based Paradigm for Industry* (New York: The Free Press, 1992), pp. 5–6.

28. Bell, *The Coming of Post-Industrial Society,* pp. xvi, xix–xx.

29. Quinn, *Intelligent Enterprise,* p. 30.

30. Peter Martin, "Revolution Again," *Financial Times,* June 4, 1998.

31. Ibid.

32. Bell, *The Coming of Post-Industrial Society,* p. xvi.

33. Taichi Sakaiya, *The Knowledge-Value Revolution, or, A History of the Future,* trans. George Fields and William Marsh (Tokyo: Kodansha International, 1991), p. 60.

34. Thomas E. Weber, "Talking Toasters: Companies Gear Up for Internet Boom in Things That Think," *Wall Street Journal,* August 27, 1998, p. A1.

35. Ibid.

36. Teresa Riordan, "Throw Away That Cell Phone," *New York Times,* November 8, 1999, p. C4.

37. Carl Shapiro and Hal R. Varian, *Information Rules: A Strategic Guide to the Network Economy* (Boston: Harvard Business School Press, 1999), pp. 14, 19; Larry Downes and Chunka Mui, *Unleashing the Killer App: Digital Strategies for Market Dominance* (Boston: Harvard Business School Press, 1998), p. 51.

38. Downes and Mui, *Unleashing the Killer App,* p. 51.

39. Ibid.; Shapiro and Varian, *Information Rules,* pp. 19–20; Encyclopaedia Britannica, Inc., "Why Subscribe to BritannicaOnline?" http://www.eb.com/whysub.htm.

40. Eleanor A. Gossen and Suzanne Irving, "Ownership Versus Access and Low-Use Periodical Titles," *Library Resources & Technical Services* 39, no. 1 (January 1995): 43.

41. Roger Brown, "The Changing Economic Environment—Access vs. Ownership: Access Where? Own What?—A Corporate View," *Serials: The Journal of the United Kingdom Serials Group* 8, no. 2 (July 1995): 125–29.

42. Ethan Bronner, "For More Textbooks, A Shift From Printed Page to Screen," *New York Times,* December 1, 1998, p. A26.

43. Ibid.

44. Jeffrey F. Rayport and John J. Sviokla, "Managing in the Marketplace," *Harvard Business Review,* December 1994, p. 144.

45. Joan Magretta, "Growth Through Global Sustainability: An Interview with Monsanto's CEO, Robert B. Shapiro," *Harvard Business Review,* January–February 1997, p. 83.

46. Ibid.

47. Thomas J. Bierma, Frank L. Waterstraat, and Joyce Ostrosky, "Shared Savings and Environmental Management Accounting: Innovation Chemical Supply Strategies," in Martin Bennett and Peter James, eds., *The Green Botton Line: Environmental Accounting for Management—Current Practice and Future Trends* (Sheffield, UK: Greenleaf Publishing, 1998), pp. 268–69; Jill Kauffman Johnson, Allen White, and Shelly Hearn, "From Solvents to Services: Restructuring Chemical Supplier Relationships to Achieve Environmental Excellence," *Proceedings of the 1997 Institute of Electrical and Electronics Engineers International Symposium on Electronics and the Environment,* May 5–7, 1997, pp. 322–25.

48. Bierma et al., "Shared Savings and Environmental Management Accounting," p. 270.

49. Paul Hawken, Amory Lovins, and Hunter Lovins, *Natural Capitalism: Creating the Next Industrial Revolution* (Boston: Little, Brown and Co., 1999), p. 136.

50. Mack Hanan, *Sales Shock! The End of Selling Products, the Rise of CoManaging Customers* (New York: AMACOM, 1996), p. 119.

51. James F. Moore, *The Death of Competition: Leadership and Strategy in the Age of Business Ecosystems* (New York: HarperCollins, 1996), p. 251; Hanan, *Sales Shock!,* p. 57.

52. Claudia H. Deutsch, "Services Becoming the Goods in Industry: Not Enough Profit in Making Things," *New York Times,* January 7, 1997, p. D4.

53. Ibid.

54. Ibid.

55. Ibid.

56. Ibid.

57. Steven L. Goldman, Roger N. Nagel, and Kenneth Preiss, *Agile Competitors and Virtual Corporations* (New York: Van Nostrand Reinhold, 1995), p. 12.

58. Neil Gross, Peter Coy, and Otis Port, "The Technology Paradox: How Companies Can Thrive as Prices Dive," *Business Week,* March 6, 1995, pp. 76–77.

59. Kevin Kelly, *New Rules for the New Economy: 10 Radical Strategies for a Connected World* (New York: Viking, 1998), p. 57.

60. Gross et al., "The Technology Paradox," p. 77.

Chapter Six

1. Stanley M. Davis and Christopher Meyer, *Blur: The Speed of Change in the Connected Economy* (Oxford: Capstone Publishing Ltd., 1998), p. 48.

2. Don Peppers and Martha Rogers, *The One to One Future: Building Relationships One Customer at a Time* (New York: Doubleday, 1993), p. 394.

3. Ibid.

4. Don Tapscott, *The Digital Economy: Promise and Peril in the Age of Networked Intelligence* (New York: McGraw-Hill, 1996), p. 245.

5. Peppers and Rogers, *The One to One Future*, p. 15.

6. Carl Sewell and Paul Brown, *Customers for Life: How to Turn That One-Time Buyer Into a Lifetime Customer* (New York: Doubleday/Currency, 1990).

7. William H. Davidow and Michel S. Malone, *The Virtual Corporation: Structuring and Revitalizing the Corporation for the 21st Century* (New York: HarperCollins, 1992), p. 230; Hyatt Resorts, "Discover Camp Hyatt," http://www.hyatt.com/resorts/camp/index.html.

8. Peppers and Rogers, *The One to One Future*, pp. 45–46.

9. Kevin Kelly, *New Rules for the New Economy: 10 Radical Strategies for a Connected World* (New York: Viking, 1998), pp. 118–19.

10. Peter Schwartz, "R-Tech," *Wired* 4, no. 6 (June 1996), http://www.hotwired.com/collections/virtual_communities/4.06–r_tech_pr.html.

11. Ibid.

12. Robert C. Blattberg and Rashi Glazer, "Marketing in the Information Revolution," in Robert C. Blattberg, John D. Little, and Rashi Glazer, eds., *The Marketing Information Revolution* (Boston: Harvard Business School Press, 1994), p. 9.

13. James Rule, "My Mailbox Is Mine," *Wall Street Journal*, August 15, 1990, p. A8.

14. Mack Hanan, *Sales Shock! The End of Selling Products, the Rise of CoManaging Customers* (New York: AMACOM, 1996), p. 107.

15. Ibid.

16. Peter F. Drucker, *The Practice of Management* (Oxford: Butterworth-Heinemann, 1954, 1993), pp. 35–36.

17. Theodore Levitt, "Marketing Myopia," *Harvard Business Review* 38 (July–August 1960): 45–56.

18. B. Joseph Pine II, *Mass Customization: The New Frontier in Business Competition* (Boston: Harvard Business School Press, 1993), pp. 146–49.

19. Ibid., pp. 141–45, 196–99.

20. Richard Cross and Janet Smith, *Customer Bonding* (Lincolnwood, IL: NTC Business Books, 1995), pp. 56–59; Larry Downes and Chunka Mui, *Unleashing the Killer App: Digital Strategies for Market Dominance* (Boston: Harvard Business School Press, 1998), pp. 112, 116–18; Hallmark, "Reminder Service," http://www.hallmark. com.

21. Cross and Smith, *Customer Bonding*, p. 190.

22. Ibid., p. 162.

23. Ibid., pp. 162–63.

24. Downes and Mui, *Unleashing the Killer App*, p. 101.

25. Ibid.

26. Cross and Smith, *Customer Bonding*, pp. 121–22.

27. Ibid., pp. 149, 153.

28. Ibid., p. 154.

29. Ibid., pp. 154, 156; Winnebago Industries, "Winnebago-Itasca Travelers Club," http://www.winnebagoind.com/witclub.htm; Winnebago Industries, "Member Benefits," http://www.winnebagoind.com/witbenefits.htm.

Chapter Seven

1. Evan McKenzie, *Privatopia: Homeowner Associations and the Rise of Residential Private Government* (New Haven, CT: Yale University Press, 1996), p. 12.

2. James L. Winokur, "Choice, Consent, and Citizenship in Common Interest Communities," in Stephen E. Barton and Carol J. Silverman, eds., *Common Interest Communities: Private Governments and the Public Interest* (Berkeley: Institute of Governmental Studies, 1994), p. 88.

3. McKenzie, *Privatopia,* pp. 176–77.

4. Ibid., p. 177.

5. Edward J. Blakely and Mary Gail Snyder, *Fortress America: Gated Communities in the United States* (Washington, DC: Brookings Institution Press, 1997), p. 63.

6. Russ Rymer, "Back to the Future: Disney Reinvents the Company Town," *Harper's Magazine* 293, no. 1757 (October 1996): 65.

7. Ibid., p. 66.

8. Ibid., p. 69.

9. Ebenezer Howard, *Garden Cities of Tomorrow* (Cambridge, MA: MIT Press, 1965), p. 76; McKenzie, *Privatopia,* pp. 3–4.

10. McKenzie, *Privatopia,* pp. 29–31.

11. Urban Land Institute / Federal Housing Administration, *The Homes Association Handbook,* Technical Bulletin no. 50 (Washington, DC: Urban Land Institute, 1964), p. vi.

12. Bettina Drew, "Celebration: A New Kind of American Town," *Yale Review* 86, no. 3 (July 1998): 60.

13. Curtis C. Sproul, "The Many Faces of Community Associations Under California Law," in Barton and Silverman, eds., *Common Interest Communities,* pp. 45–46.

14. McKenzie, *Privatopia,* p. 127.

15. Ibid., p. 128.

16. Ibid., p. 142.

17. Richard Louv, *America II* (New York: Penguin, 1982), p. 93.

18. William K. Stevens, "Condominium Associations: New Form of Local Government," *Los Angeles Daily Journal,* September 8, 1998, p. 22; "Court Finds Wife Too Young for Retirement Condo," *United Press International,* December 11, 1987; "Couple Sues to Lift Ban on Condo Door," *United Press International,* October 8, 1989; John Singh, "Fat Dog Isn't Welcome in the Land of Fat Cats," *Orlando Sentinel Tribune,* March 12, 1992, p. B4; John Singh, "Scales of Justice Tip in Favor of Pudgy Dog in Subdivision," *Orlando Sentinel Tribune,* March 17, 1992, p. B3.

19. McKenzie, *Privatopia,* p. 129.

20. Ibid., p. 147.

21. David Dillon, "Fortress America: More and More of Us Are Living Behind Locked Gates," *Planning* 60, no. 6 (June 1994): 10–11.

22. Frank Heflin, "Closed Gates Trouble Outsiders," *Progressive,* October 1993, p. 33.

23. David J. Kennedy, "Residential Associations as State Actor: Regulating the Impact of Gated Communities on Nonmembers," *Yale Law Journal* 105, no. 3 (December 1995): 7.

24. McKenzie, *Privatopia,* p. 126.

25. Drew, "Celebration," p. 59.

26. Danter Company, "Home Ownership Rates," http://www.danter.com/statistics/homeown.htm.

27. Christy Fisher, "New Markets for Landlords," *American Demographics,* November 1995, pp. 48, 50.

28. Ibid., p. 50.

29. Coates and Jarratt, Inc., for the National Multi Housing Council and the Na-

tional Apartment Association, *The Future of the Apartment Industry* (Washington, DC: National Multi Housing Council and National Apartment Association, 1995), p. 39.

30. Ibid., p. 53.

31. John R. Knight and Cynthia Fiery Eakin, "A New Look at the Home Ownership Decision," *Real Estate Issues,* Summer 1998, p. 23.

32. Steven Bergsman, "Now That Time-Shares Have Come Into Respectability, They're Also Coming to Town—Downtown," *Barrons* 76 (June 1996): 58; "The $5 Billion Swapshops: Timeshare Holidays," *The Economist* 340, no. 7979 (August 1996): 53.

33. Jon Bigness, "Time-Share Firm Purchase Is Set by HFS," *Wall Street Journal,* October 8, 1996, p. A3; "The $5 Billion Swapshops," p. 53.

34. Mitchell Pacelle, "Developers Market Time Shares as Classy Vacation for the Rich," *Wall Street Journal,* August 30, 1995, p. B1.

35. Ibid.

36. Bergsman, "Now That Time-Shares Have Come Into Respectability," p. 58.

37. "The $5 Billion Swapshops," p. 53.

38. Ibid.; Elizabeth Razzi, "Time Shares Grow Up: The Entry of Disney, Hilton and Marriott Is Helping to Erase the Industry's Hard-Sell Reputation," *Kiplinger's Personal Finance Magazine,* October 1995, p. 69.

39. Georg W. F. Hegel, *Hegel's Philosophy of Right,* trans. with notes by Thomas M. Knox (Oxford: Clarendon, 1942), p. 38.

40. Ibid., pp. 40–41.

41. Siegfried Sassoon, *Memoirs of a Fox-Hunting Man* (London: Faber, 1928), p. 14.

42. Joshua Meyrowitz, *No Sense of Place: The Impact of Electronic Media on Social Behavior* (New York: Oxford University Press, 1985), p. 115.

43. Erwin Schrodinger, *My View of the World,* trans. Cecily Hastings (Cambridge: Cambridge University Press, 1964), p. 22.

Chapter Eight

1. Arnold Toynbee, *Lectures on the Industrial Revolution of the 18th Century* (London/New York: Longmans, Green and Co, 1937).

2. Sarah Sanderson King, *Human Communication as a Field of Study* (New York: State University of New York Press, 1989), p. 111.

3. Lee Thayer, *On Communication: Essays in Understanding* (Norwood, NJ: Ablex, 1987), p. 45.

4. Quoted in Warren I. Sussman, *Culture As History: The Transformation of American Society in the Twentieth Century* (New York: Pantheon Books, 1973), p. 252.

5. Ibid.

6. John Fiske, *Introduction to Communication Studies,* 2nd ed. (New York: Routledge, 1990), p. 2.

7. Herbert I. Schiller, *Culture Inc.: The Corporate Takeover of Public Expression* (New York: Oxford University Press, 1989), p. 31.

8. Daniel Bell, *The Coming of Post-Industrial Society* (New York: Basic Books, 1973), p. 12.

9. Mike Featherstone, *Consumer Culture and Postmodernism* (London: Sage Publications, 1991), p. 114.

10. Quoted in Carl Eugene Loeffler, "Virtual Polis: A Networked Virtual Reality Application," in Carl Eugene Loeffler and Tim Anderson, eds., *The Virtual Reality Casebook* (New York: Van Nostrand Reinhold, 1994), p. 60.

11. Alvin Toffler, *Future Shock* (New York: Bantam Books, 1970), pp. 234, 236–37.

12. Norman K. Denzin, *Images of Postmodern Society: Social Theory and Contemporary Cinema* (London: Sage, 1991), p. 44.

13. James Ogilvy, "This Postmodern Business," *Marketing and Research Today* 18 (February 1990): 14.

14. Ibid., p. 20.

15. Ibid.

16. B. Joseph Pine and James Gilmore, *The Experience Economy: Work Is Theatre and Every Business a Stage* (Cambridge, MA: Harvard Business School Press, 1999), p. 100.

17. Ibid., p. 16.

18. Ibid., pp. 14–15.

19. Larry Krotz, *Tourists: How Our 'Fastest Growing Industry Is Changing the World* (Boston: Faber and Faber, 1996), p. 214.

20. World Travel and Tourism Council, "Travel & Tourism Set to Boost Worldwide Economic Growth," press release, April 8, 1998, http://www.wttc.org, "Travel & Tourism and Information Technology Join Forces for 21st Century Growth and Job Creation," press release, January 22, 1998, http://www.wttc.org.

21. Krotz, *Tourists,* p. 11; World Travel & Tourism Council, "New Figures Show Travel & Tourism's Long-Term Potential—Governments Urged to Build It into Asian Economic Recovery," press release, February 2, 1998, http://www.wttc.org.

22. World Travel & Tourism Council, "The Travel & Tourism Satellite Account: World Economic Impact," http://www.wttc.org.

23. World Travel & Tourism Council, "Travel & Tourism Set to Boost Worldwide Economic Growth."

24. William F. Theobald, *Global Tourism: The Next Decade* (Oxford: Butterworth-Heinemann, 1994), p. 4.

25. World Travel & Tourism Council, "Millennium Vision: Strategic Economic and Employment Priority," http://www.wttc.org..

26. World Travel & Tourism Council, "Travel & Tourism Taxation: A 20th Century Vicious Circle," http://www.wttc.org.

27. Barbara Crossette, "Surprises in the Global Tourism Boom," *New York Times,* April 12, 1998, section 4, p. 5.

28. Krotz, *Tourists,* pp. 11–12.

29. Theobald, *Global Tourism,* p. 7.

30. Krotz, *Tourists,* p. 6.

31. Ibid., p. 48; Daniel J. Boorstin, *The Image: A Guide to Pseudo-Events in America* (New York: Harper & Row, 1961), p. 87.

32. Boorstin, *The Image,* p. 87; Krotz, *Tourists,* pp. 50–51.

33. Krotz, *Tourists,* p. 51.

34. Boorstin, *The Image,* pp. 88–89.

35. Mark Kurlansky, *A Continent of Islands: Searching for the Caribbean Destiny* (Reading, MA: Addison-Welsey, 1992), pp. 20–21.

36. Krotz, *Tourists,* pp. 56–60.

37. Ibid., pp. 57–58.

38. Boorstin, *The Image,* p. 88.

39. Dean MacCannell, *The Tourist: A New Theory of the Leisure Class* (New York: Schocken Books, 1989), p. 100.

40. Krotz, *Tourists,* p. 223.

41. Ibid.

42. Kreg Lindberg and Jeremy Enriquez, "An Analysis of Ecotourism's Economic

Contribution to Conservation and Development in Belize," report prepared for the World Wildlife Fund (U.S.) and the Ministry of Tourism and the Environment (Belize), 1994.

43. World Travel & Tourism Council, "Millennium Vision."

44. Ibid.

45. Tom Kenworthy, "The Rich Find a Home on the Range," *Washington Post,* March 13, 1994, p. A12.

46. Quoted in Kenworthy, "The Rich Find a Home on the Range," p. A12.

47. International Council of Shopping Centers, "Shopping Centers Rank High in U.S. Tourist Attractions," *ICSC News,* June 1999, http://www.icsc.org/srch/about/impactofshoppingcenters/shoppingcentersrank.html.

48. International Council of Shopping Centers, "Did You Know That . . ." *ICSC News,* June 1999, http://www.icsc.org/srch/about/impactofshoppingcenters/didyouknow.html.

49. Ibid.

50. William Severini Kowinski, *The Malling of America: An Inside Look at the Great Consumer Paradise* (New York: Morrow, 1985), pp. 349–50.

51. Joan Didion, "On the Mall," in *The White Notebook* (New York: Simon & Schuster, 1979), p. 34.

52. Margaret Crawford, "The World in a Shopping Mall," in Michael Sorkin, ed., *Variations on a Theme Park: The American City and the End of Public Space* (New York: Farrar, Straus and Giroux, 1992), p. 21.

53. Kowinski, *The Malling of America,* p. 62.

54. Crawford, "The World in a Shopping Mall," p. 9.

55. Jennifer Stoffel, "Where America Goes for Entertainment," *New York Times,* August 7, 1988, section 3, p. 11F; Kowinski, *The Malling of America,* p. 71; International Council of Shopping Centers, "Did You Know That . . ."

56. Kowinski, *The Malling of America,* p. 61.

57. Crawford, "The World in a Shopping Mall," p. 3.

58. Tracy C. Davis, "Theatrical Antecedents of the Mall That Ate Downtown," *Journal of Popular Culture* 24, no. 4 (Spring 1991): 4.

59. Crawford, "The World in a Shopping Mall," p. 4.

60. Davis, "Theatrical Antecedents of the Mall That Ate Downtown," pp. 1, 4, 7–9.

61. Ibid., p. 5.

62. Leslie Kaufman, "Sony Builds a Mall, But Don't Call It That," *New York Times,* July 25, 1999, section 3, pp. 1–12.

63. Kowinski, *The Malling of America,* p. 355.

64. Ibid.

65. Ibid.

66. Ibid., p. 356.

67. Ibid.

68. Ibid., p. 357.

69. Neal Gabler, *Life the Movie: How Entertainment Conquered Reality* (New York: Alfred A. Knopf, 1998), p. 205.

70. Ibid., pp. 205–6.

71. Mark Landler, "Are We Having Fun Yet? Maybe Too Much," *Business Week,* March 14, 1994, p. 66; Michael J. Mandel, Mark Landler, Ronald Gover, Gail DeGeorge, Joseph Weber, and Kathy Rebello, "The Entertainment Economy: America's Growth Engines: Theme Parks, Casinos, Sports, Interactive TV," *Business Week,* March 14, 1994, p. 59.

72. Mandel et al., "The Entertainment Economy," p. 59.

73. Manuel Castells, *The Information Age: Economy, Society, and Culture* (Cambridge, MA: Blackwell Publishers, 1996), vol. 1, *The Rise of the Network Society,* p. 366; Mandel et al., "The Entertainment Economy," p. 59.

74. Walter Russell Mead, "At Your Service: The New Global Economy Takes Your Order," *Mother Jones* 22, no. 2 (March–April 1998): 35.

75. Mandel et al., "The Entertainment Economy," p. 61.

76. Ibid., p. 60.

77. Quoted in Peter C. Marzio, *The Democratic Art: Pictures for a 19th-Century America: Cromolithography, 1840–1900* (Boston: Godine, 1979), p. 5.

78. Ibid., p. 104.

79. Lewis Palmer, "The World in Motion," *Survey* 22 (1909): 357.

80. Stuart Ewen and Elizabeth Ewen, *Channels of Desire: Mass Images and the Shaping of American Consciousness* (New York: McGraw-Hill, 1982), p. 87.

81. Michael M. Davis, *The Exploitation of Pleasure: A Study of Commercial Recreations in New York City* (New York: Russell Sage Foundation, 1911), table 8, p. 30.

82. Gabler, *Life the Movie,* p. 57.

83. Mandel et al., "The Entertainment Economy," p. 60.

84. John Kao, *Jamming: The Art and Discipline of Business Creativity* (New York: HarperCollins, 1996), p. 96.

85. Ibid., p. 189.

86. Ibid., p. 190.

87. Pine and Gilmore, *The Experience Economy,* pp. 140, 143–56.

88. Tom Peters, *Liberation Management: Necessary Disorganization for the Nanosecond Nineties* (New York: Alfred A. Knopf, 1992), pp. 640, 741, 743.

89. Kao, *Jamming,* pp. 66–67.

90. Stephen J. Grove and Raymond F. Fisk, "The Dramaturgy of Services Exchange: An Analytical Framework for Services Marketing," in Leonard L. Berry, G. Lynn Shostack, and Gregory D. Upah, eds., *Emerging Perspectives on Services Marketing* (Chicago: American Marketing Association, 1983), p. 45.

91. Stephen J. Grove and Raymond F. Fisk, "The Service Experience as Theater," *Advances in Consumer Research* 19 (1992): 456.

92. Hillel M. Finestone and David B. Conter, "Acting in Medical Practice," *The Lancet* 344, no. 8925 (September 1994): 801.

93. Grove and Fisk, "The Dramaturgy of Services Exchange," p. 47.

94. Quoted in Steve Barth, "Exporting the Fantasy," *World Trade,* March 1998, p. 43.

Chapter Nine

1. Dentsu Institute for Human Studies/DataFlow International, *Media in Japan* (Tokyo: DataFlow International, 1994), p. 67.

2. *Nielsen Media Research News* (New York: A. C. Nielsen Company, 1990).

3. Manuel Castells, *The Information Age: Economy, Society, and Culture* (Cambridge, MA: Blackwell Publishers, 1996), vol. 1. *The Rise of the Network Society,* p. 339.

4. Linda M. Harasim, ed., *Global Networks: Computers and International Communication* (Cambridge, MA: MIT Press, 1993), p. 67.

5. Kevin Kelly, *Out of Control: The Rise of Neo-Biological Civilization* (Reading, MA: Addison-Wesley, 1994), pp. 340–50.

6. Mark Slouka, paraphrasing Nicholas Negroponte, in *War of the Worlds: Cy-*

berspace and the High-Tech Assault on Reality (New York: Basic Books, 1995), pp. 69–70.

7. Castells, *The Rise of the Network Society,* p. 373.

8. Brenda Laurel, *Computers as Theatre* (Reading, MA: Addison-Wesley, 1991).

9. Randall Walser, "Elements of a Cyberspace Playhouse," *Proceedings of National Computer Graphics Association '90,* 1990.

10. Howard Rheingold, *Virtual Reality* (New York: Simon and Schuster, 1991), p. 386.

11. Slouka, *War of the Worlds,* p. 75.

12. Rheingold, *Virtual Reality,* pp. 17, 19.

13. Ibid., p. 46.

14. Kevin J. Clancy and Robert S. Shulman, *Marketing Myths That Are Killing Business: The Cure for Death Wish Marketing* (New York: McGraw-Hill, 1994), pp. 140, 171.

15. Bruce Horovitz, "Accounting for Taste: Designers Tally Profits," *USA Today,* May 14, 1997, p. B1.

16. A. Fuat Firat and Alladi Venkatesh, "Postmodernity: The Age of Marketing," *International Journal of Research in Marketing* 10 (1993): 244.

17. Stephen Brown, *Postmodern Marketing* (New York: Routledge, 1995), pp. 129–30.

18. Firat and Venkatesh, "Postmodernity," p. 245.

19. Alfred L. Schreiber and Barry Levinson, *Lifestyle and Event Marketing: Building the New Customer Partnership* (New York: McGraw Hill, 1994), p. 2.

20. Ibid., p. 5.

21. Ibid., p. 2.

22. Ibid., p. 75.

23. Ibid., p. 103.

24. Ibid., p 239.

25. Ronald Collins, "Clutter," *Columbia Journalism Review,* November–December 1991, p. 49.

26. Richard Cross and Janet Smith, *Customer Bonding* (Lincolnwood, IL: NTC Business Books, 1995), pp. 4, 14, 15, 86; Robert W. McChesney, "The Political Economy of Global Communication," in McChesney et al., eds., *Capitalism and the Information Age: The Political Economy of the Global Communication Revolution* (New York: Monthly Review Press, 1998), pp. 13–14, 20; Mary Kuntz and Joseph Wever, "The New Hucksterism," *Business Week,* July 1, 1996, p. 82.

27. David Lieberman, "Networks of the Net: Media Powerhouses Buy Into New World Order," *USA Today,* June 19, 1998, Money section, p. 1B.

28. Ibid.

29. John Markoff, "Internet Service Is Planning $6 Billion Deal to Buy Excite," *New York Times,* January 19, 1999, p. 1.

30. Lieberman, "Networks of the Net," Money section, p. 1B.

31. Ibid.

32. Elihu Katz and Paul F. Lazarsfeld, *Personal Influence: The Part Played by People in the Flow of Mass Communication* (Glencoe, IL: The Free Press, 1995), p. 119.

33. Castells, *The Rise of the Network Society,* p. 171.

34. Kurt Lewin, *Field Theory in Social Science: Selected Theoretical Papers* (New York: Harper & Row, 1951), p. 186; Kurt Lewin, "Channels of Group Life: Social Planning and Action Research," *Frontiers of Group Dynamics* (New York: Harper & Row, 1946), pp. 145–46.

35. Pamela J. Shoemaker, *Communication Concepts 3: Gatekeeping* (Newbury Park, CA: Sage Publications, 1991), p. 4.

36. Steven E. Clayman and Ann Reisner, "Gatekeeping in Action: Editorial Conferences and Assessments of Newsworthiness," *American Sociological Review* 63 (April 1998): 179; Diana Crane, *The Production of Culture: Media and the Urban Arts* (Newbury Park, CA: Sage Publications, 1992), p. 67.

37. Crane, *The Production of Culture*, p. 71.

38. Diana Crane, *The Transformation of Avant Garde: The New York Art World, 1940–1985* (Chicago: University of Chicago Press, 1987), p. 114.

39. Mike Featherstone, *Consumer Culture and Postmodernism* (London: Sage Publications, 1991), p. 35.

40. Ibid., p. 44.

41. Youth Intelligence, "Youth Intelligence," media kit, 1998, p. 2.

42. Malcolm Gladwell, "The Coolhunt," *The New Yorker*, March 17, 1997, p. 78.

43. Venessa Grigoridis, "How to Totally Know What's Cool," *Cosmopolitan*, March 1999, p. 215.

44. Darius Sanai, "Hunters on Trail of Cool," *European*, July 20–26, 1998, p. 30.

45. J. D. Heiman, "Cool Occupation: Trend Spotter," *US*, March 1999, p. 73.

46. Ibid., p. 74.

47. Ibid.

48. Norman K. Denzin, *Images of Postmodern Society: Social Theory and Contemporary Cinema* (London: Sage Publications, 1991), p. 9.

49. Quoted in Daniel Burstein and David Kline, *Road Warriors: Dreams and Nightmares Along the Information Highway* (New York: Dutton, 1995), p. 299.

50. United Nations Development Program, *Human Development Report, 1999* (New York: Oxford University Press, 1999), pp. 33–34.

51. Ibid.

52. Wade Davis, "The Issue Is Whether Ancient Cultures Will Be Free to Change on Their Own Terms," *National Geographic*, August 1999, p. 65.

53. Ibid.

54. Burstein and Kline, *Road Warriors*, p. 298.

Chapter Ten

1. Arnold Toynbee, *A Study of History*, vol. 8 (London: Oxford University Press, 1954), p. 338; Barry Smart, *Modern Conditions, Postmodern Controversies* (New York: Routledge, 1992), p. 164.

2. John H. Randall, *The Making of the Modern Mind: A Survey of the Intellectual Background of the Present Age* (Boston: Houghton Mifflin, 1940), pp. 223–24; Francis Bacon, "Novum Organum," in *The Works of Francis Bacon*, vol. 4 (London: J. Rivington and Sons, 1778), pp. 114, 246, 320, 325; Francis Bacon, "The Masculine Birth of Time," in *The Philosophy of Francis Bacon: An Essay on Its Development from 1603–1609*, ed. Benjamin Farrington (Liverpool, England: Liverpool University Press, 1964), pp. 62, 92–93; Francis Bacon, "Description of the Intellectual Globe," in *The Works of Francis Bacon*, vol. 5 (London: J. Rivington and Sons, 1778), p. 506; William Leiss, *The Domination of Nature* (Boston: Beacon Press, 1972), p. 58; Carolyn Merchant, *The Death of Nature: Women, Ecology and the Scientific Revolution* (San Francisco: Harper and Row, 1980), p. 172.

3. Marquis de Condorcet, *Outlines of an Historical View of the Progress of the Human Mind* (London: J. Johnson, 1795), pp. 4–5.

4. Bertrand Russell, *Our Knowedge of the External World, as a Field for Scientific Method in Philosophy* (1914; reprint ed., London: Routledge, 1995).

5. R. G. Collingwood, *The Idea of Nature* (Oxford: Oxford University Press, 1945), p. 146.

6. Quoted in Alfred North Whitehead, *The Principles of Natural Knowledge,* 2nd ed. (Cambridge: Cambridge University Press, 1925), p. 54.

7. Collingwood, *The Idea of Nature,* p. 146.

8. Alfred North Whitehead, *Nature and Life* (New York: Greenwood Press, 1968), p. 27.

9. José Ortega y Gasset, *Meditaciones del Quijote* (Madrid: Ediciones de la Residencia de Estudiantes, 1914).

10. Werner Heisenberg, *Physics and Philosophy: Encounters and Conversations* (New York: Harper, 1958), p. 58.

11. William Bergquist, *The Postmodern Organization: Mastering the Art of Irreversible Change* (San Fransisco: Jossey-Bass, 1993), p. 24.

12. Jean Baudrillard, *Simulations,* trans. Paul Foss, Paul Patton, and Philip Beitchman (New York: Semiotext(e), 1983).

13. Ellen Edwards, "Plugged-In Generation," *The Washington Post,* November 18, 1999, p. A1.

14. Steve Levy, "Ad Nauseam—How MTV Sells Out Rock and Roll," *Rolling Stone,* December 8, 1983, p. 33.

15. E. Ann Kaplan, *Rocking Around the Clock: Music Television, Postmodernism, and Consumer Culture* (New York: Methuen, 1987), p. 46.

16. Jean Baudrillard, "The Ecstasy of Communication," in *The Anti-Aesthetic: Essays on Postmodern Culture,* ed. Hal Foster (Port Townsend, WA: Bay Press, 1983), pp. 127–30.

17. O. B. Hardison, Jr., *Disappearing Through the Skylight: Culture and Technology in the Twentieth Century* (New York: Viking, 1989), p. 321.

18. Jean Baudrillard, *Xerox and Infinity,* trans. Agitac (Paris: Touchepas, 1988), p. 7; Baudrillard, *Simulations,* p. 148.

19. Donald M. Lowe, *History of Bourgeois Perception* (Chicago: University of Chicago Press), p. 71.

20. Orison Swett Marden, *Masterful Personality* (New York: Thomas Y. Crowell Co., 1921), pp. 1, 3, 17, 23, 33, 68, 291; Warren I. Sussman, *Culture As History: The Transformation of American Society in the Twentieth Century* (New York: Pantheon Books, 1972), p. 279.

21. Georg Simmel, *Georg Simmel on Individuality and Social Forms: Selected Writings,* ed. Donald N. Levine (Chicago: University of Chicago Press, 1971), p. 393.

22. Ibid., p. 376.

23. Michael R. Wood and Louis A. Zurcher, Jr., *The Development of a Post Modern Self: A Computer-Assisted Comparative Analysis of Personal Documents* (Westport, CT: Greenwood Press, 1988), p. 125.

24. Philip Rieff, *The Triumph of the Therapeutic: Uses of Faith After Freud* (Chicago: University of Chicago Press, 1987), p 22.

25. Ibid., p. 23.

26. Christopher Lasch, *The Culture of Narcissism: American Life in an Age of Diminishing Expectations* (New York: W. W. Norton, 1979), pp. 30, 33.

27. Ibid., p. 30.

28. Ibid.

29. The following works were used in the discussion of reprogramming the

mind, pp. 203–208: Donald M. Lowe, *History of Bourgeois Perception* (Chicago: University of Chicago Press, 1982); David Crowley and Paul Heyer, eds. *Communication in History: Technology, Culture, Society* (New York: Longman, 1991); Harold A. Innis, *Empire and Communications,* rev. ed. (Toronto: University of Toronto Press, 1972); Marshall McLuhan, *Understanding Media: The Extensions of Man* (Cambridge, MA: MIT Press, 1994); Walter J. Ong, *Orality and Literacy: The Technologizing of the Word* (New York: Methuen, 1982); Elizabeth L. Eisenstein, *The Printing Revolution in Early Modern Europe* (Cambridge: Cambridge University Press, 1983).

30. Roland Barthes, *Image, Music, Text,* trans. Stephen Heath (New York: Noonday Press, 1977), p. 148.

31. Michael Heim, *Electric Language: A Philosophical Study of Word Processing* (New Haven, CT: Yale University Press, 1987), p. 215.

32. Ibid., p. 221.

33. Jean-François Lyotard, *The Postmodern Condition: A Report on Knowledge,* trans. Geoff Bennington and Brian Massumi (Minneapolis: University of Minnesota Press, 1984), p. 15.

34. Kenneth J. Gergen, *The Saturated Self: Dilemmas of Identity in Contemporary Life* (New York: Basic Books, 1991), pp. 70–80.

35. Ibid., p. 79.

36. Ibid., p. 7.

37. Ibid., pp. 17, 146–47.

38. Ibid.

39. Jean Baudrillard, *The Ecstasy of Communication,* ed. Sylvére Lotringer, trans. Bernard and Caroline Schutze (New York: Semiotext (e), 1988), p. 16.

40. Sherry Turkle, *Life on the Screen: Identity in the Age of the Internet* (New York: Simon & Schuster, 1995), p. 267.

41. Ibid., p. 12.

42. Ibid., p. 14.

43. Robert Jay Lifton, *The Protean Self: Human Resilience in an Age of Fragmentation* (New York: Basic Books, 1993), p. 17.

44. Ibid., p. 9.

45. Nicolas Evreinoff, *The Theater in Life,* trans. Alexander I. Nazaroff (New York: Benjamin Blom, 1927), p. 27.

46. Ibid.

47. Neal Gabler, *Life the Movie: How Entertainment Conquered Reality* (New York: Alfred A. Knopf, 1998), p. 8.

48. Martha Stewart, *USA Today,* Life section, January 17, 1996.

49. Daniel Boorstin, *The Image: A Guide to Pseudo-Events in America* (New York: Harper and Row, 1961), p. 240.

50. Dennis Brissett and Charles Edgley, "The Dramaturgical Perspective," in Dennis Brissett and Charles Edgley, eds., *Life As Theater: A Dramaturgical Sourcebook,* 2nd ed. (New York: Aldine de Gruyter, 1990), pp. 15, 16.

51. R. S. Perinbanayagam, *Signifying Acts: Structure and Meaning in Everyday Life* (Carbondale, IL: Southern Illinois University Press, 1985), p. 63.

52. Ibid., pp. 62–63.

53. R. S. Perinbanayagam, "Dramas, Metaphors, and Structures," *Symbolic Interaction* 5, no. 2 (1982): 266.

1. Daniel Bell, *Sociological Journeys: Essays 1960–1980* (London: Heinemann, 1980), pp. 43, 51.

2. Jean-François Lyotard, *The Postmodern Condition: A Report on Knowledge* (Minneapolis: University of Minnesota Press, 1984), p. 14.

3. Robert McChesney, "The Political Economy of Global Communication," in Robert McChesney, Ellen Meiksins Wood, and John Bellamy Foster, eds., *Capitalism and the Information Age: The Political Economy of the Global Communication Revolution* (New York: Monthly Review Press, 1998), pp. 12–13.

4. "The Power Center," *Vanity Fair,* September 1995, p. 271.

5. Laura Landro and Elizabeth Jensen, "All Ears: Walt Disney's Deal for ABC Makes Show Business a Whole New World," *Wall Street Journal,* August 1, 1995, p. A1; Disney Online, "The Walt Disney Company 1998 Factbook," www.disney.go.com/investors/factbook98.

6. Ben Bagdikian, *The Media Monopoly,* 5th ed. (Boston: Beacon Press, 1997), p. xxv; Disney Online, "The Walt Disney Company 1998 Factbook."

7. Steve Fainaru, "Multi-Media Man, *Boston Globe,* January 22, 1995, pp. 77–78.

8. Bagdikian, *The Media Monopoly,* pp. xvi–xvii.

9. Steven E. Miller, *Civilizing Cyberspace: Policy, Power, and the Information Superhighway* (New York: Addison-Wesley, 1996), p. 149.

10. McChesney, "The Political Economy of Global Communication," pp. 14–15; Bernard Simon, "Seagram to Hold On to 15% Stake in Time Warner," *Financial Times,* June 1, 1995, p. 18.

11. Ibid., p. 15.

12. Mark Landler, "Communications Pact to Favor Growing Giants," *New York Times,* February 18, 1997, p. B1.

13. Edmund L. Andrews, "Economic Boom Seen in World Telecom Pact: Political and Business Leaders Hail Accord to End Monopolies," *Herald Tribune,* February 17, 1997, p. 1.

14. Ibid.

15. Landler, "Communications Pact to Favor Growing Giants," p. B1.

16. Ibid.

17. Mike Mills, "British Telecom, AT&T Join Forces: $10 Billion Global Alliance to Offer Range of Phone, Internet, Data Services," *Washington Post,* July 27, 1998, p. A1.

18. Michael Lindemann, "Telecoms Operators Launch Global Alliance," *Financial Times,* February 1, 1996, p. 16.

19. Ibid.

20. Peter Golding, "Global Village or Cultural Pillage? The Unequal Inheritance of the Communications Revolution," in *Capitalism and the Information Age,* p. 78.

21. Andrews, "Economic Boom Seen in World Telecom Pact," p. 1.

22. Bagdikian, *The Media Monopoly,* p. ix.

23. U.S. Foreign Relations Subcommittee, 1977, cited in Robert E. Babe, *Information and Communication in Economics* (Boston: Kluwer Academic Publishers, 1994), p. 293.

24. William Greider, *One World, Ready or Not: The Manic Logic of Global Capitalism* (New York: Simon & Schuster, 1997), p. 21; Office of Technology Assessment, U.S. Congress, *Multinationals and the National Interest: Playing by Different Rules,* September 1993.

25. Esther Dyson, George Gilder, George Keyworth, and Alvin Toffler, *Cyberspace*

and the American Dream: A Magna Carta for the Knowledge Age (Washington, DC: Progress and Freedom Foundation, 1994), p. 16.

26. Jill Hills, "The U.S. Rules. OK? Telecommunications Since the 1940s," in *Capitalism and the Information Age,* p. 118.

27. Ibid.

28. Ibid.

29. Leo Herzel, "'Public Interest' and the Market in Color Television, Regulation 18," *University of Chicago Law Review,* no. 18 (1951): 802–16.

30. George A. Keyworth, Jeffrey Eisenbach, Thomas Lenard, and David E. Colton, *The Telecom Revolution: An American Opportunity* (Washington, DC: Progress and Freedom Foundation, 1995), pp. 6–7.

31. Ibid., p. 6.

32. The Progress & Freedom Foundation's FCC Working Group, "Broadcast Spectrum: Putting People First," *Progress on Point: Periodic Commentaries on the Policy Debate* 1, no. 9 (January 1996): 3.

33. Diane Coyle, *The Weightless World: Strategies for Managing the Digital Economy* (Cambridge, MA: MIT Press, 1997), p. 16.

34. Ibid.

35. Jean-Marie Guéhenno, *The End of the Nation-State,* trans. Victoria Elliot (Minneapolis: University of Minnesota Press, 1995), p. 19.

36. Miller, *Civilizing Cyberspace,* p. 206.

37. Nathaniel C. Nash, "Group of 7 Defines Policies About Telecommunications," *New York Times,* February 27, 1995, p. D1.

38. International Telecommunications Union, "Report on the State of World Communications," *ITU Newsletter* 1 (1994): 9–12.

39. Peter Golding, "World Wide Wedge: Division and Contradiction in the Global Information Infrastructure," *Monthly Review* 48, no. 3 (July/August 1996): 82.

40. Trevor Haywood, *Info-Rich/Info-Poor: Access and Exchange in the Global Information Society* (West Sussex, UK: Bowker-Saur, 1995), p. 123.

41. Michael Connors, *The Race to the Intelligent State: Towards the Global Information Economy of 2005* (Oxford: Blackwell Business, 1993), p. 18.

42. United Nations Educational, Scientific and Cultural Organization, *UNESCO Statistical Yearbook* (Paris: UNESCO, 1995).

43. United Nations Development Program, *Human Development Report, 1999* (New York: Oxford University Press, 1999), p. 63.

44. Quoted in Golding, "World Wide Wedge," p. 70.

45. United Nations Development Program, *Human Development Report, 1996* (New York: Oxford University Press, 1996).

46. Robert Taylor, "Market Fallout Will Lift Jobless Total: World Unemployment Third of All Workers Affected Says ILO Report," *Financial Times,* September 24, 1998, p. 8.

47. Golding, "World Wide Wedge," p. 70.

48. Khozem Merchant, "World Heads for Grotesque Inequalities," *Financial Times,* July 16, 1996, p. 4.

49. United Nations Development Program, *Human Development Report, 1998* (New York: Oxford University Press, 1998).

50. Barbara Crossette, "Hope, and Pragmatism for U.N. Cities Conference," *New York Times,* June 3, 1996, p. A3.

51. United Nations Development Program, *Human Development Report, 1998.*

52. Ibid.

53. Coyle, *The Weightless World,* p. 11.

54. "Number of Americans in Poverty Up for Third Year, Health Care Drops, Census Bureau Announces," *Commerce News,* October 4, 1993; "Number of Poor Americans Rises for 3rd Year," *Washington Post,* October 5, 1993, p. A6.

55. Bob Herbert, "Bogeyman Economics," *New York Times,* April 4, 1997, p. A29.

56. Lester C. Thurow, "What Boom? Two-Thirds of USA Stuck in 1973," *USA Today,* November 12, 1998.

57. G. Pascal Zachary, "Economists Say Prison Boom Will Take Toll," *Wall Street Journal,* September 29, 1995, p. B1.

58. Daniel Burstein and David Kline, *Road Warriors: Dreams and Nightmares Along the Information Highway* (New York: Dutton, 1995), p. 325.

59. Suneel Ratan, "A New Divide Between Haves and Have-Nots," *Time,* special issue on cyberspace, Spring 1995, p. 25.

60. Miller, *Civilizing Cyberspace,* p. 113; Lee de Forest, quoted in Jesse Drew, "Media Activism and Radical Democracy," in James Brook and Iain A. Boal, eds., *Resisting the Virtual Life: The Culture and Politics of Information* (San Francisco: City Lights Books, 1995), p. 74.

61. Howard Besser, "From Internet to Information Superhighway," in *Resisting the Virtual Life,* p. 60.

62. Walton S. Baer, *Cable Television: A Summary Overview of Local Decisionmaking* (Santa Monica, CA: Rand,1973), p. 6.

Chapter Twelve

1. Crawford MacPherson, *Democratic Theory: Essays in Retrieval* (Oxford: Clarendon, 1973), p. 125.

2. Ibid., p. 133.

3. Ibid.

4. Ibid., p. 135.

5. Ibid., p. 139.

6. Ibid.

7. Ibid.

8. Ibid., p. 140.

9. Independent Sector, "In Brief: America's Nonprofit Sector," pamphlet, Spring 1998, pp. 5, 6, 11–12, 16.

10. Lester M. Salamon, Helmut K. Anheier, et al., "The Emerging Sector Revisited: A Summary (Revised Estimates)," The Johns Hopkins Comparative Nonprofit Sector Project, Phase II (Baltimore: Center for Civil Society Studies, 1999), p. 4.

11. Robert Jay Lifton, *The Protean Self: Human Resilience in an Age of Fragmentation* (New York: Basic Books, 1993), p. 214.

12. Ibid.

13. David Throsby, "The Role of Music in International Trade and Economic Development," *World Culture Report: Culture, Creativity and Markets, 1998* (Paris: United Nations Educational, Scientific and Cultural Organization, 1998), p. 196.

14. Ibid., p. 206.

15. Ibid., p. 159.

16. Throsby, "The Role of Music in International Trade and Economic Development," pp. 154, 159.

17. John Tagiabue, "'Bagels' and 'Dirty Water': Fast-Food Chains Take U.S. Marketing to Europe," *New York Times,* August 27, 1999, pp. C1, C3.

18. Ibid., p. C3.

19. Roger Cohen, "Fearful Over the Future, Europe Seizes on Food," *New York Times,* August 29, 1999, section 4, p. 1.

20. Ibid., p. 3.

21. United Nations Development Program, *Human Development Report, 1999* (New York: Oxford University Press, 1999), p. 33.

22. Johan Huizinga, *Homo Ludens: A Study of the Play Element in Culture* (Boston: Beacon Press, 1955), p. ix.

23. Ibid., p. 46.

24. Ibid., p. 47; Edward Norbeck, "The Study of Play—Johan Huizinga and Modern Anthropology," in David F. Lancy and B. Allan Tindall, eds., *The Anthropological Study of Play: Problems and Prospects—Proceedings of the First Annual Meeting of the Association for the Anthropological Study of Play* (Cornwall, NY: Leisure Press, 1976), p. 6.

25. Friedrich Schiller, *On the Aesthetic Education of Man, In a Series of Letters,* trans. and ed. Elizabeth M. Wilkinson and L. A. Willoughby (Oxford: Clarendon Press, 1967).

26. Jean-Paul Sartre, *The Writings of Jean-Paul Sartre,* vol. 2 (Evanston, IL: Northwestern University Press, 1974).

Bibliography

Adorno, Theodor W. *The Culture Industry: Selected Essays on Mass Culture.* London: Routledge, 1991.

Agnew, Jean-Christophe. *Worlds Apart: The Market and the Theater in Anglo-American Thought, 1550–1750.* Cambridge: Cambridge University Press, 1986.

Anders, George. *Health Against Wealth: HMOs and the Breakdown of Medical Trust.* New York: Houghton Mifflin, 1996.

Anderson, Walter Truett, ed. *The Truth About the Truth: De-Confusing and Re-Constructing the Postmodern World.* New York: Tarcher/Putnam, 1995.

Antonelli, Cristiano. *The Economics of Information Networks.* New York: Elsevier Science Publishing Co., 1992.

Ariès, Philippe. *Centuries of Childhood: A Social History of Family Life.* Translated by Robert Baldick. New York: Knopf, 1962.

Ariès, Philippe, and Georges Duby, eds. *A History of Private Life: Revelations of the Medieval World.* Cambridge, MA: Harvard University Press, Belknap Press, 1988.

Babe, Robert E. *Communication and the Transformation of Economics.* Boulder, CO: Westview Press, 1995.

———. *Information and Communication in Economics.* Boston: Kluwer Academic Publishers, 1994.

Bacon, Francis. *The Works of Francis Bacon,* vol. 4. London: J. Rivington and Sons, 1778.

———. *The Works of Francis Bacon,* vol. 5. London: J. Rivington and Sons, 1778.

Baer, Walter S. *Cable Television: A Summary Overview for Local Decisionmaking.* Santa Monica, CA: Rand, 1973.

Bagdikian, Ben. *The Media Monopoly.* 5th ed. Boston: Beacon Press, 1997.

Bailey, James. *After Thought: The Computer Challenge to Human Intelligence.* New York: Basic Books, 1996.

Baker, Michael, ed. *Perspectives on Marketing Management,* vol. 4. New York: Wiley, 1994.

Barker, Francis. *The Tremulous Private Body: Essays on Subjection.* New York: Methuen, 1984.

Barthes, Roland. *Image, Music, Text.* Translated by Stephen Heath. New York: Noonday Press, 1977.

Barton, Stephen E., and Carol J. Silverman, eds. *Common Interest Communities: Private Governments and the Public Interest.* Berkeley, CA: Institute of Governmental Studies Press, University of California, 1994.

Baudrillard, Jean. *The Ecstasy of Communication.* Edited by Sylvére Lotringer. Translated by Bernard Schutze and Caroline Schutze. New York: Semiotext (e), 1988.

———. *Selected Writings.* Stanford, CA: Stanford University Press, 1988.

———. *Simulations.* Translated by Paul Foss, Paul Patton, and Philip Beitchman. New York: Semiotext(e), 1983.

———. *Xerox and Infinity.* Translated by Agitac. Paris: Touchepas, 1988.

Bauman, Zygmunt. *Intimations of Postmodernity.* London: Routledge, 1992.

Beaglehole, Ernest. *Property: A Study in Social Psychology.* New York: Macmillian, 1932.

Bell, Daniel. *The Coming of Post-Industrial Society.* New York: Basic Books, 1973.

———. *Sociological Journeys: Essays 1960–1980.* London: Heinemann, 1980.

Benamou, Michel, and Charles Caramello. *Performance in Postmodern Culture.* Madison, WI: Coda Press, 1977.

Benedikt, Michael, ed. *Cyberspace: First Steps.* Cambridge, MA: MIT Press, 1991.

Beniger, James R. *The Control Revolution: Technological and Economic Origins of the Information Society.* Cambridge, MA, and London: Harvard University Press, 1986.

Bennett, Martin, and Peter James, eds. *The Green Bottom Line: Environmental Accounting for Management—Current Practice and Future Trends.* Sheffield, UK: Greenleaf Publishing, 1998.

Benson, Lee. *Turner and Beard: American Historical Writing Reconsidered.* Westport, CT: Greenwood, 1980.

Bergquist, William. *The Postmodern Organization: Mastering the Art of Irreversible Change.* San Francisco: Jossey-Bass, 1993.

Berke, Michael. *Selling Equipment Leasing.* New York: AMACOM, 1994.

Berle, Adolf A., and Gardiner C. Means. *The Modern Corporation and Private Property.* 1932. Reprint. New York: Harcourt, Brace and World, 1968.

Berry, Leonard T., G. Lynn Shostack, and Gregory D. Upah, eds. *Emerging Perspectives on Services Marketing.* Chicago: American Marketing Association, 1983.

Blackstone, Sir William. *Commentaries on the Laws of England,* vol. 1. Philadelphia: Robert H. Small, 1825.

Blakely, Edward J., and Mary Gail Snyder. *Fortress America: Gated Communities in the United States.* Washington, DC: Brookings Institution Press, 1997.

Blattberg, Robert C., John D. C. Little, and Rashi Glazer, eds. *The Marketing Information Revolution.* Boston: Harvard Business School Press, 1994.

Bocock, Robert. *Consumption.* New York: Routledge, 1993.

Bolter, Jay David. *Writing Space: The Computer, Hypertext, and the History of Writing.* Hillsdale, NJ: Lawrence Erlbaum Associates, 1991.

Boorstin, Daniel J. *The Image: A Guide to Pseudo-Events in America.* New York: Harper & Row, 1961.

Bourdieu, Pierre. *Distinction: A Social Critique of the Judgement of Taste.* Translated by Richard Nice. Cambridge, MA: Harvard University Press, 1984.

Bradley, Stephen. *Globalization, Technology, and Competition: The Fusion of Computers and Telecommunications in the 1990s.* Cambridge, MA: Harvard Business School Press, 1993.

Branscomb, Anne Wells. *Who Owns Information? From Privacy to Public Access.* New York: Basic Books, 1994.

Braverman, Harry. *Labor and Monopoly Capital: The Degradation of Work in the Twentieth Century.* New York: Monthly Review Press, 1974.

Brissett, Dennis, and Charles Edgley, eds. *Life As Theater: A Dramaturgical Sourcebook.* 2nd ed. New York: Aldine de Gruyter, 1990.

Brodsky, Ira. *Wireless: The Revolution in Personal Telecommunications.* Boston: Artech House, 1995.

Brook, James, and Iain A. Boal, eds. *Resisting the Virtual Life: The Culture and Politics of Information.* San Francisco: City Lights Books, 1995.

Brown, Stephen. *Postmodern Marketing.* New York: Routledge, 1995.

Burke, Kenneth. *Dramatism and Development.* Barre, MA: Clarke University Press, Barre Publishers, 1972.

Burstein, Daniel, and David Kline. *Road Warriors: Dreams and Nightmares Along the Information Highway.* New York: Dutton, 1995.

Burt, Richard, and John Michael Archer, eds. *Enclosure Acts: Sexuality, Property, and Culture in Early Modern England.* Ithaca, NY: Cornell University Press, 1994.

Butler, Richard, and Douglas Pearce. *Change in Tourism: People, Places, Processes.* New York: Routledge, 1995.

Campbell, Colin. *The Romantic Ethic and the Spirit of Modern Consumerism.* New York: Basil Blackwell, 1987.

Capra, Fritjof. *The Web of Life: A New Scientific Understanding of Living Systems.* New York: Anchor, 1996.

Carrithers, Michael, Steven Collins, and Steven Lukes, eds. *The Category of the Person: Anthropology, Philosophy, History.* New York: Cambridge University Press, 1985.

Casey, Edward S. *The Fate of Place: A Philosophical History.* Berkeley and Los Angeles: University of California Press, 1997.

Castells, Manuel. *The Rise of the Network Society.* The Information Age: Economy, Society, and Culture, vol. 1. Cambridge MA: Blackwell Publishers, 1996.

———. *The Informational City: Information Technology, Economic Restructuring, and the Urban Regional Process.* London: Basil Blackwell, 1989.

Chandler, Alfred D., Jr. *The Visible Hand: The Managerial Revolution in American Business.* Cambridge, MA: Harvard University Press, Belknap Press, 1977.

Cheney, George. *Rhetoric in an Organizational Society: Managing Multiple Identities.* Columbia, SC: University of South Carolina Press, 1991.

Cheska, Alyce Taylor, ed. *Play as Context: 1979 Proceedings of the Association for the Anthropological Study of Play.* West Point, NY: Leisure Press, 1981.

Clegg, Stewart R. *Modern Organizations: Organization Studies in the Postmodern World.* Newbury Park, CA: Sage Publications, 1990.

Clement, Wallace, and Glen Williams. *The New Canadian Political Economy.* Kingston, Ontario, Canada: McGill-Queen's University Press, 1989.

Coase, R. H. *Essays on Economics and Economists.* Chicago: University of Chicago Press, 1994.

Collingwood, Robin G. *The Idea of Nature.* Oxford: Clarendon Press, 1945.

Combs, James E., and Michael Mansfield, eds. *Drama in Life: The Uses of Communication in Society.* New York: Hastings House, 1976.

Condorcet, Marquis de. *Outlines of an Historical View of the Progress of the Human Mind.* London: J. Johnson, 1795.

Coyle, Diane. *The Weightless World: Strategies for Managing the Digital Economy.* Cambridge, MA: MIT Press, 1997.

Crane, Diana. *The Production of Culture: Media and the Urban Arts.* Newbury Park, CA: Sage Publications, 1992.

———. *The Transformation of Avant Garde: The New York Art World, 1940–1985.* Chicago: University of Chicago Press, 1987.

Cross, Gary. *Time and Money: The Making of Consumer Culture.* New York: Routledge, 1993.

Cross, Richard, and Janet Smith. *Customer Bonding.* Lincolnwood, IL: NTC Business Books, 1995.

Crowley, David, and Paul Heyer, eds. *Communication in History: Technology, Culture, Society.* New York: Longman, 1991.

Csikszentmihalyi, Mihaly, and Eugene Rochber-Halton. *The Meaning of Things: Domestic Symbols and the Self.* New York: Cambridge University Press, 1981.

Cummings, Nicholas A., Janet L. Cummings, and John N. Johnson. *Behavioral Health in Primary Care: A Guide for Clinical Integration.* Madison, CT: Psychosocial Press, 1997.

Curran, James, and Michael Gurevitch, eds. *Mass Media and Society.* 2nd. ed. New York: Arnold, 1996.

Czitrom, Daniel. *Media and the American Mind: From Morse to McLuhan.* Chapel Hill, NC: University of North Carolina Press, 1982.

Dahlman, Carl J. *The Open Field System and Beyond: A Property Rights Analysis of an Economic Institution.* New York: Cambridge University Press, 1980.

Davidow, William H., and Michael S. Malone. *The Virtual Corporation: Structuring and Revitalizing the Corporation for the 21st Century.* New York: HarperCollins, 1992.

Davidson, Martin P. *The Consumerist Manifesto: Advertising in Postmodern Times.* New York: Routledge, 1992.

Davis, Stan, and Christopher Meyer. *Blur: The Speed of Change in the Connected Economy.* Oxford: Capstone Publishing Ltd., 1998.

Debord, Guy. *The Society of the Spectacle.* New York: Zones Books, 1994.

Delany, Paul, and George P. Landow, eds. *Hypermedia and Literary Studies.* Cambridge MA: MIT Press, 1991.

Denzin, Norman K. *Images of Postmodern Society: Social Theory and Contemporary Cinema.* London: Sage Publications, 1991.

Dicke, Thomas S. *Franchising in America: The Development of a Business Method, 1840–1980.* Chapel Hill, NC: University of North Carolina Press, 1992.

Dittmar, Helga. *The Social Psychology of Material Possessions: To Have Is to Be.* New York: St. Martin's, 1992.

Dobb, Maurice. *Studies in the Development of Capitalism.* New York: International Publishers, 1963.

Douglas, Mary. *In the Active Voice.* London: Routledge & Kegan Paul, 1982.

Douglas, Mary, and Baron Isherwood. *The World of Goods.* New York: Basic Books, 1979.

Downes, Larry, and Chunka Mui. *Unleashing the Killer App: Digital Strategies for Market Dominance.* Boston: Harvard Business School Press, 1998.

Drucker, Peter F. *Post-Capitalist Society.* New York: HarperBusiness, 1993.

———. *The Practice of Management.* 1954. Reprint. Oxford: Butterworth-Heinemann, 1993.

Dyson, Esther. *Release 2.0: A Design for Living in the Digital Age.* New York: Broadway Books, 1997.

Dyson, Esther, George Gilder, George Keyworth, and Alvin Toffler. *Cyberspace and the American Dream: A Magna Carta for the Knowledge Age.* Washington, DC: The Progress and Freedom Foundation, 1994.

Eisenschitz, Tamara S. *Information Transfer Policy: Issues of Control and Access.* London: Library Association Publishing, 1993.

Eisenstein, Elizabeth L. *The Printing Revolution in Early Modern Europe.* Cambridge: Cambridge University Press, 1983.

Ely, James W., Jr. *The Guardian of Every Other Right: A Constitutional History of Property Rights.* Oxford: Oxford University Press, 1992.

Estabrooks, Maurice. *Electronic Technology, Corporate Strategy, and World Transformation.* Westport, CT: Quorum Books, 1995.

Evreinoff, Nicolas. *The Theatre in Life.* Translated by Alexander I. Nazaroff. New York: Benjamin Blom, 1927.

Ewen, Stuart. *All Consuming Images: The Politics of Style in Contemporary Culture.* New York: Basic Books, 1988.

———. *Captains of Consciousness: Advertising and the Social Roots of the Consumer Culture.* New York: McGraw-Hill, 1976.

Ewen, Stuart and Elizabeth. *Channels of Desire: Mass Images and the Shaping of American Consciousness.* New York: McGraw-Hill, 1982.

Farrington, Benjamin, ed. *The Philosophy of Francis Bacon: An Essay on Its Development from 1603–1609.* Liverpool, England: Liverpool University Press, 1964.

Featherstone, Mike. *Consumer Culture and Postmodernism.* London: Sage Publications, 1991.

Felstead, Alan. *The Corporate Paradox: Power and Control in the Business Franchise.* London: Routledge, 1993.

Fiksdal, Susan. *The Right Time and Pace: A Microanalysis of Cross-Cultural Gatekeeping Interviews.* Norwood, NJ: Ablex Publishing Corporation, 1990.

Fiske, John. *Introduction to Communication Studies.* 2nd ed. New York: Routledge, 1990.

———. *Understanding Popular Culture.* Boston: Unwin Hyman, 1989.

Ford, Henry. *My Life and Work.* Salem, NH: Ayer Company, 1987.

Foster, Hal, ed. *The Anti-Aesthetic: Essays in Postmodern Culture.* Seattle: Bay Press, 1983.

Fox, Richard Wightman, and T. J. Jackson Lears, eds. *The Culture of Consumption: Critical Essays in American History, 1880–1980.* New York: Pantheon, 1983.

Gabler, Neal. *Life the Movie: How Entertainment Conquered Reality.* New York: Knopf, 1998.

Gaines, Jane M. *Contested Culture: The Image, the Voice, and the Law.* Chapel Hill, NC: University of North Carolina Press, 1991.

Garnham, Nicholas. *Contribution to a Political Economy of Mass-Communication.* London: Academic Press, 1979.

Garnham, Nicholas, and Fred Inglis, eds. *Capitalism and Communication: Global Culture and the Economics of Information.* London: Sage Publications, 1990.

Gates, Bill. *The Road Ahead.* New York: Viking Penguin, 1995.

Gelernter, David. *Mirror Worlds, or, The Day Software Puts the Universe in a Shoebox: How It Will Happen and What It Will Mean.* Oxford: Oxford University Press, 1991.

Gergen, Kenneth J. *The Saturated Self: Dilemmas of Identity in Contemporary Life.* New York: Basic Books, 1991.

Gilder, George. *Microcosm: The Quantum Revolution in Economics and Technology.* New York: Simon & Schuster, 1989.

Goffman, Erving. *The Presentation of Self in Everyday Life.* New York: Doubleday, 1959.
———. *Relations in Public: Microstudies of the Public Order.* New York: Basic Books, 1971.

Goldman, Steven L., Roger N. Nagel, and Kenneth Preiss. *Agile Competitors and Virtual Organizations: Strategies for Enriching the Customer.* New York: Van Nostrand Reinhold, 1995.

Goldstein, Paul. *Copyright's Highway: From Gutenberg to the Celestial Jukebox.* New York: Hill and Wang, 1994.

Grant, James. *Money of the Mind: Borrowing and Lending in America from the Civil War to Michael Milken.* New York: Farrar, Straus & Giroux, 1992.

Greider, William. *One World, Ready or Not: The Manic Logic of Global Capitalism.* New York: Simon & Schuster, 1997.

Guéhenno, Jean-Marie. *The End of the Nation-State.* Translated by Victoria Elliott. Minneapolis: University of Minnesota Press, 1995.

Gumpert, Gary. *Talking Tombstones and Other Tales of the Media Age.* New York: Oxford University Press, 1987.

Gurevitch, Michael, Tony Bennett, James Curran, and Janet Woollacott, eds. *Culture, Society, and the Media.* New York: Methuen, 1982.

Habermas, Jurgen. *The Structural Transformation of the Public Sphere: An Inquiry into a Category of Bourgeois Society.* Cambridge, MA: MIT Press, 1989.

Hampton, Benjamin B. *History of the American Film Industry: From Its Beginnings to 1931.* New York: Dover, 1970.

Hanan, Mack. *Sales Shock! The End of Selling Products, the Rise of CoManaging Customers.* New York: AMACOM, 1996.

Harasim, Linda M., ed. *Global Networks: Computers and International Communication.* Cambridge, MA: MIT Press, 1993.

Hardison, O. B., Jr. *Disappearing Through the Skylight: Culture and Technology in the Twentieth Century.* New York: Viking, 1989.

Harvey, David. *The Condition of Postmodernity: An Enquiry into the Origins of Cultural Change.* Cambridge, MA: Blackwell, 1990.

Hawken, Paul, Amory Lovins, and Hunter Lovins. *Natural Capitalism: Creating the Next Industrial Revolution.* New York: Little, Brown & Co., 1999.

Hawthorne, Nathaniel. *The House of the Seven Gables.* Boston: Ticknor, Reed, and Fields, 1851.

Hayward, Philip, and Tana Wollen, eds. *Future Visions: New Technologies of the Screen.* London: BFI Publishing, 1993.

Healy, Jane M. *Endangered Minds: Why Children Don't Think and What We Can Do About It.* New York: Simon & Schuster, 1990.

Heer, Friedrich. *The Medieval World: Europe, 1100–1350.* Translated by Janet Sondheimer. London: Weidenfeld & Nicolson, 1962.

Heilbroner, Robert L. *The Making of Economic Society.* Englewood Cliffs, NJ: Prentice-Hall, 1962.

Heim, Michael. *Electric Language: A Philosophical Study of Word Processing.* New Haven, CT: Yale University Press, 1987.
———. *The Metaphysics of Virtual Reality.* Oxford: Oxford University Press, 1993.

Heisenberg, Werner. *Physics and Philosophy: Encounters and Conversations.* New York: Harper, 1958.

Herman, Edward S., and Robert W. McChesney. *The Global Media: The New Missionaries of Corporate Capitalism.* Herndon, VA: Cassell, 1997.

Hoffman, Charles. *The Depression of the Nineties: An Economic History.* Westport, CT: Greenwood, 1970.

Hollowell, Peter G., ed. *Property and Social Relations.* London: Heinemann, 1982.

Hornbrook, Adrian, ed. *World Leasing Yearbook 1995.* Sussex, UK: Grange Press, 1995.

Horney, Karen. *The Neurotic Personality of Our Time.* New York: W. W. Norton, 1937.

Howard, Ebenezer. *Garden Cities of Tomorrow.* Cambridge, MA: MIT Press, 1965.

Huizinga, Johan. *Homo Ludens: A Study of the Play Element in Culture.* Boston: Beacon Press, 1955.

Hunt, E. K. *Property and Prophets.* New York: Harper & Row, 1972.

Innis, Harold A. *Empire and Communications.* 1950. Reprint. Rev. ed. Toronto, Ontario, Canada: University of Toronto Press, 1972.

Jameson, Fredric. *Postmodernism: Or the Cultural Logic of Late Capitalism.* Durham, NC: Duke University Press, 1991.

Jones, Steven G., ed. *Cybersociety: Computer-Mediated Communication and Community.* Thousand Oaks, CA: Sage Publications, 1995.

Jussawalla, Meheroo. *The Economics of Intellectual Property in a World Without Frontiers: A Study of Computer Software.* Westport, CT: Greenwood, 1992.

Kamath, Kundapur V., Sanjiv A. Kerkar, and Tumu Viswanath. *The Principles and Practices of Leasing.* Croydon, Surrey, England: Lease Asia, 1990.

Kao, John. *Jamming: The Art and Discipline of Business Creativity.* New York: Harper-Collins, 1996.

Kaplan, Ann E. *Rocking Around the Clock: Music Television, Postmodernism, and Consumer Culture.* New York: Methuen, 1987.

Katz, Elihu, and Paul F. Lazarsfeld. *Personal Influence: The Part Played by People in the Flow of Mass Communications.* Glencoe, IL: The Free Press, 1955.

Kelly, Kevin. *New Rules for the New Economy: 10 Radical Strategies for a Connected World.* New York: Viking, 1998.

———. *Out of Control: The Rise of the Neo-Biological Civilization.* Reading, MA: Addison-Wesley, 1994.

Kern, Stephen. *The Culture of Time and Space 1880–1918.* Cambridge, MA: Harvard University Press, 1983.

Keynes, John Maynard. *The General Theory of Employment, Interest and Money.* New York: Harcourt, Brace, 1935.

Keyworth, George A., Jeffrey Eisenbach, Thomas Lenard, and David E. Colton. *The Telecom Revolution: An American Opportunity.* Washington, DC: The Progress and Freedom Foundation, 1995.

King, Sarah Sanderson, ed. *Human Communication as a Field of Study.* Albany: NY: State University of New York Press, 1989.

Kowinski, William Severini. *The Malling of America: An Inside Look at the Great Consumer Paradise.* New York: Morrow, 1985.

Krotz, Larry. *Tourists: How Our Fastest Growing Industry Is Changing the World.* Boston: Faber and Faber, 1996.

Kumon, Shumpei, and Henry Rosovsky, eds. *Cultural and Social Dynamics.* The Political Economy of Japan, vol. 3. Stanford, CA: Stanford University Press, 1992.

Kurlansky, Mark. *A Continent of Islands: Searching for the Caribbean Destiny.* Reading, MA: Addison-Wesley, 1992.

Kurtzman, Joel. *The Death of Money: How the Electronic Economy Has Destabilized the World's Markets and Created Financial Chaos.* New York: Simon & Schuster, 1993.

Lafargue, Paul. *The Evolution of Property from Savagery to Civilization.* New York: Scribner, 1901.

Lancy, David F., and B. Allan Tindall, eds. *The Anthropological Study of Play: Problems and Prospects—Proceedings of the First Annual Meeting of the Association for the Anthropological Study of Play.* Cornwall, NY: Leisure Press, 1976.

Landow, George P. *Hypertext: The Convergence of Contemporary Critical Theory and Technology.* Baltimore: Johns Hopkins University Press, 1992.

Lanham, Richard A. *The Electronic Word: Democracy, Technology, and the Arts.* Chicago: University of Chicago Press, 1993.

Lasch, Christopher. *The Culture of Narcissism: American Life in an Age of Diminishing Expectations.* New York: W. W. Norton, 1979.

Laurel, Brenda. *Computers As Theatre.* Reading, MA: Addison-Wesley, 1991.

Leach, William. *Land of Desire: Merchants, Power, and the Rise of a New American Culture.* New York: Pantheon, 1993.

Leiss, William. *The Domination of Nature.* Boston: Beacon Press, 1974.

Levin, David Michael. *The Body's Recollection of Being: Phenomenological Psychology and the Deconstruction of Nihilism.* London: Routledge and Kegan Paul, 1985.

Lewin, Kurt. *Field Theory in Social Science: Selected Theoretical Papers.* New York: Harper & Row, 1951.

———. *Frontiers of Group Dynamics.* New York: Harper & Row, 1946.

Lifton, Robert Jay. *The Protean Self: Human Resilience in an Age of Fragmentation.* New York: Basic Books, 1993.

Lipman-Blumen, Jean. *The Connective Edge: Leading in an Interdependent World.* San Francisco: Jossey-Bass, 1996.

Locke, John. *Of Civil Government: Two Treatises.* New York: E. P. Dutton, 1924.

———. *Two Treatises of Government,* vol. 2. Edited by Peter Laslett. New York: Mentor, 1963.

Loeffler, Carl Eugene, and Tim Anderson, eds. *The Virtual Reality Casebook.* New York: Van Nostrand Reinhold, 1994.

Louv, Richard. *America II.* New York: Penguin, 1983.

Love, John F. *McDonald's: Behind the Arches.* London: Bantam Press, 1987.

Lowe, Donald M. *History of Bourgeois Perception.* Chicago: University of Chicago Press, 1982.

Lury, Celia. *Cultural Rights: Technology, Legality, and Personality.* London: Routledge, 1993.

Lyotard, Jean-François. *The Postmodern Condition: A Report on Knowledge.* Translated by Geoff Bennington and Brian Massumi. Minneapolis: University of Minnesota Press, 1984.

MacCannell, Dean. *The Tourist: A New Theory of the Leisure Class.* New York: Schocken Books, 1989.

McChesney, Robert W. *Corporate Media and the Threat to Democracy.* New York: Seven Stories Press, 1997.

McChesney, Robert W., Ellen Meiksins Wood, and John Bellamy Foster, eds. *Capitalism and the Information Age: The Political Economy of the Global Communication Revolution.* New York: Monthly Review Press, 1998.

Macfarlane Alan. *The Origins of English Individualism: The Family, Property, and Social Transition.* New York: Cambridge University Press, 1979.

McIlwain, Charles H. *The Growth of Political Thought in the West, from the Greeks to the End of the Middle Ages.* New York: Macmillan, 1932.

McKenna, Regis. *Real Time: Preparing for the Age of the Never Satisfied Customer.* Boston: Harvard Business School Press, 1997.

———. *Relationship Marketing: Successful Strategies for the Age of the Customer.* Reading, MA: Addison-Wesley, 1991.

McKenzie, Evan. *Privatopia: Homeowner Associations and the Rise of Residential Private Government.* New Haven, CT: Yale University Press, 1996.

McLuhan, Marshall. *Understanding Media: The Extensions of Man.* Cambridge, MA: MIT Press, 1994.

McLuhan, Marshall, and Bruce R. Powers. *The Global Village: Transformations in World Life and Media in the 21st Century.* New York: Oxford University Press, 1989.

MacPherson, Crawford. *Democratic Theory: Essays in Retrieval.* Oxford: Clarendon Press, 1973.

Malabre, Alfred L. *Beyond Our Means: How Reckless Borrowing Now Threatens to Overwhelm Us.* New York: Vintage, 1987.

Mandel, Ernest. *Late Capitalism.* Translated by Joris De Bres. London: NLB, 1976.

Marchand, Roland. *Advertising the American Dream: Making Way for Modernity, 1920–1940.* Berkeley, CA: University of California Press, 1985.

Marcuse, Herbert. *Eros and Civilization: A Philosophical Inquiry into Freud.* New York: Vintage, 1962.

Marden, Orison Swett. *Masterful Personality.* New York: T. Y. Crowell, 1921.

Martin, James. *Cybercorp: The New Business Revolution.* New York: AMACOM, 1996.

Marvin, Carolyn. *When Old Technologies Were New: Thinking About Electric Communication in the Late Nineteenth Century.* New York: Oxford University Press, 1988.

Marzio, Peter C. *The Democratic Art: Pictures for a 19th-Century America: Chromolithography, 1840–1900.* Boston: Godine, 1979.

Masuda, Yoneji. *The Information Society as Post-Industrial Society.* Washington, DC: World Future Society, 1980.

Medoff, James, and Andrew Harless. *The Indebted Society: Anatomy of an Ongoing Disaster.* Boston: Little, Brown and Co., 1996.

Merchant, Carolyn. *The Death of Nature: Women, Ecology and the Scientific Revolution.* San Francisco: Harper & Row, 1980.

Meyrowitz, Joshua. *No Sense of Place: The Impact of Electronic Media on Social Behavior.* New York: Oxford University Press, 1985.

Miller, Daniel. *Material Culture and Mass Consumption.* London: Basil Blackwell, 1987.

Miller, Steven E. *Civilizing Cyberspace: Policy, Power, and the Information Superhighway.* New York: Addison-Wesley, 1996.

Molnar, Alex. *Giving Kids the Business: The Commercialization of America's Schools.* Boulder, CO: Westview Press, 1996.

Moore, James F. *The Death of Competition: Leadership and Strategy in the Age of Business Ecosystems.* New York: HarperCollins, 1996.

Morris, Colin. *The Discovery of the Individual, 1050–1200.* New York: Harper & Row, 1972.

Mosco, Vincent. *The Pay-Per Society: Computers and Communication in the Information Age.* Norwood, NJ: Ablex Publishing Company, 1989.

Mosco, Vincent, and Janet Wasko. *The Political Economy of Information.* Madison, WI: University of Wisconsin Press, 1988.

Munzer, Stephen R. *A Theory of Property.* New York: Cambridge University Press, 1990.

Nedelsky, Jennifer. *Private Property and the Limits of American Constitutionalism: The Madisonian Framework and Its Legacy.* Chicago: University of Chicago Press, 1990.

Negroponte, Nicholas. *Being Digital.* New York: Knopf, 1995.

Nourse, Edwin G. *America's Capacity to Produce*. Washington, DC: The Brookings Institution, 1934.

Oakley, Francis. *The Medieval Experience: Foundations of Western Cultural Singularity*. New York: Scribner, 1974.

O'Connor, James. *Accumulation Crisis*. New York: Basil Blackwell, 1984.

Ong, Walter J. *Orality and Literacy: The Technologizing of the Word*. New York: Methuen, 1982.

Ortega y Gasset, José. *Meditaciones del Quijote*. Madrid: Ediciones de la Residencia de Estudiantes, 1914.

Pagels, Heinz R. *The Dreams of Reason: The Computer and the Rise of the Sciences of Complexity*. New York: Simon & Schuster, 1988.

Papert, Seymour. *The Children's Machine: Rethinking School in the Age of the Computer*. New York: Basic Books, 1993.

Patterson, Marvin, and Sam Lightman. *Accelerating Innovation: Improving the Process of Product Development*. New York: Van Nostrand Reinhold, 1993.

Pellegrini, Anthony, ed. *The Future of Play Theory: A Multidisciplinary Inquiry into the Contributions of Brian Sutton-Smith*. Albany, NY: State University of New York Press, 1995.

Pelton, Joseph N. *Wireless and Satellite Telecommunications: The Technology, the Market and the Regulations*. Upper Saddle River, NJ: Prentice Hall, 1995.

Pennock, J. Roland, and John W. Chapman, eds. *Property*. New York: New York University Press, 1980.

Peppers, Don, and Martha Rogers. *The One to One Future: Building Relationships One Customer at a Time*. New York: Doubleday, 1993.

Perinbanayagam, Robert S. *Signifying Acts: Structure and Meaning in Everyday Life*. Carbondale, IL: Southern Illinois University Press, 1985.

Perlman, Kalman I. *The Leasing Handbook*. Washington, DC: Office of Project and Facilities Management, U.S. Dept. of Energy, 1990.

Peters, Tom. *Liberation Management: Necessary Disorganization for the Nanosecond Nineties*. New York: Knopf, 1992.

Pine, B. Joseph II. *Mass Customization: The New Frontier in Business Competition*. Boston: Harvard Business School Press, 1993.

Pine, B. Joseph II, and James Gilmore. *The Experience Economy: Work Is Theatre and Every Business a Stage*. Cambridge, MA: Harvard Business School Press, 1999.

Polanyi, Karl. *The Great Transformation: The Political and Economic Origins of Our Time*. Boston: Beacon Press, 1957.

Porter, Michael E., ed. *Competition in Global Industries: Coalitions and Global Strategy*. Boston: Harvard Business School Press, 1986.

Quinn, James Brian. *Intelligent Enterprise: A Knowledge and Service Based Paradigm for Industry*. New York: The Free Press, 1992.

Radin, Margaret Jane. *Reinterpreting Property*. Chicago: University of Chicago Press, 1993.

Randall, John H. *The Making of the Modern Mind: A Survey of the Intellectual Background of the Present Age*. Boston: Houghton Mifflin, 1940.

Reeve, Andrew. *Property*. London: Macmillan Education Ltd., 1986.

Rein, Irving J., Philip Kotler, and Martin R. Stoller. *High Visibility*. New York: Dodd, Mead, 1987.

Rheingold, Howard. *Virtual Reality*. New York: Simon & Schuster, 1991.

Rieff, Philip. *The Triumph of the Therapeutic: Uses of Faith After Freud*. Chicago: University of Chicago Press, 1987.

Rifkin, Jeremy. *Biosphere Politics: A New Consciousness for a New Century.* New York: Crown, 1991.

———. *The Biotech Century: Harnessing the Gene and Remaking the World.* New York: Tarcher/Putnam, 1998.

———. *The End of Work: The Decline of the Global Labor Force and the Dawn of the Post-Market Era.* New York: Putnam, 1995.

Rifkin, Jeremy, and Nicanor Perlas. *Algeny.* New York: Viking, 1983.

Rifkin, Jeremy, and Ted Howard. *The Emerging Order: God in the Age of Scarcity.* New York: Putnam, 1979.

Rochberg-Halton, Eugene. *Meaning and Modernity: Social Theory in the Pragmatic Attitude.* Chicago: University of Chicago Press, 1986.

Rose, Carol M. *Property and Persuasion: Essays on the History, Theory, and Rhetoric of Ownership.* Boulder, CO: Westview Press, 1994.

Rothbard, Murray N. *America's Great Depression.* Princeton, NJ: Van Nostrand, 1963.

Rowles, Graham D., and Russell J. Ohta, eds. *Aging and Milieu: Environmental Perspectives on Growing Old.* New York: Academic Press, 1983.

Russell, Bertrand. *Our Knowledge of the External World, as a Field for Scientific Method in Philosophy.* 1914. Reprint. London: Routledge, 1995.

Ryan, Bill. *Making Capital from Culture: The Corporate Form of Capitalist Cultural Production.* New York: Walter de Gruyter, 1992.

Sassoon, Siegfried. *Memoirs of a Fox-Hunting Man.* London: Faber, 1928.

Schechner, Richard. *Between Theater and Anthropology.* Philadelphia: University of Pennsylvania Press, 1985.

Schiller, Friedrich. *On the Aesthetic Education of Man, in a Series of Letters.* Translated and edited by Elizabeth M. Wilkinson and L. A. Willoughby. Oxford: Clarendon Press, 1967.

Schiller, Herbert I. *Culture, Inc.: The Corporate Takeover of Public Expression.* New York: Oxford University Press, 1989.

———. *Mass Communications and American Empire.* 2nd ed. Boulder, CO: Westview Press, 1992.

Schlatter, Richard. *Private Property: The History of an Idea.* New York: Russell & Russell, 1973.

Schneider, Kenneth R. *Autokind vs. Mankind: An Analysis of Tyranny, a Proposal for Rebellion, a Plan for Reconstruction.* New York: Schocken, 1972.

Schneirov, Richard. *Labor and Urban Politics: Class Conflict and the Origins of Modern Liberalism in Chicago, 1864–97.* Chicago and Urbana, IL: University of Illinois Press, 1998.

Schreiber, Alfred L., and Barry Lenson. *Lifestyle and Event Marketing: Building the New Customer Partnership.* New York: McGraw-Hill, 1994.

Schrodinger, Erwin. *My View of the World.* Translated by Cecily Hastings. Cambridge: Cambridge University Press, 1964.

Sewell, Carl, and Paul Brown. *Customers for Life: How to Turn That One-Time Buyer into a Lifetime Customer.* New York: Doubleday/Currency, 1990.

Shapiro, Carl, and Hal R. Varian. *Information Rules: A Strategic Guide to the Network Economy.* Boston: Harvard Business School Press, 1999.

Sherman, Andrew J., ed. *The Franchising Handbook.* New York: American Management Association, 1993.

Shilling, A. Gary. *Deflation: Why It's Coming, Whether It's Good or Bad, and How It Will Affect Your Investments, Business, and Personal Affairs.* Short Hills, NJ: Lakeview Publishing Co., 1998.

Shoemaker, Pamela J. *Gatekeeping: Communication Concepts*, vol. 3. Newbury Park, CA: Sage Publications, 1991.

Shulman, Seth. *Owning the Future: Staking Claims on the Knowledge Frontier*. Boston: Houghton Mifflin, 1999.

Simmel, Georg. *Georg Simmel on Individuality and Social Forms: Selected Writings*. Edited by Donald N. Levine. Chicago: University of Chicago Press, 1971.

————. *The Philosophy of Money*. London: Routledge & Kegan Paul, 1978.

Sklar, Martin J. *The United States as a Developing Country: Studies in U.S. History in the Progressive Era and the 1920s*. New York: Cambridge University Press, 1992.

Slater, Gilbert. *The English Peasantry and the Enclosure of Common Fields*. London: Archibald Constable & Co., Ltd., 1907.

Slouka, Mark. *War of the Worlds: Cyberspace and the High-Tech Assault on Reality*. New York: Basic Books, 1995.

Smart, Barry. *Modern Conditions: Postmodern Controversies*. New York: Routledge, 1992.

Smith, Adam. *An Inquiry into the Nature and Causes of the Wealth of Nations*, vol. 1. Edited by Edwin Cannon. London: Methuen, 1961.

————. *Lectures on Jurisprudence*. Oxford: Oxford University Press, 1978.

Smith, Preston G., and Donald G. Reinersten. *Developing Products in Half the Time*. New York: Van Nostrand Reinhold, 1995.

Smuts, Robert W. *Women and Work in America*. New York: Schocken, 1971.

Soja, Edward W. *Postmodern Geographies: The Reassertion of Space in Critical Social Theory*. London: Verso Publishers, 1989.

Sorkin, Michael, ed. *Variations on a Theme Park: The American City and the End of Public Space*. New York: Farrar, Straus & Giroux, 1992.

Springler, Claudia. *Electronic Eros: Bodies and Desire in the Postindustrial Age*. Austin, TX: University of Texas Press, 1996.

Stanworth, John, and Brian Smith. *The Barclays Guide to Franchising for the Small Business*. Oxford: Blackwell, 1991.

Stephenson, William. *The Play Theory of Mass Communication*. Chicago: University of Chicago Press, 1967.

Stewart, Thomas A. *Intellectual Capital: New Wealth of Organizations*. New York: Doubleday/Currency, 1997.

Stigler, George. *Trends in Output and Employment*. New York: National Bureau of Economic Research, 1947.

Strasser, Susan. *Satisfaction Guaranteed: The Making of the American Mass Market*. New York: Pantheon, 1989.

Sussman, Warren I. *Culture as History: The Transformation of American Society in the Twentieth Century*. New York: Pantheon Books, 1972.

Sveiby, Karl Erik. *The New Organizational Wealth: Managing and Measuring Knowledge-Based Assets*. San Francisco: Berrett-Koehler Publishers, 1997.

Sweezy, Paul M. *The Theory of Capitalist Development: Principles of Marxian Political Economy*. New York: Oxford University Press, 1942.

Tapscott, Don. *The Digital Economy: Promise and Peril in the Age of Networked Intelligence*. New York: McGraw-Hill, 1996.

Tate, William E. *The English Village Community and the Enclosure Movement*. London: Gollancz, 1967.

Tawney, Richard H. *The Acquisitive Society*. New York: Harcourt, Brace and Howe, 1920.

Thayer, Lee. *On Communication: Essays in Understanding*. Norwood, NJ: Ablex, 1987.

Theobald, William F. *Global Tourism: The Next Decade*. Oxford: Butterworth-Heinemann, 1994.

Toffler, Alvin. *Future Shock.* New York: Bantam, 1970.

Toffler, Alvin and Heidi. *Creating a New Civilization: The Politics of the Third Wave.* Washington, DC: The Progress & Freedom Foundation, 1994.

Toynbee, Arnold. *Lectures on the Industrial Revolution of the 18th Century.* London and New York: Longmans, Green and Company, 1937.

———. *A Study of History,* vol. 8. London: Oxford University Press, 1954.

Tuan, Yi-Fu. *Segmented Worlds and Self: Group Life and Individual Consciousness.* Minneapolis: University of Minnesota Press, 1982.

Turkle, Sherry. *Life on the Screen: Identity in the Age of the Internet.* New York: Simon & Schuster, 1995.

Turner, Frederick Jackson. *The Frontier in American History.* New York: Holt, 1920.

Turner, Victor. *The Anthropology of Performance.* New York: Performing Arts Journal Publications, 1986.

———. *From Ritual to Theater: The Human Seriousness of Play.* New York: Performing Arts Journal Publications, 1982.

Umiker-Sebeok, Jean, ed. *Marketing and Semiotics: New Directions in the Study of Signs for Sale.* New York: Mouton de Gruyter, 1987.

Varela, Francisco J., Evan Thompson, and Eleanor Rosch. *The Embodied Mind: Cognitive Science and Human Experience.* Cambridge, MA: MIT Press, 1991.

Veblen, Thorstein. *Essays in Our Changing Order.* Edited by Leon Ardzrooni. New York: Viking, 1943.

Weber, Max. *The Protestant Ethic and the Spirit of Capitalism.* Translated by Talcott Parsons. New York: Scribner, 1958.

Whitehead, Alfred North. *Nature and Life.* 1934. Reprint. New York: Greenwood, 1968.

———. *The Principles of Natural Knowledge.* 2nd ed. Cambridge: Cambridge University Press, 1925.

———. *Science and the Modern World: Lowell Lectures, 1925.* New York: Macmillan, 1927.

Whiteley, Richard, and Dianne Hessan. *Customer Centered Growth: Five Proven Strategies for Building Competitive Advantage.* New York: Addison-Wesley, 1996.

Wiener, Norbert. *Cybernetics: Or, Control and Communication in the Animal and the Machine.* Cambridge, MA: MIT Press, 1961.

———. *The Human Use of Human Beings: Cybernetics and Society.* Boston: Houghton Mifflin, 1954.

Wikse, John R. *About Possession: The Self as Private Property.* University Park, PA: Pennsylvania State University Press, 1977.

Williams, William Appleman. *The Contours of American History.* Cleveland: World Publishing Co., 1961.

Wolf, Michael J. *The Entertainment Economy: How Mega-Forces Are Transforming Our Lives.* New York: Times Books, Random House, 1999.

Wood, Michael R., and Louis A. Zurcher, Jr. *The Development of a Postmodern Self: A Computer-Assisted Comparative Analysis of Personal Documents.* Westport, CT: Greenwood, 1988.

Woolley, Benjamin. *Virtual Worlds: A Journey in Hype and Hyperreality.* New York: Blackwell, 1992.

Zurcher, Louis A., Jr. *The Mutable Self: A Self-Concept for Social Change.* Newbury Park, CA: Sage Publications, 1977.

Authorship, 205; hypertext and, 207
Automation, 9, 262
Automobiles, 21; dealerships, 44, 58; leasing of,
    74–76; ownership of, 73–74
Autonomy, 208–9, 240, 264; postmodern views
    of, 191
Awareness bonding, 109

Bacon, Francis, 188, 190
Bagdikian, Ben, 223
Bankruptcies, 40
Banks: and leasing of equipment, 43; and personal
    loans, 38
Barnevik, Percy, 84
Barthes, Roland, 207
Baudrillard, Jean, 196, 197, 210
Bell, Daniel, 76, 84, 141, 219
Benetton, 173–74
Bergquist, William, 194
Bergson, Henri, 192
Bermuda, telecommunications in, 229–30
Biodiversity, preservation of, 257–58
Biological resources, 66. See also Genes
Bioprospecting, 65
Black market, 256
Blackstone, William, 77
Blattberg, Robert C., 100
Bloomingdale, Alfred, 38
Blur: The Speed of Change in the Connected Econ-
    omy, Davis and Meyer, 97
Body tissues, patented, 69–70
Book publishing, gatekeeping in, 181–82
Book value, and market value, 51–52
Books, 206; ownership of, 87–88
Boorstin, Daniel J., 150, 215
Bourgeois class, 198–99, 200
Braverman, Harry, 81, 83
Buckingham, Jane Rinzer, 183–84
Burger King Kids Club, 110
Burke, Kenneth, 165
Burns, Robert, 151
Busch, Lawrence, 68–69
Business, 5; changes in, 256; format franchising,
    58–64; services, 82–83
Business Week, 94, 177
Buyer's market, 106; services in, 91

Cable television, 34, 233–34
California, prison spending in, 231–32
Campbell, Kim, 167
Canclini, Néstor Garcia, 250
Capital: intellectual, 5, 51, 52–53, 55; physical, 41–
    44; social, 11, 245, 256, 258, 265
Capital equipment leasing, 43
Capitalism, 3–4, 7, 81, 102, 198, 202, 243–45, 258;
    changes in, 50, 55, 56–64, 76–77, 94–95, 114,
    137–67; and commercial relationships,
    96–97; cultural, 7, 8, 10–11, 137–67, 220,
    248, 260; and cultural production, 177;

management tools, 204; and marketing,
    171–72; mass production and, 82; and ser-
    vice economy, 82–85
Cash-free society, 36
Castells, Manuel, 19, 170, 179
Celebration (Disney's planned community),
    116–17
Channels of Desire, Ewen and Ewen, 162–63
Charge accounts, 37–38. See also Credit cards
Chemical supply industry, 89–90
Children, 99; and television, 196. See also Young
    people
Chromolithography, 161–62
Chrysler Corporation, 21, 51, 90
CIDs. See Common-interest developments
CityCarClub. See European Car Sharing Network
Civil education, 254–55
Civil society organizations (CSOs), 259–60
Class distinctions, 260
Class warfare, 257
Clinton, Bill, 221–22
Cloning (animals), 69
Club Med, 150
Coates and Jarratt, Inc., 125
Coca-Cola, 174–75
Collingwood, Robin G., 192
The Coming of Post-Industrial Society, Bell, 83
Commerce: cultural, 138; in cyberspace, 17, 34;
    network-based, 50
Commercial contracts, 241–42
Commercial relationships, 100, 111–13, 241
Commercialization of culture, 140
Commodification: of communications, 140, 205;
    of culture, 8–9; of experience. See Commod-
    ification of experience; of living space,
    116–17; of passion, 145; of relationships, 10,
    96–113, 241–42; of time, 112
Commodification of experience, 97, 98, 112,
    145–60, 165, 170–71, 219, 260; in common-
    interest developments, 119; in cyberspace,
    170–71; and empathy, 246–47; movies and,
    162–63; in shopping malls, 154–60; tourism
    as, 146–53
Common-interest developments (CIDs), 115–23,
    132
Commons, enclosure of cultural, 140
Communications, 11, 138–40, 144; commodifica-
    tion of, 140, 205; global network, 16–17;
    market control of, 220–21; technology,
    147–48, 203–4, 218–19
Communications Act of 1934, 232–33
Communications gap, 230–32
Communities, 108–11, 123, 139, 254; gated,
    115–23; planned, 118–19; social, 243–44. See
    also Common-interest developments
Communities of interest, 109, 224
Community bonding, 109, 113
Competition in telecommunications market,
    224

Index   305

Economy, 81, 141; capitalist, 3–4; cultural, 138;
    entertainment, 161–63; hypercapitalist, 10;
    network-based, 5, 17–18, 20, 112; as theater,
    163–67. *See also* Global economy; Network
    economy
Ecosystems, electronic, 169–70
EDS corporation, 18, 45, 49
Education, new mission for, 253–55
Edvinsson, Leif, 51
Electronic devices, 21–22; disposable, 86
Electronic marketplace, 101
Electronic media, 131, 169, 196, 206–8
Electronic networks, 11, 12–13, 18–24; global,
    17–18; money transfer in, 36–37
Eli Lilly, 92
Elite class as cultural intermediaries, 182–85
Empathy, 245–47; education and, 255
Employment, changes in, 8–9. *See also* Work
Encarta, 87
Encyclopaedia Britannica, 86–87
Energy resources, savings of, 88–89
England, enclosure acts in, 78–79
Enlightenment, philosophies of, 188–90
Entertainment, 83, 160–61, 265; in shopping
    malls, 157–59; tourism and, 149
Entertainment economy, 161–63
Entertainment industry, 7, 24–29, 160–61
Environment, service economy and, 88–90. *See
    also* Artificial environments
Equipment, leasing of, 41–44
Europe, service economy in, 84
European Car Sharing Network, 75–76
Event marketing, 174–75
Evreinoff, Nicolas, 214
Exclusion, 140; property and, 237–39, 264
The Excursionist, 148
Experience, 203; in artificial environments,
    168–71; commercialization of, 240–41;
    commodification of. *See* Commodification
    of experience; cultural, 7, 8, 29; search for,
    211–12; selling of, 172–73; social, arts and,
    142; theatricalization of, 215–16
Experience economy, 7–8, 145
The Experience Economy, Pine and Gilmore, 164
Experience industries, 145
Experiential capitalism, 149
Exploitation of workers, 48

Fantasy in postmodern era, 196
Fast-food franchises, 60, 251
FCC (Federal Communications Commission),
    225–26, 232
Featherstone, Mike, 143, 182
Felstead, Alan, 63
Feudal society, property in, 77–79
Film industry, 24–29, 162, 169, 184
Financial planning services, 103–4
Financial Times, 222
Firat, A. Fuat, 173, 174

First Amendment rights, 121–22, 159
Fisk, Raymond P., 165–66
Ford Motor Company, 74–75, 90
Format franchising, 57–64
Fourth sector (informal economy), 256
Franchising, 57–64; food distribution, 251
The Franchising Handbook, Kirkham and
    McGowan, 61
Freedom, 141, 239–40, 264; Age of Access and, 12
Fundamentalist movements, 258–60
Future, recommendations for, 252
Futurists, and cultural capitalism, 144–45

Gabler, Neal, 160, 163, 214
Gain-sharing arrangements, 90–92
Gandhi, Mohandas K., 259
Garden cities, 118
Gated communities, 115–23
Gatekeepers, 11, 104–5, 177–85; of gated com-
    munities, 115, 122
Gates, Bill, 86–87, 230
Gateways, electronic, 177–79
Geertz, Clifford, 139
General Electric, 33, 92–93
General Motors, 51
Generational differences, 12–13
Genes, 57, 64–71
Genetic engineering, 64–71; of crops, 251
Gergen, Kenneth, 208, 209–10
Geron Corporation, 71
Ghermezion, Nader, 157–58
Gilder, George, 52, 224
Gilmore, James, 145
Gingrich, Newt, 226
Glazer, Rashi, 20–21, 100
Gleick, James, 18
Global culture, homogenization of, 185
Global economy, 30, 37, 72, 114, 138, 158; cul-
    tural production of, 140, 163, 167; experi-
    ence industries in, 145; franchising and, 59;
    intangible assets of, 51; media market in,
    219; networks in, 23–24, 111; services in, 84,
    102; tourism industry in, 146–47
Global Telecommunications Agreement, 222, 225
Goffman, Erving, 215, 216
Goods, 81–82; free, with services, 93–94; services
    as, 85–91
Gordon, DeeDee, 183
Government agencies, networks and, 17
Government services, dependency on, 103
Governments, 240, 256; cyberspace and, 228
Graphics and entertainment, 161–62
Greenspan, Alan, 30
Grove, Andy, 28
Grove, Stephen J., 165–66

Hachette Filipacchi Magazines, 49
Hale, Ken, 185
Hall, Edward T., 139